automobiles of america

MILESTONES, PIONEERS, ROLL CALL, HIGHLIGHTS

fourth edition, revised

by Motor Vehicle Manufacturers Association of the United States, Inc.

(formerly Automobile Manufacturers Association of the United States, Inc.)

a savoyard book
wayne state university press, detroit, 1974

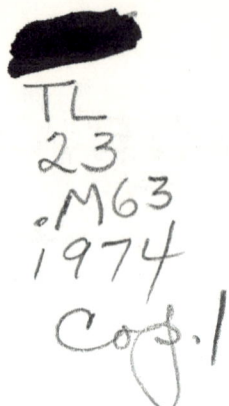

First edition © 1961, 1962
Second revised edition © 1968
Third edition, revised © 1970
Fourth edition, revised © 1974 by
Motor Vehicle Manufacturers Association
of the United States, Inc.
320 New Center Building
Detroit, Michigan 48202

All rights are reserved. No part of this book
may be reproduced without formal permission.

Published by Wayne State University Press
Detroit, Michigan 48202

Published simultaneously in Canada by
The Copp Clark Publishing Company
517 Wellington Street, West
Toronto 2B, Canada

Manufactured in the United States of America.

Library of Congress Cataloging in Publication Data

Motor Vehicle Manufacturers Association of the
 United States.
 Automobiles of America.
 (A Savoyard book)
 First-3d ed., rev., by Automobile Manufacturers Association.
 1. Automobiles, American. 2. Automobile industry and trade—United
States. I. Automobile Manufacturers Association. Automobiles of America.
II. Title.   TL23.M63 1973   629.22'22'0973   73-19838

contents

Foreword, 5
Acknowledgments, 9
Milestones, 11
Pioneers, 207
Roll Call, 241
Highlights, 279
Index, 288

foreword

In the waning years of the 19th century a new age dawned —the age of the automobile.

The distribution of the world's automobiles today would indicate that the dawn's first light was seen in America. But this was not so. While no other country in the world has approached the United States in the production and use of automobiles, the indomitable machine that has revolutionized our way of life was born in Europe.

Actually, however, the automobile was not "born" in the sense of being invented by anyone. It is the product of an evolutionary process that started long before mankind ever dreamed of such a thing as an "auto age."

Automobile history can be traced to the time of Leonardo da Vinci or even as far back as the discovery of the wheel. Historians set 1769 as the year of the first self-propelled land vehicle—a cumbersome steam artillery tractor built by French Army Captain Nicolas Cugnot. In 1805, a mobile steam dredge was produced by Oliver Evans of Philadelphia. And during the first half of the last century, steam powered carriages actually were in operation on the roads of England.

But the mechanical evolution of the modern automobile really began to take form about 100 years ago when European inventors such as Eugene Langen and Nikolaus August Otto developed the internal combustion engine.

It was 1864 when Langen and Otto formed a company to produce and sell their revolutionary power plants which ran on coal gas instead of steam. An Otto engine displayed at the Paris Exposition of 1867 attracted world-wide attention. In 1876, another Otto engine was shown at the Philadelphia Centennial Exposition, stirring further interest in this country.

By 1876 Otto had developed the four-cycle engine and in 1885 successfully operated an engine on liquid fuel.

In a few years, similar engines were being made in the United States as a new and attractive source of power for lumbering, pumping, power generation and marine uses. And it wasn't long before men were tinkering with the idea of using such an engine to propel a carriage.

In this application, however, the Europeans still were ahead. Vehicles operated by internal-combustion engines were built in the 1880's by Europeans Gottlieb Daimler, Karl Benz, Wilhelm Maybach, Emile Levassor and others. Daimler and Maybach were granted a German patent on a V-2 engine as early as June 9, 1889. These two also displayed a motor vehicle at the Paris Exposition of 1889.

By this time, the word "automobile" had not even been coined. But the idea of a practical self-propelled vehicle already had captured the imagination of many men, both in Europe and the United States. New names—some uncomplimentary—were invented for the new contraptions. "Horseless carriage" perhaps was the most common early term, and "gas buggy" was coined for the gas-burning internal-combustion variety. By the time the twentieth century was well into its first decade, the terms "automobile," or "auto" and "motor car," or "car," were the common expressions.

In the beginning the gasoline car was up against stiff competition from both steam and electric-powered makes. Ultimately, however, the internal-combustion engine emerged the winner.

foreword

When the automobile appeared on the U. S. scene it was somewhat like a ship on a desert. America was virtually a roadless land. By 1900, all of the hard-surfaced roads in the United States would not have linked New York and Boston.

A few carriage routes went beyond the cities and towns. But in wet weather they turned into winding rivers of mud. When dry, they were deeply rutted and dusty. Under any conditions, they offered little encouragement to pioneers of the dawning motor age.

But, the motoring enthusiasts of that early day were a hardy, adventurous lot. By 1903, one had even managed to drive an automobile from coast to coast, clear across the roadless land.

With such audacity, motorists themselves proved the practical potentialities of motor travel and led the way to better roads.

A mere *8,000* crude automobiles were chugging over dirt roads and cobblestone streets at the turn of the century. Today some *100 million* motor vehicles of all types are in use, traveling *a trillion* miles a year on *four million* miles of roads and streets.

The family car has become an American institution. *Four-fifths of American families* now own cars on which they depend for going to and from work, shopping, and such day-to-day necessities as taking children to school. More than *80 per cent* of vacation trips are made by car.

The automotive industry, to keep pace with the growing demand for motor vehicles, has produced more than *279 million* cars, trucks and buses. The ratio of motor vehicles to population has reached *1 to 2*.

Automobiles are directly responsible for the existence in the U. S. today of more than *three-quarters* of a million business enterprises—including many types and varieties never known before the "auto age." Automotive transportation industries provide jobs for more than *12* million people, or one in every seven employed in the country.

7

Automobiles of America

This infinitely flexible and individual form of transportation has changed virtually every aspect of American life—ending isolation both in the city and on the farm, stimulating development of the land and spearheading the growth of the nation's vigorous economy.

Through the pages that follow, the uniquely American phase of automotive history is told in four parts—(1) in "Milestones," a chronological review of significant events; (2) in "Pioneers," a selection of brief biographical sketches of outstanding leaders on America's automotive frontier; (3) in "Roll Call," a listing of the hundreds of American cars and trucks that have appeared through the years; (4) in "Highlights," a few basic facts and figures that tell more precisely than words how the automobile has affected Twentieth Century America.

MOTOR VEHICLE MANUFACTURES ASSOCIATION
OF THE UNITED STATES, INC.

acknowledgments

Automobiles of America represents the work and skill of many individuals and several out-of-print publications. In addition, collections of source material at both the Motor Vehicle Manufacturers Association and the Detroit Public Library have aided immeasurably with their newspaper clippings, trade journals, catalogs, and books. Statistical data, too, reflect the valuable collection at MVMA.

Historic automotive photographs from the MVMA archives provided most of the illustrations; the following also contributed and are gratefully recognized:

    Bureau of Public Roads
    Detroit Public Library
    Henry Ford Museum
    Library of Congress
    R. E. Olds Company
    Smithsonian Institution

Too many persons bear a close relationship to the book to permit individual acknowledgment. To those who have contributed of their time and knowledge we all owe a debt, for they have helped to tell a gallant story which deserves our understanding. It is not just an industry that is reflected in these pages, but a way of economic thinking and of life.

                                                             MVMA

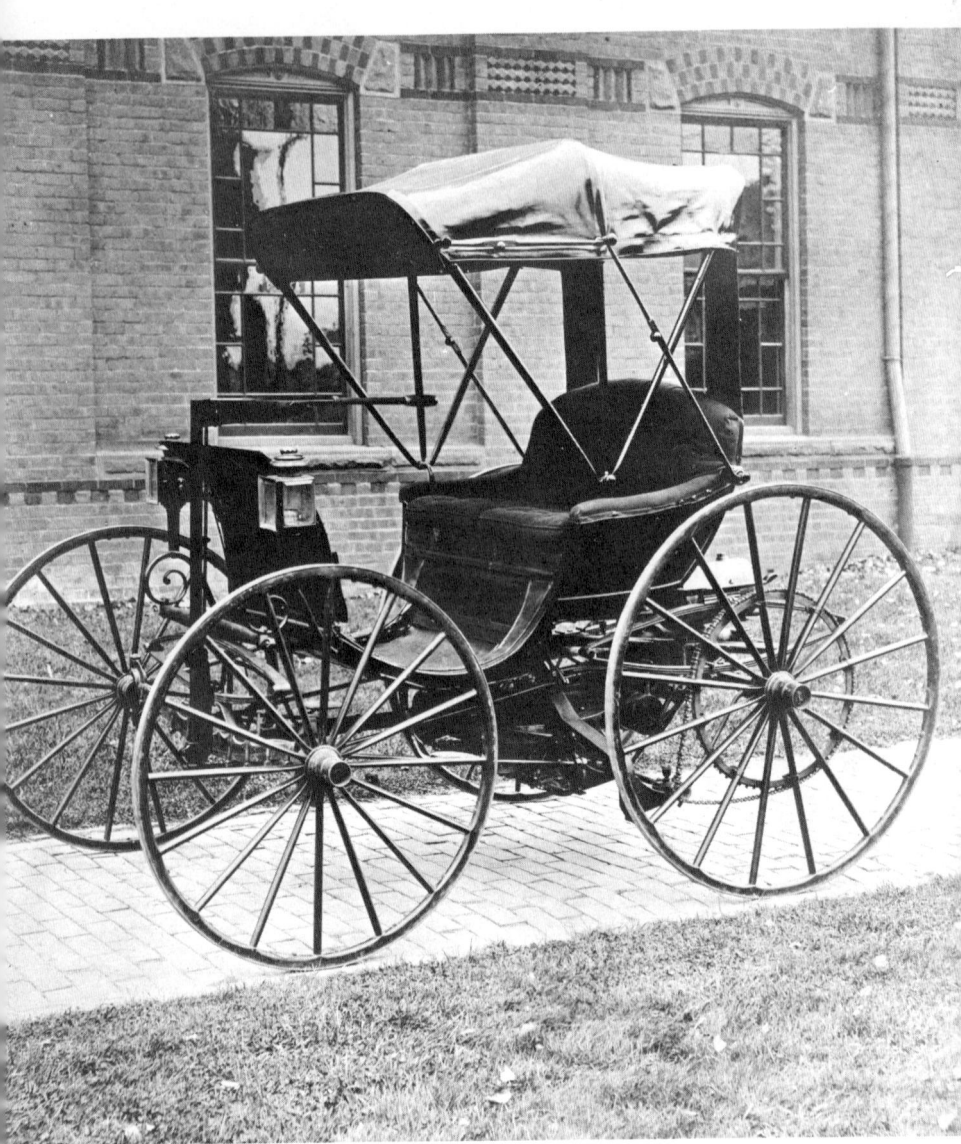

1893—America's first workable gasoline-engine vehicle. Designed by Charles E. Duryea, built and driven by J. Frank Duryea.

milestones

Along the ancient roadways of the world, milestones marked the slow progress of the traveler. And while modern America is transported more efficiently and guided by more elaborate road markers, the word "milestone" still stands for the mark of progress. To reach its present state of highway transportation efficiency, the nation had to pass many such milestones along the way. Below and on the following pages are listed many of the important milestones of automotive history in America.

Early experiments

1893 America's first successful gasoline-engine motor vehicle was in operation on Sept. 21 in Springfield, Mass. Using the designs of Charles E. Duryea, his brother J. Frank Duryea built a single-cylinder horseless carriage. The Duryea vehicle was the first American-made car to have an electric ignition and a spray carburetor, both of which J. Frank Duryea designed and built.

A national good roads movement sparked by cycling enthusiasts prompted establishment of the U. S. Office of Road Inquiry under the Department of Agriculture. This office later became the Bureau of Public Roads, under the Department of Commerce. The founding statute signed by President Benjamin Harrison read in part: "To enable the

Secretary of Agriculture to make inquiries in regard to the systems of road management throughout the United States, to make investigations in regard to the best methods of road-making, and to enable him to assist the agricultural college and experiment stations in disseminating information on this subject, ten thousand dollars."

The first brick surface on a rural road in the U. S. was laid on the Wooster Pike near Cleveland, Ohio. The four miles of brick pavement were completed in the fall of 1893 near route 71 of the Interstate Highway System.

1894 A car conceived by Elwood G. Haynes of Kokomo, Ind., was constructed by Elmer and Edgar Apperson, assisted by Jonathan Dixon Maxwell. Powered by a one-cylinder engine, the 820-pound Haynes car operated on Pumpkinvine Pike in Kokomo on July 4th, at a speed of six miles per hour.

Edward Joel Pennington probably operated one of his cars this year—there were several in existence by 1895.

1894—Elwood Haynes in his first car. It was powered by a single cylinder engine built by Clark Sintz of Grand Rapids, Mich.

1895

In September the first American company established to make gasoline cars was the Duryea Motor Wagon Company, organized by Charles E. and J. Frank Duryea.

The U. S. Patent Office granted George Baldwin Selden the patent he had applied for in 1879. The Selden Patent covered the essential features of the modern gasoline automobile. Features of special significance were: an internal combustion engine of the two-cycle type developed by George B. Brayton using liquid hydrocarbon fuel with a power shaft running faster than the road wheels, and a clutch or disconnecting device between the engine and the propelling wheels.

Hiram Percy Maxim started a motor carriage department for Pope Mfg. Co., bicycle makers of Hartford, Conn.

The first U. S. motor vehicle race in which any contestants finished was sponsored by the Chicago Times-Herald and run over a snow-drifted course in Chicago on Thanks-

Automobiles of America

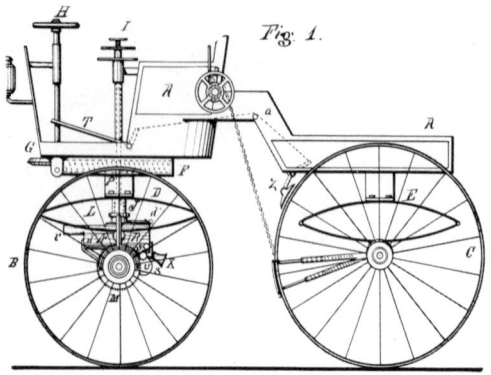

1895—The patent granted to George B. Selden was regarded for many years as a master document, covering all the essential features of the gasoline automobile.

giving Day, Nov. 28. It was won by J. Frank Duryea in a Duryea Motor Wagon at an average speed of 7½ miles per hour (considering delays for repairs) over the 55 mile course. Of the six starters, only two completed the run. Second place was won by a Mueller-Benz, driven across the finish line by Charles Brady King of Detroit, an umpire, who took over the tiller when driver Oscar Mueller collapsed from exposure an hour before the end of the race. The *Times-Herald* contest was scheduled to run on Nov. 1, but was postponed to allow entrants more time to prepare their vehicles. For those present and ready to compete the judges allowed a consolation race on Nov. 2 which was actually the first U. S. motor vehicle race. Four vehicles started, but breakdowns and accidents put all the vehicles out of the contest.

Public interest in horseless carriages heightened late in the year. The first American automotive trade journals started publication: "The Horseless Age," edited by E. P. Ingersoll of New York, and "The Motocycle," edited by E. E. Goff of Chicago. In addition, the nation's first automotive association, the American Motor League, was organized in Chicago.

1895—The Duryea entry, winner of America's first motor vehicle race. J. Frank Duryea at the tiller, with Arthur W. White, umpire, of Toronto, as passenger.

A new industry is born

1896 J. Frank Duryea, as chief engineer of the Duryea Motor Wagon Company, produced a third car. From these plans 13 cars were built that year—the first time that more than one car was made from the same design in the U. S.

George H. Morill, Jr., of Norwood, Mass., bought one

1896—Henry Ford and his experimental "Quadricycle."

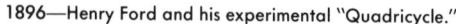

Automobiles of America

1896—The first gasoline powered car on the streets of Detroit. Charles B. King at the tiller, Oliver E. Barthel as passenger.

1896—America's first track race for motor vehicles—September at Narragansett Park, Cranston, R. I.

of the 13 Duryea Motor Wagons, and thus became the first known purchaser of an American gasoline car.

Charles Brady King drove the first car on the streets of Detroit, March 6. The car was powered with a four-cylinder, four-cycle, water-cooled engine that King designed and built.

Barnum & Bailey Circus announced an exhibition of the Duryea Motor Wagon as a parade feature on April 2.

Hiram Percy Maxim of the Pope Mfg. Co., in Hartford, Conn., built an electric motor carriage.

On Memorial Day, J. Frank Duryea won the Cosmopolitan Race (New York City to Irvington-on-the-Hudson

milestones

and return). This was the third motor vehicle race in the U. S.

Henry Ford successfully operated his two-cylinder, four horsepower, "Quadricycle" in Detroit on June 4.

The French word, "automobile," first began to appear in published references to motor vehicles in the U. S.

America's first motor vehicle track races were run at Narragansett Park, R. I., on Sept. 7. Seven vehicles were entered, two electrics and five Duryeas, but two of the Duryeas were disqualified. All five heats, one mile each, were won by a Riker Electric Stanhope. Average for the first mile was 26.8 miles per hour. Second prize went to a Morris and Salom Electrobat. The race was so dull that spectators demanded, "Get a horse!" This was probably the origin of the famous phrase.

1896—Alexander Winton and five companions in his first experimental car.

Automobiles of America

Alexander Winton of Cleveland produced an experimental two-seater motor carriage in September.

During the same month, Ransom Eli Olds drove a one-cylinder, six horsepower car on the streets of Lansing, Mich. He had been experimenting with steam-powered vehicles since 1886.

Two Duryea cars participated in the Emancipation Day run from London to Brighton on Nov. 14. This event celebrated repeal of England's "red flag" laws, and marked the first appearance of American motor vehicles in Europe.

1897 The first automotive press preview and open house in the U. S. was held at the Pope Mfg. Co., in Hartford, Conn., on May 13. Invitations were sent to journalists to see the Pope plant and try out the firm's automobiles.

1897—The Stanley twins in their famous Stanley Steamer.

milestones

A Winton car was driven a mile in one minute and 48 seconds in Cleveland (on Memorial Day), and from Cleveland to New York in 10 days (July 28–Aug. 7).

Olds Motor Vehicle Company was organized on Aug. 21 —the first automobile company in Michigan. Studebaker Brothers, carriage-makers since 1852, began experimenting with motor vehicles.

Louis S. Clarke and William Morgan of Pittsburgh, Pa., organized Pittsburgh Motor Vehicle Co., Oct. 21.

Pope Manufacturing Co., Hartford, Conn., began marketing Columbia Mark III Electric Phaetons.

Gilbert Loomis, a mechanic from Westfield, Mass., who built his own one-cylinder car, took out automobile insurance. The premium was $7.50 for $1,000 worth of liability insurance on a policy used for horse-drawn vehicle liability.

1898—Hiram Percy Maxim and Bert Holcomb in a Mark VIII Pope-Columbia.

Automobiles of America

1898 William E. Metzger of Detroit established the first independent automotive dealership.

The earliest known franchised dealership for U. S. cars was opened by H. O. Koller in Reading, Pa., to sell Winton motor vehicles.

Electric cab service was initiated in New York City.

Haynes was the first U. S. motor vehicle manufacturer to use aluminum alloy.

Winton introduced a Commercial Delivery Wagon, and built a quantity of one-cylinder passenger cars.

John Wilkinson built his first four-cylinder, valve-in-head, air-cooled motor, from which Franklin engines later evolved.

1899 Experiments in collecting mail with motor vehicles were conducted in Buffalo, Cleveland and Washington by the U. S. Post Office Department.

The Automobile Club of America was organized.

The U. S. Army purchased its first electric vehicles for general transportation assignments.

Alexander Winton drove one of his cars from Cleveland to New York in 47 hours and 37 minutes driving time.

R. E. Olds organized his second company, the Olds Motor Works, and moved operations from Lansing to Detroit.

A Haynes-Apperson car was delivered from the factory in Kokomo, Ind., to Brooklyn in 21 days.

Electric delivery wagons were put into use by New York and Boston stores.

Freelan O. Stanley, driving a Stanley Steamer built by himself and his twin brother, Francis E., climbed Mt. Washington, N. H., in August.

Rollin White adopted the flash boiler, developed in Europe, for experiments with steam cars.

20

milestones

A. L. Dyke of St. Louis, Mo., established the first automobile parts and supply business in the U. S.

Mrs. John Howell Phillips of Chicago was the first woman known in the U. S. to receive a driver's license.

American Motor Company, New York City, opened a garage with "competent mechanics always on hand to make repairs when necessary."

Pittsburgh Motor Vehicle Company became the Autocar Company on Aug. 28.

Percy Owen opened the first automobile salesroom in New York City at 120 Broadway, on Nov. 1. The firm sold Winton cars.

James Ward Packard completed and ran his first car in Warren, Ohio on Nov. 6. With his brother, Warren D., and George L. Weiss, of Cleveland as partners, he formed the New York and Ohio Co., to build the Packard car.

Back Bay Cycle & Motor Company of Boston, opened a stable for "renting, sales, storage and repair of motor vehicles."

The Stanley Brothers sold their steam car rights to Mobile and Locomobile.

"Motor Age" published its first issue in September.

1899—The Mobile Steamer had center steering because it was felt the car could be controlled more easily.

Automobiles of America

1900 The First National Automobile Show was held Nov. 3–10 in New York City's Madison Square Garden under the sponsorship of the Automobile Club of America. An estimated 48,000 visitors saw displays by 40 automobile and 11 parts and accessory exhibitors. There were about 300 types of vehicles exhibited, with prices ranging from $280 to $4,000. The exhibits were valued at $565,000. The Mobile Company of America built a 200-foot

1900—First National Automobile Show at New York's old Madison Square Garden featured test drives on obstacle courses.

ramp extending 53 feet in height to the Garden roof for demonstrating the hill climbing ability and good brakes of the steamers.

Mack introduced a bus which ran eight years as a bus and was then converted into a truck, to run nine more years.

1900—The first truck built by White was a steamer which introduced "horseless" delivery service.

President McKinley was the first U. S. President to ride in an automobile.

New York City acquired a motor-driven ambulance.

The Saturday Evening Post carried its first automobile advertising.

The publication "Automobile Topics" made its appearance.

Gasoline engines were located under a hood for the first time in the U. S. by several American automobile manufacturers.

John Brisben Walker drove his steam car to the top of Pikes Peak.

Special kerosene lamps for automobiles were offered by the R. E. Dietz Co., New York City, featuring a 20 candle-power reflected clear white flame capable of casting a 200-foot beam. One of the primary advantages of the Dietz lamp was that it produced a steady light even over rough roads.

A gasoline car defeated electric and steam cars for the first time in a free-for-all race at Washington Park race track in Chicago.

Engineer's certificates were issued by New York City as drivers' licenses. Harold T. Birnie was the first to receive one of these driving permits on May 15.

23

Automobiles of America

Carl Breer at the age of 17 built his first motor vehicle. (Later Breer was one of the engineers for the first Chrysler car.)

The National Association of Automobile Manufacturers was organized.

The G & J, designed by Thomas Jeffery, was the forerunner of the Rambler—the car had the engine in the front and left side steering.

Several automobile manufacturers started to use governors and float-free carburetors.

1901 Two events occurred early in the year that destined the gasoline engine to win out over steam and electric. Near Beaumont, Tex., Spindletop, the fabulous gusher, came in Jan. 10. The price of crude petroleum dropped below five cents a barrel. Nearly two months later

1901—Possibilities of long-distance automobile touring were demonstrated in the New York-to-Buffalo endurance run.

milestones

1901—George N. Pierce in a Pierce Motorette, forerunner of the Pierce-Arrow.

the second event favoring the gasoline engine was a fire that destroyed the Detroit factory of the Olds Motor Works. The only thing saved was an experimental curved-dash roadster. In order to get back in business after the disaster, the firm had no choice but to use that one car as a model and to subcontract orders for parts and sub-assemblies to small shops in the Detroit area. Most of the operators of these shops thus became automobile manufacturers, and, in consequence, Detroit became the Motor City.

The New York-to-Buffalo endurance run demonstrated the possibility of long-distance automobile touring. As a result, automobile Blue Books with route directions were started. The Automobile Club of America launched a program to place roadside touring signs from New York to Boston.

Connecticut passed laws regulating speed and the registrations of motor vehicles.

The steering wheel had virtually ousted the tiller or lever steering system.

R. E. Olds built 425 curved-dash Oldsmobiles to become the first mass-producer of gasoline automobiles in the world.

David Dunbar Buick, inventor and manufacturer of bathroom appliances, organized Buick Auto-Vim & Power Company, Detroit.

First Jones speedometers used, on Oldsmobiles.

New York State's licenses for motor vehicles added nearly a thousand dollars to the state treasury in the first year.

A total of 88 exhibitors displayed their products at the Second National Automobile Show, Nov. 2–9, in Madison Square Garden. The 1901 show displayed cars that marked the end of the horseless carriage, with the almost universal introduction of the French body type, the tonneau, which was fastened into the car behind the driver's seat and carried two passengers in a pair of seats resembling cut-down barrels.

There was a tendency toward multiple cylinders in the cars exhibited at the show. Water cooling was almost universal among the show cars, and detachable tires became more popular. Improvements were also noted in ignition systems, with the magneto generator coming into more general use.

Roy Dikeman Chapin drove an Oldsmobile from Detroit to New York, covering the distance in 7½ days, at an average of 14 miles per hour.

Electric Vehicle Company, owner of the Selden Patent, threatened suits against automobile manufacturers not licensed by the firm.

milestones

A gasoline storage facility for direct service to automobiles became available at an automobile storage and repair station in New York City. The bulk gasoline tank was outside the building as a safety precaution, and connected to the basement by pipe from which gasoline could be dispensed by a self-measuring device, thus eliminating all handling and pouring of the inflammable fluid.

1902 The popularity of the tonneau body type continued to increase, not only for gasoline cars, but for steam and electric vehicles as well.

The American Automobile Association was organized in Chicago, March 4. The national organization was proposed

1902—The curved-dash Oldsmobile.

27

Automobiles of America

four months previously by Frank G. Webb, treasurer of the Long Island Automobile Club.

Thomas B. Jeffery Company introduced the Rambler car and built 1,500 cars during the year.

A 60-day guarantee on new automobiles was adopted by the National Association of Automobile Manufacturers (112 members).

An ordinance was passed in Chicago permitting drivers to wear spectacles, but not *pince-nez* eyeglasses.

Louis S. Clarke, of Autocar Co., designed porcelain spark plug insulation, and patented the double reduction principle in the rear axle construction.

The Motor Mart was established in New York City to buy and sell used cars.

Max Grabowsky organized the Rapid Motor Vehicle Company (in later years it became GMC) to build one-cylinder trucks.

T. H. Shevlin was arrested in Minneapolis for speeding in excess of ten miles an hour and fined $10.

Jonathan Dixon Maxwell joined Charles Brady King to manufacture the Silent Northern, which introduced an integral engine and transmission assembly, three-point suspension of this power unit, and running boards. Maxwell also designed a siphon cooling system which Benjamin and Frank Briscoe manufactured.

Cadillac Automobile Company was formed; the first car was completed Oct. 17.

Oldsmobile production passed the 2,000 mark for the year.

Ohio Automobile Company, successor to the New York and Ohio Co., changed its name to Packard Motor Car Company.

J. Stevens Arms & Tool Company began manufacture of a two-cylinder car called the Stevens-Duryea, designed by J. Frank Duryea.

milestones

The Locomobile became the first American gasoline car with a four-cylinder, water-cooled, front-mounted engine.

Electric Vehicle Company was given the right by court decision to make and use Sterling Elliott's steering knuckle. Elliott's principle of steering is still employed on motor vehicles. The principle enables both front wheels to turn instead of the axle, when the steering device is moved.

Packard was granted a patent on Nov. 4 for a gearshift "H" slot, which later became standard for American automobiles.

1903 Sponsorship of the Third National Automobile Show was shared by the Automobile Club of America and the National Association of Automobile Manufacturers. Cars displayed at the Jan. 17-24 show had several features not seen at the earlier Paris auto show, such as mechanical valves (Rambler and Oldsmobile), compensating carburetors, square "bonnets" and honeycomb radiators. The French style tonneau bodies with a pair of rear seats and closed cars with a "glass front" were feature attractions at the 1903 show.

Cadillac made its first appearance at the 1903 show with a 7.3 horsepower, one-cylinder runabout.

The Ford Motor Company was incorporated with a capitalization of $150,000 in stock; $100,000 issued, and $28,000 paid in cash. Henry Ford, who, as chief engineer of the Detroit Automobile Company, had made several successful racing cars, was named vice president and chief engineer. Original shareholders included John and Horace Dodge, who took stock in exchange for tooling their machine shop to build motors, Albert Strelow, who accepted stock as payment for his carpenter shop which Ford wanted as an assembly plant, Alex Y. Malcolmson, a coal dealer who invested $7,000, Charles J. Woodall and James

29

1903—The first transcontinental automobile trip was completed by Dr. H. Nelson Jackson and his chauffeur, Sewall K. Crocker, in this two-cylinder Winton from San Francisco to New York City in 63 days.

1903—Barney Oldfield at the tiller of Ford's "999" racer.

milestones

Couzens, Malcolmson's employes, John S. Gray, banker and candy manufacturer, John W. Anderson and Horace H. Rackham, attorneys, Vernon Fry, real estate salesman, and Charles H. Bennett, inventor and manufacturer of windmills and air rifles.

The first transcontinental automobile trips were made during the summer of 1903. First to make the long drive was Dr. H. Nelson Jackson of Burlington, Vt., and his chauffeur Sewall K. Crocker. The pair drove a used Winton car, leaving San Francisco on May 23 and arriving in New York on July 26. The second cross-country automobile traveler was Tom Fetch, who, starting June 20, drove a single-cylinder Packard ("Old Pacific") from San Francisco to New York in 53 days. L. L. Whitman and E. T. Hammond made the third San Francisco to New York trip in an Oldsmobile (July 6–Sept. 17).

Packard moved to Detroit, and into the world's first reinforced concrete factory building, designed by Albert Kahn.

The Association of Licensed Automobile Manufacturers was organized. It included the Electric Vehicle Co., the Winton Company, and eight other manufacturers; George H. Day was appointed manager.

The Buick Motor Company was organized with a loan of $1,500 in cash and $2,000 in materials, advanced by Benjamin Briscoe, Jr., and Frank Briscoe. The new firm began making cars with valve-in-head engines.

"MoToR" magazine began its career.

Peerless adopted pressed steel frame construction—one of the major technical improve-

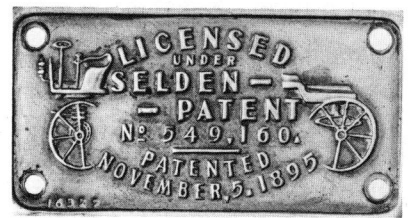

1903—The Selden Patent Plate. Until 1911, almost every manufacturer of gasoline-propelled vehicles had to pay royalties to holders of this patent through the Association of Licensed Automobile Manufacturers.

31

1903—Overland, forerunner of the Willys line.

ments during the year. Three other manufacturers used the frame construction shortly afterward.

A power steering arrangement was used in a heavy duty Columbia Electric Motor Truck. A separate electric motor furnished the power.

Ford was sued as an infringer of the Selden patent.

White Steamers made perfect scores in the 650-mile reliability trials held by the Automobile Club of Great Britain and Ireland.

B. A. Gramm perfected a power take-off.

General adoptions this year: T-head cylinders, sliding gear transmissions, mechanically-operated intake valves, and shock absorbers.

Berner Eli ("Barney") Oldfield, former cycle racer, began to achieve fame as the driver of Henry Ford's racer, "999." His chief competitors were Wridgeway, in a Peerless, Fosdick, in a Winton, Carl Fisher, in a Mohawk, Walter C.

Baker, in the "Torpedo Kid," and Charles Schmidt, in a Packard.

The Brownlow-Latimer Federal Good Roads Bill, first of its kind to be introduced in Congress, received strong support from the automotive industry and automobile clubs across the nation. The bill died in committee.

1904 The Fourth National Automobile Show, held Jan. 16–23, was larger than any of its predecessors, with 185 exhibitors, including 87 automobile exhibits. A "convertible" of sorts made its appearance at this show: a touring car, to which could be attached a glass-sided, solid top, called "California top" for use in inclement weather.

Automatic lubrication was another feature found on some cars, including the Autocar. Some models featured a fan to cool the water pipes used in the engine cooling system. Standard quick-demountable rims appeared on many new cars.

Studebaker sold its first gasoline motor vehicle.

R. E. Olds sold his interest in the Olds Motor Works, and organized the Reo Motor Car Company.

The Detroit Y.M.C.A. established a school for automobile mechanics.

Carl Graham Fisher and James A. Allison organized the Prest-O-Lite Company to perfect a safe method of using acetylene gas for automobile headlights.

Leland & Faulconer Manufacturing Company was merged with Cadillac Automobile Company and the name was changed to the Cadillac Motor Car Company.

The first White bus appeared.

A disastrous fire at the Cadillac plant delayed production and forced the company to return dealer deposits on 1,500 cars.

1904—Electric cars were popular among women.

1904—A 1,258-mile motor tour from New York to St. Louis was the forerunner of the famous Glidden Tours.

1904—A test run conducted by an express company showed motor trucks made more deliveries in better time, went farther and occupied less ground space than horses.

1904—The First Vanderbilt Cup Race was held on Long Island.

Pope-Hartford was criticized by competitors for including lamps as standard equipment.

The Fischer car was equipped with an air brake system for the rear wheels and drive sprockets. An auxiliary engine powered the air compressor.

The National Association of Retail Automobile Dealers was formed.

Ford Motor Company opened its first branch (on Jefferson Avenue, Detroit).

One of the earliest cars in the U. S. to attempt an automatic transmission was the Sturtevant. The car featured a centrifugal clutch which had low and high speed ranges. The Sturtevant also featured an air brake system.

A motor tour of 1,258 miles was organized to drive from New York to the Louisiana Purchase Exposition in St. Louis. Of the 71 cars that started, only 59 reached St. Louis. Col. Augustus Post, general chairman of the pilgrimage, gave the signal to start the 17-day motor trip on July 25. One of the tourists, Charles Glidden, impressed with the tour, later proposed what became the famous Glidden Tours.

The first Vanderbilt Cup Race was held Oct. 8 on Long Island.

Automobiles of America

1905 The trend toward large gasoline cars was noticeable at the Fifth National Automobile Show at Madison Square Garden—177 were gasoline cars, 4 steam cars and 31 electrics, including 9 electric trucks. Only one car (Waltham Buckboard) had wire spokes—all others had artillery type wheels with wood or steel spokes. The French tonneau with a rear door had been replaced by longer bodies with side doors. Comfort and ease in riding were stressed in the new models; speed was secondary.

1905—Two Oldsmobiles, "Old Scout" and "Old Steady," completed a transcontinental race from New York to Portland in 44 days.

1905—Motor cars provided new mobility, brought the country close to city folks.

1905—Lined up in front of the Mt. Washington Hotel in New Hampshire are 36 of the cars, including four non-contestants, in the first Glidden Tour. The tour covered 870 miles from New York City to Bretton Woods, N. H. and return.

Cape or folding tops were introduced by several manufacturers, and some replaced the canopy tops.

The first Glidden tour of 870 miles was routed from New York to the White Mountains and return. Percy Pierce with a Pierce-Arrow won the award.

The Society of Automobile Engineers was formed.

Cars were sold on the installment plan.

The American Motor Car Manufacturers Association was organized.

Two Oldsmobiles completed a transcontinental race from New York to Portland, Oregon, in 44 days.

The Ariel car offered a motor air cooled in winter and water cooled in summer.

Bus operations were started on New York's First Avenue.

The Holsman Motor Buggy offered 48-inch wheels; the Stearns boasted a 119-inch wheelbase.

A bill was introduced in the 59th Congress to regulate the operation of automobiles and other motor vehicles by the states. This, the first attempt by the Federal government to regulate motor vehicles, died in committee.

The Diamond T Company was organized by C. A. Tilt.

Motor trucks were introduced by many automobile makers, including Packard, Oldsmobile, Maxwell, and Mitchell.

Innovations during the year included: Gabriel exhaust horn, Weed tire chains, Goodyear universal rims to take either clincher or straight side tires, power tire pump, and ignition lock.

1906

Cars displayed at the Sixth National Automobile Show indicated that manufacturers were striving to develop better and stronger materials—chrome-nickel steel, phosphor bronze and high carbon steel were prominent. The Marmon cast aluminum body was an example of attempts to build lighter cars.

A Stanley Steamer, with Fred Marriott driving, ran a mile in $28\frac{1}{5}$ seconds, averaging 127.66 m.p.h., at Ormond Beach, Fla., Jan. 27.

Buick included a storage battery as standard equipment.

Six-cylinder cars were the talk of the country. National, Stevens-Duryea, Ford, Franklin and Pierce-Arrow offered six's.

Motor vehicles aided in relief operations following the San Francisco earthquake and fire. Walter C. White organized a caravan of White trucks in Los Angeles to carry help and supplies to the victims of the stricken city.

Prest-O tire tanks were introduced for tire inflation; each

1906—Fred Marriott became the first human to travel more than two miles a minute when the streamlined Stanley Steamer "Rocket" averaged 127.66 mph at Ormond-Daytona Beach on Jan. 27.

tank had the capacity to inflate 25 tires of 34 × 4 size up to 80 pounds pressure.

In addition to the craze for six-cylinder cars, a wide variety of engines was offered by some manufacturers.

Reo had its first four-cylinder car; Olds introduced a two-cycle engine; Maxwell built a 12-cylinder racer; and Adams-Farwell offered three- and five-cylinder rotary engines, an innovation which later influenced rotary aviation engines.

Front bumpers appeared on some cars, but not as standard equipment.

L. L. Whitman drove a Franklin from New York to San Francisco in 15 days, 2 hours, 15 minutes.

Backed by Edwin Ross Thomas, Buffalo manufacturer, Roy D. Chapin, Howard E. Coffin, Frederick O. Bezner

1906—Motor vehicles were used extensively in relief and rescue operations following the earthquake and fire that destroyed much of San Francisco.

1906—The date "1877" on the car represents the year in which the invention was conceived. Patent Office rules permitted the inventor to assert a date of invention two years prior to the date of his patent application—in Selden's case, 1879.

and James J. Brady, former Olds employees, organized the E. R. Thomas-Detroit Company.

Automobile plants in Detroit produced 550 to 600 cars a week. Packard alone built an average of six cars a day.

1907 Technical advances noted by the press at the Seventh National Automobile Show, Jan. 12–19, were the prevalence of selective transmissions, a gain in six-cylinder engines, larger brakes (some equipped with

1907—An air-cooled Franklin light runabout crosses a stream that flows over an early road.

camel's hair cloth covering on the friction surfaces—forerunner of modern asbestos brake lining), improved body finishes (up to 30 coats of paint), and twin carburetors (on the Stearns, Columbia and Matheson).

The first motor truck show was staged in Chicago.

International Harvester Company built its first automotive vehicle in January, 1907, in Chicago. The truck plant then was moved to Akron, Ohio, in October, 1907.

Oakland Motor Car Company was organized by Edward M. Murphy, buggy builder, of Pontiac, Mich., to make a two-cylinder car designed by Alanson P. Brush. Nineteen

1907—Maxwell, along with other manufacturers, designed cars especially for doctors. This is the "Doctor Model."

Automobiles of America

1907—One of the first International motor trucks was an "Auto Wagon" produced in 1907. All models through 1915 were right-hand drive.

years later Oakland introduced a companion car, the Pontiac, which survived the parent.

Gasoline economy runs were much in vogue; one of the most popular was conducted in Chicago.

Henry Ford purchased 60 acres of land in Highland Park, Mich., and started construction of a new factory.

Hewitt introduced a V-8 limousine, the first U. S. production touring car with an eight-cylinder engine.

A Reo crossed and re-crossed the continent, negotiating such climbs as Mt. Hood and Raton Range.

The Association of Licensed Automobile Manufacturers presented a formula for figuring horsepower; the formula was adopted by many states as a basis for taxation.

Oldsmobile employed nickel plating for trim parts that had hitherto been brass.

Humps were purposely built into streets at Glencoe, Ill., to discourage speeding.

Buick adopted a four-cylinder engine with a sliding-gear transmission, and won the Dead Horse Hill Climb at Worcester, Mass.

A Franklin was driven 1,060 miles from New York to Chicago in 39 hours, 36 minutes.

A bill was introduced in Congress providing for regulation of speed, identification and registration of motor vehicles engaged in interstate travel. Supported by motor vehicle manufacturers and automobile clubs, it died before it reached the floor of the House of Representatives.

Engine timing gears were enclosed in many cars. Mud aprons were becoming more general under the engine.

Autocar introduced a truck with a shaft-driven axle.

Despite the business depression, both Packard and Ford made profits of more than a million dollars.

1908 Wheelbases on most of the new models were longer, and manufacturers moved the rear seats toward the center of the car to provide more comfort. The four-cylinder vertical engine was almost standard at the Eighth National Automobile Show. Most of the cars exhibited offered sliding gear transmissions. Other mechanical improvements included the increased accessibility of parts, bigger and better brakes, better enclosed clutches, and easier controls.

General Motors Company was incorporated in New Jersey by William Crapo Durant, with William Eaton as first president.

1908—One of the first 800 Ford Model T's.

1908—The famous Thomas Flyer, winner of the New York to Paris race.

Cadillac became the first American car manufacturer to win the Dewar Trophy, awarded by the Royal Automobile Club of Great Britain for the greatest contribution to advancement of the industry. Cadillac was honored for interchangeability of parts.

The Model T Ford made its first appearance on Oct. 1.

1908—A Thomas taxi cab in Central Park. The meter was an innovation.

milestones

A four-cylinder, 60-horsepower Thomas Flyer won the New York-to-Paris Race, which began in Times Square on Feb. 12, headed westward, and ended 170 days later in Paris. The Thomas car drove a total of 13,341 miles in 88 days with an average of 151 miles per day.

J. M. Murdock of Johnstown, Pa., was the first motorist to drive his family across the U. S. They left Los Angeles on April 24 and arrived in New York on May 26.

The Columbia Mark XLVI used a gasoline engine to drive an electric generator. From this generator, separate electric motors propelled the wheels. The aim of this "gasolect" car was to provide a smooth flow of power by eliminating the conventional gear shift transmission.

Buick, Oldsmobile and Oakland became units of General Motors.

C. Harold Wills developed the use of vanadium steel for Ford.

Pierce-Arrow won fourth successive victory in the fourth Glidden Tour.

1908—The J. M. Murdocks in their Packard.

John North Willys was made president and general manager of Overland, which became Willys-Overland.

Fred J. and Charles T. Fisher organized Fisher Body Company.

Rapid Motor Vehicle Company (trucks) became part of General Motors.

Autocar discontinued passenger car production to concentrate on 1½ ton trucks of 97 in. wheelbase, with engines under the seat.

Otto Zachow and William Besserdich, of Clintonville, Wis. developed the first successful four-wheel drive motor vehicle.

Innovations: Stewart magnetic speedometers; Charles Y. Knight's invention of sleeve-valve engines; left-hand steering; silent timing chains; motor-driven horns; baked enamel finishes; helical gears.

The Commercial Car Manufacturers Association was formed, with G. M. Weeks as president and Walter Wardrop as manager.

1909 At the Ninth National Automobile Show, more emphasis was placed on pleasing the public than on booking orders from dealers. Four-cylinder cars ac-

1909—Mrs. John R. Ramsey and three companions in a Maxwell touring car were the first women to drive an automobile across the U. S.

1909—The first Hudson.

counted for 71 per cent of the gasoline automobiles, 27 per cent were six-cylinder, and only two single-cylinder models were displayed. Air self-starters were found on several of the cars exhibited. Another new feature was a steering wheel with the under side corrugated so the driver's hand would not slip.

First rural mile of concrete pavement in the U. S. opened July 4 in Wayne County, Mich. The pavement was constructed on Woodward Avenue (now U. S. 10) between Six Mile and Seven Mile Roads, at a cost of $13,534.59.

Louis Chevrolet, famous racer, began work on a six-cylinder passenger car of his own design in his Detroit shop.

The Selden Patent was sustained as valid and infringed upon by Ford.

Mrs. John R. Ramsey became the first woman to drive across the U. S. She left New York in a Maxwell car with three women companions on June 9, and arrived in San Francisco 53 days later.

W. S. Seaman & Company (later Seaman Body Corp.) built the first automobile bodies in Milwaukee.

Carl Graham Fisher and his associates completed the first Indianapolis Speedway. After the first races on Aug. 19, the track was paved with brick for a two-day meet in December.

The Hudson Motor Car Company was organized.

Cadillac was one of many companies that became part of General Motors during 1909. General Motors paid its first preferred stock dividend.

Gramm trucks featured overdrive transmissions.

The White Company built a gasoline engine car to replace the famous White Steamer.

The 1909 Glidden Tour from Detroit to Denver and back to Kansas City covered 2,636 miles—the longest Glidden Tour up to that time.

Fabric tops, often called "one-man tops," appeared on the market.

The year was marked by an acceleration of earlier trends in engineering, production techniques and uses of materials: magnetos showed a steady gain; cellular radiators were gradually displacing tubular ones; high-tension ignition systems were used on the majority of cars instead of the make-and-break system; selective gearsets had a 10-to-1 lead over the progressive type. The fashion was to cast cylinders in pairs, but the block casting was getting under way in small models; and there was a large increase in the use of chrome nickel steel and vanadium steel.

At the end of the year there were 290 different makes of automobiles produced at 145 cities in 24 states. Detroit had 25 different car makes and a total of 45 makes were produced in Michigan. Chicago had the second highest number with 14 different brands, then Indianapolis with 12 and Cleveland with 10. Indiana rated second among states with 44 and Ohio third with 39 makes.

1910

A new type of automobile body made its first appearance in the U. S. at the 10th National Automobile Show, the *torpedo*. This new body resembled a bathtub on wheels. The dashboard and its instruments were brought up closer to the driver, by means of a cowl, and the sides were extended upward, in some cases almost to shoulder height. Previously, motorists and their passengers had perched on cars, high and exposed; now they could sit in them, low and sheltered.

The year witnessed a trend toward standardization: many car makers changing transmission, motor starting or some other detail to bring their cars in line with the rest of the field. Clutches, however, still showed great variety—and little efficiency. Haynes used a contracting band; E-M-F had a leather-faced cone with cork insert; Rambler used the Borg & Beck single plate clutch; and Knox, Thomas and Stevens-Duryea featured a multiple-disc clutch.

Several important marketing changes took place. The Owen car, designed by Ralph Owen, offered as standard equipment: top, windshield, electric horn, electric-acetylene headlamps, electric-oil side lamps and an electric tail lamp.

1910—The Owen offered a top, windshield, electric horn, headlamps and a tail lamp as standard equipment.

1910—Motorists had their problems—poor roads, flat tires and almost no protection from the weather.

Another make, the Overland, announced its model "38" as a completely equipped car at $1,000 and was the first car in this class to carry as standard equipment at list price a top, windshield, lamps and magneto.

Benjamin Briscoe started the $16,000,000 United States Motor Car Corporation by combining and affiliating 130 separate companies with the firm. Some of these included Columbia Motor Car Company (successor to the Electric Vehicle Company that controlled the Selden patent), Brush Runabout Company, Alden Sampson Company, Dayton Motor Car Company and Maxwell-Briscoe Motor Company. (Over-expansion and lack of working capital forced United States Motor Car Company into receivership in September, 1912.)

Major Henry Souther headed the first Standardization Committee of the Society of Automobile Engineers after having directed standardization of parts as an activity of the A.L.A.M.

Reo announced its Speed Wagon, a low-priced light delivery truck.

Four Wheel Drive Auto Company, Clintonville, Wis., began manufacture of four-wheel drive vehicles.

milestones

Racing at Indianapolis Speedway this year featured a three-day series ending May 31, a three-day meet ending July 4, and two days of racing on Sept. 3 and 4.

American LaFrance Fire Engine Company, a fire engine manufacturer for 75 years, produced its first fire-fighting motor vehicle.

Automobile production started at the Ford Motor Company, Highland Park plant.

G. A. Schacht produced a complete line of trucks, from a 1,000-pound delivery unit to a three-ton chain-drive chassis.

Patents were issued on the Knight valve principle which was the forerunner of the Knight engine to be introduced in the U. S. in 1911.

Central Oil Co. built what may have been the first drive-in gasoline station with an island, in Detroit.

1911—The first transcontinental motor truck trip was made by a Saurer truck.

1911

The four-door car became popular at the 1911 National Automobile Show—nearly every manufacturer exhibited a model.

The first truck show in Madison Square Garden was held during the second week of the 11th National Automobile Show. The commercial phase of the show had 286 exhibitors, including 27 gasoline vehicles, 7 electric displays, and 18 motorcycle stands.

The hazards of starting engines by hand-cranking were reflected in the devices offered during the year as hopeful solutions of the problem. An Amplex had a compressed-air starter; also available for nearly all cars was the Geiszler Starting Device, an apparatus that was supposed to start the engine with an electric charge.

The Selden Patent, previously sustained in the U. S. District Court, was declared "valid but not infringed" by Ford and other manufacturers, in the U. S. Court of Appeals. (The payment of royalties that disrupted the early industry had come to an end.)

The first transcontinental motor-truck trip was made by a Saurer truck. The tour started on March 4 from Denver to Los Angeles and then to San Francisco. The truck was

1911—A Mack fire truck equipped with the first Gould pump.

then shipped by railroad back to Pueblo, Colorado, where the eastward leg of the journey began on June 12 under its own power for New York.

Pierce-Arrow added a five-ton truck to its line of passenger cars.

Diamond T Motor Car Company discontinued making passenger cars to concentrate on trucks.

General Motors Truck Company was formed by combining the Rapid and Reliance Truck Companies.

Hudson offered a "simplified chassis" (including a new four-cylinder block engine with cross-shaft in front carrying magneto and water pump) and multiple disc clutch.

International Motor Company (Mack) was formed by consolidation of Mack Bros. Motor Car Co., Saurer Motor Company, and Hewitt Motor Company.

Edward N. Hines originated painted center lines on highways in Wayne County (Detroit), Mich.

Chevrolet Motor Company of Michigan was organized in November, and production began.

The first 500-mile Indianapolis Speedway Race was won by Ray Harroun in a six-cylinder Marmon "Wasp," which introduced the first use of a rearview mirror in the U.S. Time: 6 hours, 42 minutes, 8 seconds.

For the first time, securities of automotive companies were listed on the New York Stock Exchange.

The Studebaker Corporation was formed, and manufacture of electric vehicles was discontinued to allow concentration on gasoline cars.

Knight sleeve-valve engines were introduced on the American market by Stearns, Stoddard-Dayton, and Columbia.

1912 The 12th National Automobile Show was sponsored by the new Automobile Board of Trade, formed to succeed the A.L.A.M. which disbanded in 1911.

1912—First Brockway truck.

The self-starter was the vogue at the 1912 show. There were 13 types of acetylene starters on display, 6 compressed air, 7 electric, 14 mechanical, 2 gasoline and 1—the Winton—exhaust gas.

At the commercial display, during the second week of the National Automobile Show, a five-ton Sampson coal truck was equipped with a compressed air device for dumping. Pope-Hartford's new truck, the first built by the company, had a tilting cab for access to the motor located under the seat. The new General Motors Trucks were exhibited for the first time.

Steward Motor Corporation was formed to make cars and trucks.

A Packard truck was the first truck to cross the continent from the East Coast to the Pacific Coast. It carried a three-ton load from New York to San Francisco in 46 days.

Cadillac adopted an electric starter developed by Charles F. Kettering of the Dayton Engineering Laboratories Company (Delco), along with a generator-battery lighting system.

milestones

The all-steel body developed by Edward Gowen Budd (an open car model), was offered by Oakland and Hupmobile.

Engine temperature indicator, the Boyce Moto-Meter, was introduced.

Chicago adopted an ordinance limiting horn use.

Electric car makers organized and held separate shows.

George A. Brockway, famous carriage-builder, organized the Brockway Motor Company to build trucks.

Philadelphia held a commercial wagon parade in which 500 trucks participated.

1913 A single ticket at the 13th National Automobile Show was good for the double showings in both Madison Square Garden and Grand Central Palace. The

1913—The Model T's popularity led the way to mass production. This overhead body drop at the Ford Highland Park (Mich.) plant was **one of** the features which speeded output.

popular priced cars were on display at the Palace and the high-priced and high-powered cars were at the Garden. A general trend toward sloping fronts and hoods was noticed at the 1913 show, along with strides toward smoother lines and longer curves. Designers went back to colonial days and Louis XIV coaches for the popular coupes, which flared out at the top.

Dealers, worried about used car sales, asked the National Association of Automobile Manufacturers to investigate.

The National Automobile Chamber of Commerce was organized (predecessor of the Automobile Manufacturers Association, Inc.) through a merger of the Automobile Board of Trade and the National Association of Automobile Manufacturers.

A standard 90-day warranty for passenger cars and commercial vehicles was recommended to its members by the NACC.

Chevrolet operations were moved to Flint and merged with the Little Motor Car Company.

Installment paper was used in automobile financing.

Cadillac won the Dewar Trophy for the second time. The award was given for the development of the electric starter.

Wire wheels were offered as standard equipment on several production cars.

The Bendix drive for electric starters was shown for the first time.

Ford production attained a rate of a thousand cars a day.

Kissel Kar introduced a new wrap-around windshield on several of its 1913 models, though it wasn't called by that name.

The National Association of Automobile Advertising Men was organized.

Packard used forced feed lubrication and worm bevel gears.

The first Chevrolet assembly plant was opened.

milestones

The Thomas B. Jeffery Company introduced the four-wheel-drive Quad truck.

Carl Graham Fisher, who was promoting an ocean-to-ocean highway, turned his pledges over to the Lincoln Highway Association.

Pierce-Arrow put headlamps on the mudguards.

Spaulding touring cars were equipped with folding backs on front seats in order to convert into beds. Electric reading lamps and air mattresses were included.

Gulf Oil Company was the first U. S. petroleum firm to distribute free road maps.

1914 The 14th National Automobile Show at Grand Central Palace in New York City was sponsored by the newly formed National Automobile Chamber of Commerce.

1914—First stop sign used to control traffic was in Detroit.

57

Automobiles of America

A novelty of the 1914 show was the display of cyclecars. There were five such showings of these tiny one- and two-passenger vehicles. One cyclecar, the Argo, was priced at $295. The first cyclecars had appeared in 1913, and had been dismissed as "toys" and "a silly fad" by most motorists and vehicle manufacturers. After their formal debut at the National Automobile Show, the market for them expanded enormously. The craze was, however, short-lived; few of the little "economy" vehicles remained on the market after 1915.

During the show week Henry Ford announced a $5 minimum daily wage (including a profit-sharing plan) for all non-salary employees over 22 years of age, and an eight-hour day.

Chevrolet discontinued its six-cylinder model, and began making four-cylinder cars.

Cadillac developed and introduced a V-8 high-speed automobile engine.

The Rambler's name was changed to Jeffery.

Horace and John Dodge started production of the Dodge automobile.

Alfred Reeves became general manager of the National Automobile Chamber of Commerce.

Hand brake at driver's left was introduced by Packard.

Maxwell offered an adjustable driver's seat.

A Detroit ordinance prohibited gasoline pumps at curbs.

The first stop sign to control traffic was installed in Detroit.

Electric traffic lights were installed in Cleveland, Ohio, in August.

Henry Ford announced plans to rebate between $40 to $60 to each purchaser of a new Ford Model T providing the Ford Motor Company sold more than 300,000 cars from August 1914 to August 1915.

The traffic department of the National Automobile

Chamber of Commerce suggested dimensions of automobile box cars to railroad companies. The NACC also drafted a road-building code, setting forth the views of the automobile manufacturers on highway conditions.

The Society of Automobile Engineers organized several research committees to study gas-electric vehicles, kerosene carburetors, greases, engine characteristics, governors, and non-electric continuous torque transmission.

Buick changed to a six-cylinder engine.

1915 The outstanding feature of the 1915 National Automobile Show was the eight-cylinder engine. Cadillac, King, Briggs-Detroiter and Remington all offered such engines. Cadillac introduced a V-8 several months before.

Another auto show attraction was the "sociable" body offered by Packard, Winton, Kline and Kissell, with the corridor or salon body with an aisle between the two front seats allowing passengers to move freely between front and back seats. Another novel car was the Gadabout roadster with a wicker body. The National had another original seating arrangement—four armchairs that could be moved on casters in any direction.

There were no cyclecars exhibited at the 1915 show, thus signaling the end of the short-lived fad.

Briscoe and Owen offered convertible roadsters on which the top, when down, was completely concealed at the rear of the body.

Packard added a 12-cylinder model, the "Twin Six," America's first, and the first automobile engine with aluminum pistons.

Franklin put the spare tire in the trunk of its roadster model.

Ford production passed one million cars.

Automobiles of America

1915—This Saxon, priced $395, illustrates the trend to light cars in this period.

General Motors declared its first dividend ($50 a share) on common stock.

The Liberty Bell was transported from Philadelphia to the Panama-Pacific Exposition by a White Truck.

A solid metal wheel was offered on the Jeffery truck.

Demountable rims replaced the clincher types.

Cadillac offered tilt-beam headlamps.

Oldsmobile offered a top and windshield as standard equipment.

World War I began to create material shortages.

During this year a great wave of five-cent jitneys arose in various cities that had been hit by transit strikes.

Automobiles were admitted to Yellowstone National Park on Aug. 1 over a carefully prepared one-way route.

Truck production began to assume importance as the war in Europe demonstrated the worth of motor trucks.

milestones

Ford Motor Company refunded $50 to those who purchased Model T's between August 1914 and August 1915. Checks were distributed Aug. 15.

Prism lenses for headlights made their first appearance.

There were approximately 450 automotive and auto parts manufacturers in the U. S. by the end of 1915.

1916 New models displayed at the 16th National Automobile Show generally featured lower prices and more powerful engines. Most of the cars were under $1,250, including many six-cylinder models. Five manufacturers—Enger, Haynes, National, Packard and Pathfinder—exhibited 12-cylinder models.

New design features noted at the 1916 show included the slanted windshields, and double-cowl bodies, in which

1915—The Briscoe featured a "cyclops-eye" headlight.

Automobiles of America

"tonneau cowls" separated front and back seats. Increased use of wire wheels was also noted.

Studebaker displayed a gold chassis reportedly worth $25,000 at the 1916 National Automobile Show. The most unusual car exhibited, however, was the light-weight Marmon 34, with aluminum body and fenders, aluminum engine castings and other aluminum parts. The seven-passenger touring car, with a wheelbase of 136 inches, weighed only 3,540 pounds.

Charles W. Nash left General Motors to take over the Thomas B. Jeffery Company and form Nash Motors Company.

A General Motors one-ton truck established a record for an endurance run by hauling a load of canned milk from Seattle to New York in 30 days.

The number of makes offering V-8 engines grew to 18

1916—Passage of the Federal Road Aid Act was the beginning of a nation-wide system of interstate highways.

models. They included: Abbott, Apperson, Briscoe, Cadillac, Cole, Daniels, Hollier, Jackson, King, Monarch, Oakland, Oldsmobile, Peerless, Pilot, Ross, Scripps-Booth, Standard and Stearns-Knight.

The Fordson Tractor was announced by Ford Motor Company.

Ford bought a factory site on the banks of the Rouge River in Dearborn, Mich.

The U. S. Army used a fleet of trucks as a supply train for an expeditionary force in Mexico.

The National Automobile Chamber of Commerce passed a resolution branding the advertisement of deferred payments as "unethical."

United Motors Corporation was formed with Alfred P. Sloan, Jr., as president.

Hand-operated windshield wipers, stop lights, and rearview mirrors appeared as standard equipment on several cars.

Cross licensing agreements pertaining to patents became effective in the auto industry.

Prices of gasoline and automobiles advanced during the year, and economy tests of stock cars became so numerous that the Society of Automobile Engineers published requirements for such tests if they were to be recognized.

The Federal Aid Road Act, signed by President Woodrow Wilson on July 11, was the first Federal law aimed at the establishment of a nation-wide system of interstate highways. The act provided for the construction of "rural public roads" and defined them as "any public road over which the United States mails now are or may hereafter be transported." Federal contributions would not exceed 50 per cent of the total cost of each project, and the matching portion would be furnished by the states. The act also put more emphasis upon the organization of a state highway department before a state could receive Federal highway aid.

1917—The first Nash-designed car had a six-cylinder valve-in-head engine.

1917

All car and truck manufacturers offered full co-operation to the government as the United States entered World War I.

Many automotive companies participated in the development and production of Liberty aircraft engines, designed by Jesse G. Vincent and E. J. Hall.

The first Nash appeared, with a six-cylinder valve-in-head engine.

Henry M. Leland, former president of Cadillac, formed the Lincoln Motor Company.

Chevrolet offered a V-8 model.

Studebaker developed and adopted an internal manifold hot-spot to vaporize the fuel mixture more efficiently.

The Society of Automobile Engineers became the Society of Automotive Engineers (S.A.E.).

Paige introduced a coupe with a rumble seat and a V-type windshield.

Hudson Motor Car Company organized the Essex Motor Car Company to manufacture a light car.

64

Several closed cars exhibited at the 1917 National Automobile Show were equipped with heaters.

Frederick Furber developed a built-in radiator shutter which was introduced by Columbia.

John North Willys and Col. Charles Clifton represented the automotive industry on the National Industrial Conference Board.

The largest truck contract was announced between Kelly-Springfield Co., and the United States Circus Corp., for 100 trucks. The circus planned to use the 3½-ton trucks instead of rail cars for transporting the tent show.

By the end of the year various boards for organizing the motor industry were formed to bring about the standardization of design for war production. The result of large war contracts was seen in a considerable number of mergers and an extraordinary number of capital stock increases.

1918 The country was in the midst of war when the 18th National Automobile Show was held at New York's Grand Central Palace. There were fuel shortages of coal and petroleum, due mainly to the nation's almost total dependence for transportation, on war-burdened railroads, and talk of the possibility that motor vehicle production would be curtailed, or even stopped altogether. As far as official Washington was concerned, motor vehicles were dispensable luxuries, and the wartime excise levies taxed them as if they were tobacco, whiskey, furs, perfume or jewelry.

Factories were turned over to war work, men drafted into the army, and women took their places at benches, machine tools, and even in repair shops. The industry's war production included shells, helmets, caissons, aircraft engines, tractors, tanks, naval craft, anti-aircraft guns, gun carriages, artillery recoil mechanisms, in addition to military vehicles.

1918—Motor trucks proved their value in the first World War. Typical are these White two-ton models shown in convoy in France.

    Because of the war, accessory and automobile manufacturers offered many new devices for prolonging the life of cars, and introduced carburetors designed to use low-grade fuels and even kerosene.

    There were heatless days and gasless Sundays to conserve fuel; everything was done to check the use of motor cars unless vehicle travel was necessary. Motorless Sundays ended Oct. 13.

    Designers borrowed from the armored cars and other military vehicles that were produced at the time. Four cars—Paige, Oldsmobile, McFarlan and Anderson—had steel wheels that resembled military wheels. Straight lines, higher hoods and the steel wheels gave many of the new models a war-like appearance.

Closed cars (which were 10 per cent of production) had more glass area in 1918, giving more visibility. More attention was given to the driver's seat of closed cars for those owners who wanted to do their own driving, their chauffeurs having become part of the war effort.

The first unit of highway construction authorized under the Federal Aid Road Act of 1916 was completed Jan. 30, from Richmond to the Alameda County line in California. The 2.55 mile road was built at a cost of $53,938.85, of which Federal aid totaled $24,244.56.

Four-wheel hydraulic brakes were developed by Malcolm Loughead of California. Along with E. A. Featherstone, D. O. Scott and Otto C. Lang, Loughead (Lockheed) formed a company to promote the patents which were used later (in 1920) on production automobiles.

Passenger car production, already curtailed by plant facility shortages, was given a government steel allocation to balance their inventories for building 50 per cent of the cars produced during the previous year. After the armistice in November, the percentage was increased to 75 per cent.

White discontinued passenger car production to concentrate on trucks.

Chevrolet became part of General Motors.

Nash became the world's largest producer of trucks this year with an Army contract for 11,494 units.

The National Automobile Dealers Association was organized in Washington in response to a call from F.W.A. Vesper to combat a threat to take all men out of the dealer shops.

As the year closed, the price situation puzzled all car makers. The fact was that cheaper materials were expected, but prices did not drop. The troubles of readjustment were at hand.

1919—Essex helped boost the popularity of the economical closed car.

1919

Few new ideas were exhibited at the 19th National Automobile Show; there was too little time after the armistice to work on new models. Some manufacturers, however, did bring out changes in design and detail, particularly better brakes, wiring, and suspension. The war had taught ways of improving these three parts. A low-priced, four cylinder Essex, made by Hudson, was the only new car at the Show. A white Daniels sport touring car displayed a golf bag attachment over the running board for the eager golfer who liked to be ready when he passed a country club.

The flat rate system of repair was tried out.

Ford produced 750,000 cars, more than one-third of the industry's total output.

1919—A Hupmobile touring car at Yosemite Falls, Calif.

General Motors Acceptance Corporation was formed.

Studebaker discontinued carriage making to concentrate on motor vehicles.

G. A. Schacht perfected a "two-range" truck transmission featuring eight forward speeds and two reverse speeds.

Henry Ford bought out minority stockholders, and Edsel Bryant Ford became president of Ford Motor Company.

Front and rear bumpers were offered as standard equipment on the Westcott touring car.

Having built and sold 30,000 small trucks since 1908, Autocar adopted a short wheelbase and engine-under-seat design for 2- and 5-ton trucks.

The world's first three-color traffic control light was installed in Detroit, and Detroit police pioneered in offering safety instruction in school classrooms.

Car makers were swamped with orders by May, but were unable to fill them because of parts and material shortages.

Strikes, rising wages, and a shortage of automobiles were major problems confronting the automotive industry in July as dealers were clamoring for new models.

General Motors bought an interest in Fisher Body Company, and Nash bought an interest in the Seaman Body Corporation.

Indirect lighting of instruments on the dash appeared on

69

some cars. Approximately 90 per cent of all passenger cars made during the year were open models, i.e., touring cars and roadsters.

1920 The first post-war National Automobile Show sponsored by the National Automobile Chamber of Commerce was held Jan. 3 through Jan. 10. Closed cars continued to gain over open cars (119 closed models in 1920 compared with 79 in the previous show). The marked change in the cars displayed was the increase in the number of owner-driven, as opposed to chauffeur-driven cars. Convertible cars had almost disappeared—only two were displayed at the show. (At that time, the term "convertible" meant a touring car or roadster which could be purchased, for about $500, a "California top"—a solid-roofed structure with glazed windows—which could be stored in a stable or garage in summer, but would replace the folding fabric top in autumn.)

Sloping windshields were evident everywhere. Also, heaters were standard equipment. Wire wheels were more numerous than wooden artillery wheels.

Buick and McFarlan offered solid metal wheels on passenger cars.

A compass and camera were offered as standard equipment on the Templar touring roadster. Flower vases were part of the standard equipment on the sedan model.

General Motors Research Corporation was organized under the direction of C. F. Kettering.

Duesenberg appeared; it was the first U. S. car with a straight-eight engine and first licensee to use hydraulic four-wheel brakes developed by Malcolm Loughead in 1918.

Packard introduced the Lanchester vibration dampener.

William C. Durant again lost control of General Motors, and Pierre S. duPont was named president.

milestones

1920—Bullet-shaped headlamps were one of the features on the Kissel. The hood ventilator cooled the engine in the summer and permitted fumes to escape.

1920—Dort touring car.

In May the manager of the Kansas City Federal Reserve Bank declined to discount any paper from member banks based on passenger car stocks. This action caused great concern within the automotive industry, for it meant a tightening of credit.

A railroad strike curtailed transportation of freight. The motor truck proved its qualities by carrying great loads of long and short haul freight. Freight embargoes also promoted driveaways and river shipments of automobiles.

In August, a bankers' committee took over the Maxwell plant.

A nation-wide program of highway research on a large scale was launched. As a result of problems in highway construction and maintenance, the Highway Research Board of the National Research Council was organized. Tests on experimental roads were conducted at Arlington, Va., Pittsburg, Calif., and near Springfield, Ill.

By October, completion of Federal-aid highway projects totaled 191 miles.

Mack had rubber engine mountings and rubber spring shackles.

1921 Most popular body type at the 21st National Automobile Show was the open touring car, seating five, six, or seven passengers. Glass windshield wings made their eastern debut—the first seen at a New York show, although they had been popular for years in Southern California.

The post-war depression brought a drastic curtailment of sales.

Studebaker developed nickel-molybdenum steel for commercial use.

Ford weathered a financial crisis with the help of dealers. Ford car production passed the five million mark, or 55.45 per cent of the industry's total output.

milestones

Hudson offered a coach, the Essex, priced at only $300 more than a touring car.

Fred M. Zeder, Owen R. Skelton and Carl Breer incorporated as consulting automotive engineers to begin design of cars with new concepts. Later the Chrysler was one of their cars.

W. C. Durant retired from General Motors directorate and organized Durant Motors, Inc.

Nickel plating appeared on radiators and lamps.

Cadillac offered thermostatic control of carburetion.

On March 4, Warren G. Harding became the first U. S. President to ride in an automobile to his inauguration. The car was a Packard Twin-Six.

1921—A distinctive feature of the Willys-Knight was the sleeve-valve engine that reportedly "improved with use."

1921—The famous Stutz Bearcat.

Cadillac moved into a new factory on Clark Avenue, Detroit, Mich.

Detroit police experimented with synchronized traffic signal lights, and raised-platform safety zones.

The General Motors Building in Detroit was opened, and became the home of many departments of the corporation.

Herbert Hoover, Secretary of Commerce, asked the National Automobile Chamber of Commerce to appoint a committee to promote automotive business in the U. S. and abroad. J. Walter Drake was made chairman, and, later that year, the Automotive Division of the Bureau of Foreign and Domestic Commerce in the Department of Commerce was organized, with Gordon Lee as the manager.

One of the innovations offered during the year was a

milestones

back-up lamp which was turned on automatically when the car was reversed. This was combined with the tail-lamp on the Wills-St. Claire.

On Dec. 9, Dr. Thomas Midgley, Jr. and associates proved effectiveness of tetraethyl lead in gasoline.

1922 A new body style at the 1922 National Automobile Show was the roadster-coupe, primarily a business car, which consisted of a roadster body with a permanent top.

Balloon tires and air cleaners were introduced on passenger cars.

1922—The Peerless, one of the heavy cars of the 'twenties.

75

Ford bought Lincoln Motor Company at a receiver's sale and began production of higher-priced cars.

Durant bought Locomobile and Mason.

The earliest known electrically interlocked traffic signal system was installed in Houston, Texas.

Charles M. Schwab gained control of Stutz.

Elwood Haynes received the John Scott medal for metallurgical achievement in stainless steel, stellite, and chrome iron.

Several cars introduced a gasoline gauge on the instrument panel.

An Oldsmobile set a record, traveling 1,000 miles in 15 hours.

Automobile insurance policies were revised to cover the actual value rather than the purchase price of a car. Declining automobile prices led many insurance firms to believe motorists were deliberately destroying their cars to collect claims covering their depreciation on their automobiles.

In October Ford Motor Company astonished the automotive industry with a $50 reduction on all models.

Motor-driven snow removal equipment opened 27,096 miles of snow-covered highways from the East Coast through the Mid-West. This was the first concerted effort by many newly established state highway departments to use the motor truck in snow removal.

1923 Most popular body styles at the 23rd National Automobile Show were the five-passenger closed car and the permanent-top phaeton. The four-door phaetons featured windows that lowered or could be removed for storage within the car.

Optimistic predictions over a peak production year proved correct. It was an all-time high record that stood until 1925. A total of 4,034,012 motor vehicles was sold by the manufacturers.

1923—The Star, Durant's bid for the light-car field, offered the first production station wagon.

Dodge offered steel closed bodies, in which sheet steel replaced wood everywhere except on the roof, which was an insert constructed of wood bows and slats covered by waterproof fabric.

Packard introduced the first mass-produced straight-eight L-head engines.

Springfield Body Corporation offered a factory-installed radio as optional equipment.

Zeder, Skelton, Breer Engineering Company joined Walter Chrysler, then board chairman of Maxwell-Chalmers Corp., to develop a new car to carry the Chrysler name.

Four-wheel brakes, foot-controlled headlamp dimmer switches and power-operated windshield wipers were adopted by several manufacturers as standard equipment.

"Ethyl" gasoline was first put on the market Feb. 2, in Dayton, Ohio, by General Motors Research Corporation.

Ford Motor Company announced a weekly purchase plan under which a customer was issued a coupon book and made at least $5 weekly payments to the local dealer. When

Somewhere West of Laramie

SOMEWHERE west of Laramie there's a broncho-busting, steer-roping girl who knows what I'm talking about. She can tell what a sassy pony, that's a cross between greased lightning and the place where it hits, can do with eleven hundred pounds of steel and action when he's going high, wide and handsome.

The truth is—the Playboy was built for her.

Built for the lass whose face is brown with the sun when the day is done of revel and romp and race.

She loves the cross of the wild and the tame.

There's a savor of links about that car—of laughter and lilt and light—a hint of old loves—and saddle and quirt. It's a brawny thing—yet a graceful thing for the sweep o' the Avenue.

Step into the Playboy when the hour grows dull with things gone dead and stale.

Then start for the land of real living with the spirit of the lass who rides, lean and rangy, into the red horizon of a Wyoming twilight.

JORDAN
JORDAN MOTOR CAR COMPANY, Inc., Cleveland, Ohio

1923—A new style of automobile advertising was pioneered by the Jordan Motor Car Company.

the total price of the car had been paid, the dealer delivered the car. The lowest price Model T was the runabout, selling at $265. (At the end of two years, more than 300,000 Ford cars were sold under the plan.)

With transmission gears locked in high, E. G. "Cannon Ball" Baker drove an Oldsmobile from New York to Los Angeles in 12½ days. The car was equipped with large gasoline tanks, and refueling enroute was accomplished by raising the rear wheels off the ground in order to keep the engine running.

Ford production exceeded two million cars during the year.

Alfred P. Sloan, Jr., became president of General Motors.

1924—Not one electric, not one steamer, as the 24th National Automobile Show made the four-acre display at the 258th Field Artillery Armory the first 100 per cent gasoline National Automobile Show. Top mechanical attractions at the show were the increased number of cars featuring four-wheel brakes and balloon tires as standard equipment.

milestones

Six-cylinder vehicles were the most prized, a sensation being the Essex Coach priced under $1,000. Also of interest was the baked-enamel finish on low-priced cars.

The Chrysler light six, introduced by Maxwell-Chalmers Corp., featured a high-compression engine (4.5-to-1), seven-

1924—Flint Six touring car sported disc wheels and front bumper.

1924—Cars let families combine city living with country pleasures. A Model T Ford.

bearing crankshaft, four-wheel hydraulic brakes and a replaceable cartridge oil filter.

In addition to Packard and Duesenberg, straight-eight engines were offered by Auburn, Hupmobile, Jordan, Rickenbacker and several engine manufacturers.

General Motors Proving Ground at Milford, Mich., was completed.

Ethyl Corporation was organized by General Motors and Standard Oil (New Jersey).

The Winton Company discontinued manufacture of automobiles. Later, the firm was reorganized to produce Diesel engines.

Major Award Trophy was presented to the White Motor Company by the U.S.S.R. for reliability and endurance.

The publication "MoToR," edited 21 years for car owners, became a trade magazine.

Ford Motor Company produced its ten-millionth car.

There was now one automobile for every seven persons in the U. S.

A Reo motor bus made a transcontinental trip.

Two-filament bulbs, permitting use of direct and diverted light, appeared in headlights of some cars.

Nash Motors bought LaFayette Motors Corp.

Hudson announced its price on a coach which was $5 more than an open car.

Ford began manufacturing accessories for Ford cars.

Adoption of S.A.E. standards saved automobile manufacturers an estimated $124 for each car produced.

1925 The most discussed mechanical aspect of new cars at the 25th National Automobile Show was the continued trend toward straight-eight engines. Balloon tires created the need for easier steering systems which were offered in 1925 models.

Other car features widely discussed were rumble seats, one-piece windshields, mohair upholstery and crank-type window lifts. Synthetic quick-drying pyroxylin finishes that could be sprayed on and baked gave the industry a wide range of colors in high-gloss finishes.

Accessories available to the automotive consumer included: balloon tire jacks, stop signals, locking radiator caps, trunk racks, all-weather enclosures for touring cars, mirrors, ash-trays, cigar lighters and heat indicators.

For the first time, more closed than open models were sold.

General Motors acquired control of the Yellow Truck and Coach Manufacturing Company.

A.C.F. acquired Fageol Motors Company of Ohio and moved operations to Detroit.

General Motors Truck Company introduced a one-ton truck with four-wheel brakes.

1925—Wills Sainte Claire had balloon tires.

Maxwell-Chalmers was reorganized as Chrysler Corporation.
Ford production exceeded 9,000 units a day.
Fisher Body acquired Fleetwood, a custom body-building company.
More than 150 electric railway systems were now operating motor buses.
Chrysler offered rubber engine mounts.
The 25-millionth U. S. motor vehicle was produced.
A national chain of drive-it-yourself stations was established.
Front and rear bumpers were now standard equipment.
Automobile Daily News began publication (later the name changed to Automotive News).
Uniform markings for Federal-aid highways were adopted. Even numbers were assigned to east-west roads, odd numbers to running north-south.

1926

A feature of 1926 models at the 26th National Automobile Show was better vision, made possible by narrower pillars. Steel posts made this possible. Another windshield feature was the "shock-proof" glass offered by Stutz and Rickenbacker. The Stutz windshield had wire running horizontally through the glass at intervals of several inches, while the Rickenbacker windshield was a sandwich of transparent celluloid between two sheets of glass.

Other engineering features of the year included heavier crankshafts, shorter strokes and faster engines.

A novel car was the new Rickenbacker sport sedan, a low car with no running boards and a fender-mounted spare tire. The radiator, wire wheels, lamps and other exterior trim were brass finished, while the bumpers (shaped to resemble airplane propellers) were brass-bound mahogany. Gold plating was used on the interior hardware.

1926—Rickenbacker sport sedan, guaranteed to do 90 m.p.h.

A few models had small glass "eyes" at the rear of the headlamps to enable the driver to see if his lights were on.

Three companion cars were introduced at the National Automobile Show. Ajax, a Nash-built six-cylinder car, and Moon's Diana had been on the road a few months earlier, but the show was their first "public" appearance. Pontiac, made by Oakland (General Motors) was first displayed at the industry-sponsored show.

E. G. "Cannon Ball" Baker drove a fully loaded two-ton GM truck from New York to San Francisco in record-breaking time of five days, 17 hours, 30 minutes.

Packard offered hypoid gears which permitted the propeller shaft to be lower, thus making it possible to lower the body line.

Ford announced plans to discontinue manufacture of Model T.

83

Automobiles of America

General Motors bought Fisher Body Corporation.
Ford inaugurated the five-day work week.
All outstanding Nash preferred stock was retired.
Dr. Graham Edgar devised the octane scale for gasoline.
Chandler offered a one-shot lubrication system.
Hot water car heaters were introduced in the U.S.
Oldsmobile introduced chromium plating.
Reo introduced the Flying Cloud models.

1927 A definite trend toward the small car was apparent at the 27th National Automobile Show. In addition to the new Erskine, made by Studebaker, other

1927—Ford introduced the famous Model A.

84

small cars included the Little Marmon, in several models and styles; the Whippet and Whippet Six, made by Willys; and the Jordan Little Playboy. Four-wheel brakes were standard equipment on virtually all the cars at the show. Air cleaners, gasoline filters, crankcase ventilators, oil filters, automatic windshield wipers, balloon tires and rear-view mirrors were all becoming common.

The Packard and Little Marmon were equipped with hypoid rear axles, devised in response to demands for lower cars.

Cadillac introduced the LaSalle V-8.

The Fageol brothers organized the Twin Coach Company.

Mack adopted a vacuum brake booster and four-wheel brakes on trucks and fire engines.

Carl Breer began the study of aerodynamics in relation to automobile body design, which led to the "Airflow" design and monocoque type of body and chassis construction.

Graham-Paige Motors Corporation succeeded Paige-Detroit Motor Car Company.

Studebaker celebrated its Diamond Jubilee.

General Motors stockholders received $134,836,081 in dividends.

Nash announced that employees owned $20,000,000 worth of stock.

An electric drive with no gear shift was developed by E. M. Frazer.

Packard built a 500-acre proving ground with a two and one half-mile concrete oval test track at Utica, Michigan.

Ford produced the last (mass-produced) Model T on May 31. A total of 15,007,033 Model T's were assembled by the company since it was introduced in 1908. After a six-month changeover period, Ford introduced the Model A.

Automobiles of America

Chrysler shareholders received $10,000,000 in dividends.

Concrete mixers, mounted on White heavy-duty trucks, appeared on the Pacific Coast.

Lockheed (Malcolm Loughead) introduced an internal expanding hydraulic brake system.

1928 Lower prices and an increase in the number of eight-cylinder cars were two predominant features of the new models in the 28th National Automobile Show. Higher compression ratios, combined with better fuel, brought about a higher horsepower average for the industry.

Cadillac introduced a synchromesh transmission, and safety plate glass in all windows.

Chandler offered Westinghouse vacuum brakes that reduced pedal pressure by two-thirds.

Most Graham-Paige models featured a four-speed transmission.

1928—Reo's Flying Cloud sport coupe with a rumble seat was typical of a popular body style of the later 1920's.

milestones

Chrysler purchased Dodge Brothers, Inc., July 30.
Studebaker acquired control of Pierce-Arrow.
Ford offered shatter-proof glass as standard equipment.
Coast-to-coast bus service began.
Brockway gained control of the Indiana Truck Corporation.
Buick celebrated its silver anniversary.
Chrysler entered the low-priced field with the Plymouth, and offered the De Soto as another new line of cars.
The publication "Fleet Owner" made its appearance.
Chevrolet reverted to six-cylinder engines instead of four's.

1929 Public interest in new automobiles reached such heights that most Manhattan hotel lobbies were packed with displays of cars during the 1929 National Automobile Show. A number of redesigned models were first displayed at the show. Auburn had one streamlined

1929—The Marquette model 30 was introduced by Buick.

1929—The Viking with a V-8 engine was Oldsmobile's companion car.

aluminum model that resembled an airplane cabin; Franklin's *le Pirate* model concealed the running boards under the doors.

Hupmobile acquired two Chandler-Cleveland plants in Cleveland.

Kleiber Motor Company experimented with Diesel-powered trucks.

More than 80,000 De Sotos were sold during the first year of production.

Tail lamps on both sides of the car were introduced.

The Aerocar, a house trailer, provided a new form of transportation and mobile living.

Cord offered front-wheel drive.

Radios were offered as optional equipment on many automobiles.

Chrysler adopted a down-draft carburetor for better fuel distribution and increased efficiency.

Nash offered an eight-cylinder engine for the first time.

Ford raised its wage scale to $7-a-day minimum.

Companion cars were offered by two major manufacturers. Oldsmobile introduced the Viking, a V-8; Buick offered the Marquette.

Motor vehicle production broke all records in 1929. Output totaled 5,337,087 units (the greatest until 1949).

Almost 90 per cent of all American cars sold in 1929 were closed models (sedans, coaches, coupes, etc.), whereas almost 90 per cent sold in 1919 had been open models.

1930

Confusion was apparent on prices of new models at the 30th National Automobile Show. Four makes had a higher price tag, while five other lines reduced prices.

Cadillac offered V-16 and V-12 engines. The new V-16 engine, rated at 185 horsepower, had a complete fuel system for each bank of cylinders, and a power brake operated by the manifold vacuum.

Studebaker introduced free-wheeling.

Graham-Paige offered rubber-cushioned chassis springs and aluminum pistons with Invar struts for reduced weight and added strength.

Chrysler offered an eight-cylinder engine for the first time.

The National Automobile Chamber of Commerce launched a plan which would withdraw 360,000 antiquated motor vehicles from use.

American Austin Car Company was organized to build the Austin Bantam.

Studebaker developed a carburetor intake silencer.

Cadillac, Chrysler, Dodge, LaSalle, Marmon and Roosevelt cars were wired for radio installation.

Pontiac developed tin plated pistons and pressed steel axle housing.

Automobiles of America

Plymouth franchises were given to all Chrysler, De Soto and Dodge dealers.

Police cars were being equipped with radios.

Cadillac offered automatic hydraulic tappet clearance adjusters.

1930—Cord featured a front-wheel-drive.

1930—Austin Bantam had a 75-inch wheel base and was powered by a 14.8 horsepower four-cylinder engine.

1931—An unlimited number of custom-built body designs were available on standardized straight-eight on Duesenberg chassis.

1931

With all business still in decline, the 31st National Automobile Show reflected the automobile manufacturers' dilemma quite clearly: whether to risk vast sums on completely new models, or reduce drastically the prices of existing models. Most of the makers had the larger, more powerful, more luxurious cars that the public had signified it most wanted until the chill of the Great Depression had set in. They now offered these big cars at reduced prices.

During National Auto Show week, the National Automobile Chamber of Commerce passed a resolution favoring the grouping of new model announcements in November and December. This plan had a twofold aim: it was hoped that buying would be stimulated in the fall and winter, rather than have it create a rush every spring. By thus changing buying habits, it was hoped that the unhappy conditions of summertime rush and wintertime decline in factory work might be changed for the better.

The Oakland line of cars was discontinued in favor of its companion car, the Pontiac, which offered eight and six-cylinder models.

A GMC truck and refrigerated trailer delivered 21 tons of California fruit to New York in 117 hours running time—

1931—The double-cowl Packard phaeton was one of the luxury cars of the period. It has been considered by many as a "classic" car.

demonstrating the efficiency of the motor truck as practical for transporting perishable goods.

Plymouth offered "floating power" rubber engine mountings designed to give the engine an independent axis.

Buick adopted an eight-cylinder engine.

Free-wheeling was available on Auburn, Chrysler, De Soto, De Vaux, Dodge, Essex, Graham, Hudson, Hupmobile, Lincoln, Marmon, Peerless, Pierce-Arrow, Plymouth, Studebaker, Willys and Willys-Knight.

Oldsmobile adopted a synchromesh transmission.

Pontiac produced a radiator grille made of pressed steel.

The 50 millionth U. S. motor vehicle was produced during the year.

A retractable hardtop convertible was patented by B. B. Ellerbeck of Salt Lake City.

A standard warranty for passenger cars for 90 days or 4,000 miles, and 90 days and/or 5,000 miles for commercial vehicles was recommended by the National Automobile Chamber of Commerce directors.

1932 The year opened in the gloomy economic climate of a deepening depression. It was destined to be the poorest auto production year since 1918. In general, the new models were heavier, but the power had not been increased correspondingly. Five makes displayed 12-cylinder models. Convertibles, both phaetons and coupes with disappearing tops, were popular at the exhibition.

Chrysler this year strove for silence with rubber-mounted engines and improvements to silence fans, air-intake and exhaust.

Ford offered a new model with a V-8 engine to replace the Model A.

Graham introduced full-skirted fenders.

Pierce-Arrow introduced hydraulic valve-lifters.

Buick, Cadillac, Chrysler, De Soto, Dodge and LaSalle offered vacuum-operated clutches. Nearly all other makes featured free wheeling, which could be engaged by a control on the dash of the car.

Inside visors began to replace outside shades in an effort to decrease wind-resistance.

Oldsmobile and Packard offered automatic chokes on their 1932 models.

Backed by Walter C. Marmon, Col. Arthur William Sydney Herrington, military transport engineer, began

1932—First year for the Ford V-8.

Automobiles of America

production of all-wheel-drive vehicles for lumber and petroleum industries.

White acquired Indiana Truck.

1933 Aerodynamic streamlining was beginning to be noticed at the 33rd National Automobile Show. The skirted fender, V-front grille, sweeping tail lines, and slanted windshield were more prominent. Economy seemed to be important. Gasoline mileage was advertised by many manufacturers, and durability was stressed by nearly all companies.

Power brakes became available on a number of makes.

Fisher bodies offered "No-Draft Ventilation," with the front section of the side windows pivoted on the top and bottom to control the flow of air inside the car.

Use of the accelerator pedal for starting the engine was adopted on several makes to eliminate a separate starter pedal on the floor.

White developed a new type of bus, a coach with under-the-floor, horizontally-opposed 12-cylinder "pancake" engine.

Valve seat inserts, independent wheel suspension, and reflex glass tail- and stop-lights were introduced.

A drive-in theater was opened in Camden, N. J.

1933—Depression and the ravages of nature combined to drive thousands to pack their belongings on the car or in trailers and leave home for better opportunities.

1934—De Soto's Airflow model.

1934

Two features that drew most attention at the 34th National Automobile Show were streamlining and the independent suspension of the front wheels. Streamlining was particularly stressed by the new and quite revolutionary De Soto and Chrysler "Airflow" models. Hupmobile and, to a degree, LaSalle also featured it. Nearly all cars had one of the three forms of independent front wheel suspension then shown.

Reo was the only car at the show with a completely automatic transmission, though several makers had automatic de-clutching devices. A low-priced Graham had a mechanical supercharger that forced air into the carburetor. Several makes had rear fender covers, then called "pants."

There was a noticeable trend to larger cars on the new models, even among those of lower price. Nearly all models were longer, wider and offered more room inside. Several were even wide enough to seat three persons comfortably in the front seat. Doors were made wider; on some models door openings were cut back over fenders to provide more room for entering and leaving the vehicle.

Chevrolet produced its 10-millionth car to celebrate its 23rd anniversary.

Chrysler and De Soto offered an automatic transmission overdrive on Airflow models.

The name of the National Automobile Chamber of Commerce was changed to the Automobile Manufacturers Association, Inc. (AMA).

Studebaker emerged from receivership.

Cadillac introduced a high output generator and voltage regulator to keep the battery fully charged for extra loads.

Reo offered a gear shift on the dash.

Radio controls, built into the instrument panel, appeared on several makes.

All General Motors cars—Cadillac, Buick, Oldsmobile, Pontiac and Chevrolet—offered the first production all-steel turret top in December for their line of 1935 models.

1935—The first Lincoln-Zephyr.

1935—Chevrolet pioneered the first all-steel station wagon body; it was on a panel delivery truck chassis.

1935

The 35th National Automobile Show was sponsored by the Automobile Merchants Association of New York after the Automobile Manufacturers Association decided to wait until November for its show in an effort to stabilize employment.

Ford Motor Company, which had not participated in national shows since early in the century, took part in the 1935 show.

Hudson and Terraplane introduced a new "electric hand" fingertip control for gear shifting. The control was mounted on the steering column.

A trend toward lower-priced cars was noticed for the 1935 model year. New models, with fewer features or less power, were announced by Chrysler, De Soto, Graham, Hudson, Hupmobile, Packard, Pontiac and Reo—all with lower prices.

An AMA report disclosed that motorists paid one of every eight tax dollars.

A trend toward two-door and four-door sedans developed.

The Keeshin Transcontinental Run was conducted to give impetus to long-distance truck transportation.

Count Alexis de Sakhnoffsky designed streamlined trucks for White.

Ford introduced the Lincoln-Zephyr.

Nash offered a new type of "sealed-in" motor with the manifold cast inside the block.

Approximately 3 million automobiles now had radios.

Pontiac produced its one-millionth car.

Chevrolet adopted a new type of frame without the X-member.

The great break with tradition characterized the 36th National Automobile Show in November. Since it had been decided that a fall show would possibly help level the peaks and valleys in the industry's sales and employment, the manufacturers moved their new-model announcements ahead two months. The innovation won plaudits from the nation's leaders. President Roosevelt saluted the industry for its leadership in the "vanguard of recovery." Sales were encouragingly better than they had been at recent shows, some exhibitors jubilantly reported that they more than doubled.

The new 1936 model cars featured hand brakes on the left of the driver to give more room in the front seat. Nash exhibited a car with twin travel beds.

1936 Automobile manufacturers were optimistic that the buying spirit at the 1936 model introduction in the previous fall would carry through the year. It turned out to be the best year since 1929.

1936—House trailers, later to be known as mobile homes, brought nature as close as the highway from home.

The AMA reported that 95 per cent of all cars were sold under $750 wholesale.

The Department of Commerce announced that 54 per cent of all U. S. families owned cars.

Reo discontinued passenger car manufacturing to concentrate on a line of commercial vehicles.

The three-millionth Buick was built.

Hudson introduced a "radical safety control," a steel torque arm which resulted in easier steering and the elimination of "nosing down" when braking. Also offered on the Hudson was a double automatic emergency braking system with a separate reserve brake system that went into use in the event the primary brakes failed.

Sloping side windows and built-in defrosters appeared on many cars.

Nash Motors Company of Kenosha, Wis., merged with Kelvinator Corporation of Detroit to form Nash-Kelvinator

Automobiles of America

Corporation. Charles W. Nash became board chairman, and George W. Mason, president.

Exhibits at the 37th National Automobile Show in November were of a more popular nature with less technical and mechanical detail than in past years. Emphasis was on the comfort and beauty of new models. House trailers were also displayed at the show as an accessory for touring and camping.

1937
The Waterman Arrowbile was one of the earliest flying automobiles.

Buick made a new-model changeover in the record time of 10 days.

Chrysler spent $22 million in plant improvements, and built more than a million cars and trucks during the year.

Ford offered a choice of 60 h.p. and 85 h.p. engines.

Steering column gearshifts were offered by several manufacturers.

1937—Cord offered a supercharged front-wheel drive model.

milestones

Several of the cars on display at the 37th National Automobile Show, Oct. 27 through Nov. 3, featured the storage battery in a location under the hood, making it more accessible and near other regularly serviced items.

Oldsmobile and Buick introduced the Automatic Safety Transmission, an automatic gearshift.

Chrysler offered an adjustable seat that moved not only back and forth, but up and down as well. Chrysler cars also offered safety padding on the back of the front seat.

Windshield washers were offered by Studebaker.

1938 The year saw one of the worst slumps in automotive history—production was down 40 per cent. New models for 1939 and the National Automobile Show in the fall were looked upon as the necessary stimulus to bring the automotive business out of its economic low.

Ford Motor Company introduced the Mercury line of cars. The new make was aimed for the medium price field, and equipped with a V-8 engine.

Studebaker spent $3.5 million in tooling for the new low-priced Champion model.

Nash introduced "conditioned air" heating and ventilation which heated and filtered fresh air from the outside, and then circulated it inside the car with a fan.

Packard offered "Econo-drive," an overdrive transmission.

Pontiac adopted "Duflex" rear springs that were used with a smaller auxiliary leaf spring for uniform riding quality under any load. A remote gearshift control on the steering column was also introduced.

Hudson introduced a 112-inch wheel-base model in the low-priced field.

Several manufacturers offered coil spring rear suspension in place of leaf springs.

101

1938—Plymouth offered a convertible top operated by vacuum power.

Chevrolet introduced a vacuum operated gearshift.

Chrysler developed "Superfinish," a method of finishing parts with no scratches more than one-millionth of an inch deep. The company also introduced a fluid coupling for the Chrysler transmission.

Ford spent $40 million for plant expansion.

New car models exhibited at the 39th National Automobile Show had several interesting features, including Buick's directional signals, and Plymouth's safety signal speedometer and vacuum operated convertible top.

Ford, Chevrolet and Dodge offered cab-over-engine trucks.

Dodge and International Harvester entered the Diesel-powered truck field.

1939 Automotive production milestones were reached during the year. The 75 millionth motor vehicle was made in the U.S. Ford produced its 27 millionth vehicle, and the 15 millionth Chevrolet was produced.

milestones

Hudson introduced "Airfoam" cushions and a hood lock release under the dash.

White built 300 scout cars for the U.S. Army.

Packard designed and built a high-speed marine engine for the U. S. Navy's famous PT boats.

Powell Crosley, Jr. introduced the Crosley, a small car.

Nearly every manufacturer held its 1940 new car announcement until the 40th National Automobile Show in October, so the impact of the new models would be strong. The Show was held 27 days earlier than in past years to facilitate the group announcement.

There was a wide range of colors on the 1940 models exhibited at the National Automobile Show, and the colors were made more lustrous by the use of metallic pigments. Two-tones were displayed at many exhibits. The most popu-

1939—Powell Crosley, Jr. and the new Crosley car.

lar body style at the Show was the four-door six passenger sedan, followed by the two-door sedan. There was great spectator interest in the new station wagon models displayed.

Sealed Beam Headlamps were generally adopted for the first time by the automotive industry for the 1940 models.

Push-button radios appeared in cars.

Oldsmobile offered "Hydra-Matic Drive," an automatic transmission.

Automatic overdrive became available on several makes of cars. Lincoln-Zephyr and several models of other makes omitted running boards or enclosed them under the door.

Oldsmobile offered all-coil-spring suspension, four-way stabilization, and knee-action front-wheel suspension on all models.

Pontiac began production of taxi-cabs.

Several models featured an under-the-seat heater for better air circulation. Heaters and defrosters were standard equipment on many 1940 models.

An air condition unit was offered by Packard.

1940 Col. Arthur W. S. Herrington invited a group of automotive engineers to Fort Benning, Ga., in March to witness demonstrations of a small armed vehicle designed and built by Capt. Robert G. Howie. This demonstration resulted in the development of the wartime one-quarter ton four-wheel-drive military vehicle, the forerunner of "Jeep" vehicles made by Willys Motors, Inc.

The war in Europe converted many U. S. automobile branch plants on the Continent to military production.

William S. Knudsen, president of General Motors, went to Washington at the invitation of President Roosevelt to direct production for national defense.

Nash introduced its "600" series, a pioneer of the mass produced unitized body.

milestones

1940—Oldsmobile offered Hydra-Matic automatic transmission as an accessory. Station wagons accounted for less than 1 per cent of total motor vehicles in the country.

 Packard contracted to build Rolls-Royce aircraft engines.
 Ford contracted to build Pratt & Whitney aircraft engines.
 Dodge built 20,000 special trucks for the U. S. Army.
 Chevrolet produced a million cars in less than ten working months.
 Cadillac discontinued the LaSalle.
 The 41st National Automobile Show in the Grand Central Palace Oct. 12-20, was the last of a series that had run without break from 1900. Before the event opened, AMA directors announced that all manufacturers had shelved plans for the 1941 show and new model introductions so

105

that time and attention, as dictated by the emerging needs, could be devoted to production for national defense.

Ford Motor Company exhibited Ford, Lincoln and Mercury cars and Ford trucks for the first time in a National Auto Show sponsored by the AMA or its predecessors.

Hydra-Matic Drive was made available on all Cadillac models. Fluid Drive became available on Dodge, De Soto, and Chrysler cars.

Interchangeable six- or eight-cylinder engines on a basic frame were offered by Oldsmobile and Pontiac. A supporting radiator frame or longer fan shroud made up the difference in shorter engines.

Chrysler introduced a safety-rim wheel that kept the tire on the rim in the event of a blowout. Two-speed electric windshield wipers were also offered by Chrysler.

Buick offered a dual compound carburetor that cut in a second carburetor when the throttle was depressed to floor.

Enclosed running boards were generally adopted throughout the industry.

The Automotive Committee for Air Defense was established on Oct. 30 to facilitate aircraft production.

A nationwide plan for financing automotive repairs on an installment basis was announced.

1941 Production records were made by at least three car makers. Plymouth made its 4 millionth unit, Dodge built its 5 millionth car and the 29 millionth Ford was produced.

The new 1942 models had a lower, longer, broader, and more massive look. Grilles were wider, bumpers heavier, and running boards were either absent or concealed.

Front fenders were extended to the middle of the front door on General Motors cars.

Hudson offered a combination automatic clutch with a

1941—The Nash Ambassador offered a folding seat which formed a bed.

semi-automatic transmission. The driver could select either the manual or semi-automatic shift with buttons on the dash.

Many makes substituted a lightweight iron alloy for pistons. Substitute materials were also used for trim and decoration.

De Soto's headlamps were concealed in the front fenders. The lamp doors disappeared upward when a knob under the instrument panel was pulled; this also turned on the lights.

National Defense

Buick built a new aviation engine plant.

Oldsmobile produced shells for the U. S. Army in a modern forge plant.

107

Automobiles of America

Chrysler achieved mass production of tanks, delivered its first anti-aircraft guns, and proceeded with scores of defense contracts.

Ford began production of combat cars.

Pontiac began work on Oerlikon anti-aircraft guns.

General Motors divisions began production of machine guns.

Studebaker took a contract to produce aircraft engines.

Willys started delivery of a reconnaissance car, soon to be popularly known as the "Jeep."

White produced half-tracks, tank destroyers, prime movers, and cargo trucks.

Naval forces from Japan struck Pearl Harbor Dec. 7—War against Japan was declared by the U. S. Congress on the following day.

The Automotive Council for War Production was organized on Dec. 31 to apply the full facilities of the automotive industry to the task of production for the armed forces.

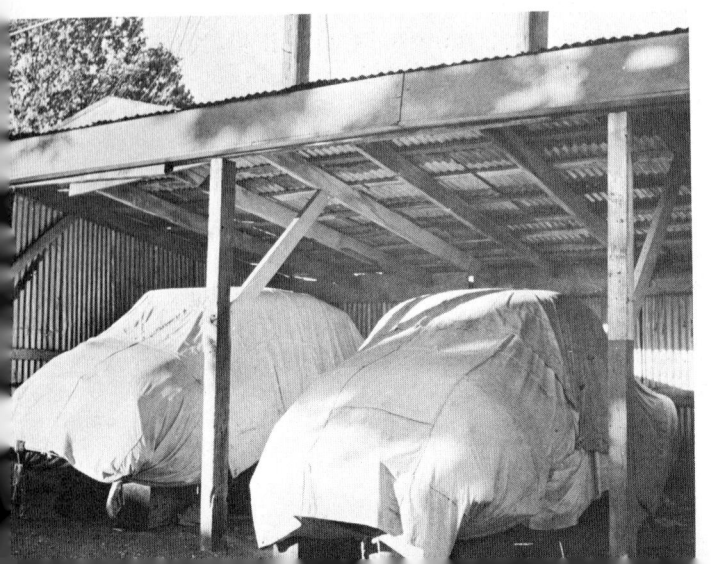

1942—Military service and rationing put many automobiles into storage for the duration of World War II.

milestones

1942 All automobile companies halted production of civilian passenger cars on Feb. 9.
Car rationing began March 2.
Production of civilian trucks halted March 3.
On May 3 the national speed limit was set at 40 m.p.h. to conserve fuel. It was later cut to 35 m.p.h.
Gasoline supplies were cut 50 per cent in 17 eastern states on May 15.
Also in May the Ford Willow Run Michigan Bomber Plant opened.
By July war output of automotive companies exceeded their peacetime production rate.
On Sept. 10 President Roosevelt ordered nation-wide gasoline rationing effective Dec. 1 to conserve fuel and rubber.
Graham-Paige began production of amphibian tanks.
Nash-Kelvinator produced Pratt & Whitney engines, Hamilton Standard propellers, Sikorsky helicopters.
Chrysler spent $40 million to increase tank production, and started a huge aircraft engine plant in Chicago.
Pontiac was the first automobile manufacturer to win the Navy "E" Award. When this award was superseded by Army-Navy "E," Chrysler Tank Arsenal was accorded the first such award in the U. S.
At the year's end the Automotive Council for War Production reported the industry's 1942 production of arms at $4,665,000,000.

1943 The Office of Price Administration (O.P.A.) banned non-essential driving in 17 eastern states in January.
O.P.A. disclosed that 25 million gasoline ration books had been issued.

Automobiles of America

By June production for war in 1,000 automotive plants had doubled in 12 months; employment total: 1,250,000.

Henry Kaiser announced plans to manufacture automobiles after the war.

William B. Stout developed a "flying automobile" for postwar production.

By November employment in U. S. plants formerly manufacturing motor vehicles and bodies reached its wartime peak and began to taper off due to demands for manpower in armed services; output of such plants was now double the rate of best peacetime year.

The Automotive Council for War Production reported 1,038 automotive plants voluntarily cooperating in the industry-wide effort to maintain maximum production, and that value of products thus made had reached a total of $13 billion.

1944 The War Production Board authorized production of 1,000,000 trucks for civilian and military use in 1944 in January.

Willys-Overland announced plans to produce a civilian version of the Jeep after the war.

The Detroit region was shown accountable for 13.6 per cent of the nation's war production.

The War Production Board announced formation of the Automobile Industry Advisory Committee to consider basic problems to be dealt with in eventual resumption of passenger car production.

Basic gasoline ration was reduced to two gallons a week.

Joseph W. Frazer, board chairman of Graham-Paige, announced plan to manufacture automobiles after the war.

In September the Office of War Information revaled that passenger cars were now being scrapped at the rate of 4,000 a day.

110

1943—Military vehicles rolled along assembly lines for the duration of the war.

1944—Automotive companies produced 57 per cent of the tanks delivered to U. S. and allied armed forces during World War II.

Automobiles of America

In November the War Production Board authorized manufacture of the first light civilian trucks since early in 1942.

It was revealed that the United States had supplied the U.S.S.R. with more than 345,000 motor vehicles.

The Automotive Council for War Production revealed that the automotive industry produced $9 billion worth of armament in 1944, and that costs to the Government had been reduced one-third since 1941.

1945 The Automobile Manufacturers Association statistics disclosed that 48 per cent of all passenger cars now in use were more than seven years old.

Crosley Corporation announced its intent to produce small cars powered with four-cylinder lightweight engines after the war.

1945—Henry Ford II drove the first civilian postwar automobile from the assembly line on July 3.

milestones

In April the War Production Board announced a program for transition to civilian motor vehicle production after V-E Day.

V-E Day became reality on May 8 when Germany surrendered to Allied Forces.

On May 11 the War Production Board announced that reconversion to motor vehicle production could begin July 1.

On May 22 all restrictions on manufacture of replacement parts were lifted.

Willow Run Plant closed on June 23 after delivering 8,685 bombers.

Ford began production of passenger cars on July 3.

Formation of Kaiser-Frazer Corporation was announced on July 26.

World War II ended with the surrender of Japan on Aug. 14.

Gasoline rationing ended the day following the Japanese surrender.

All restrictions on truck production were lifted on Aug. 20.

The Automotive Council for War Production was dissolved on Oct. 15.

Production of 1946 motor vehicles started. New models were announced by Chevrolet, Buick, Cadillac, Pontiac, Oldsmobile, Studebaker, Nash, Hudson and Packard.

A strike began in General Motors plant on Nov. 21.

SUMMARY OF AUTOMOTIVE INDUSTRY'S WAR PRODUCTION

The automotive industry contributed more material to the armed services of the United States and Allies than any other single industry. In addition to all the armored cars used, it supplied 92 per cent of the scout cars and carriers, 87 per cent of the aircraft bombs, 85 per cent of the steel

113

Automobiles of America

helmets, 75 per cent of the aircraft engines, 57 per cent of the tanks, 56 per cent of the carbines, 50 per cent of the Diesel engines, 47 per cent of the machine guns, 10 per cent of the completed aircraft, 10 per cent of the torpedoes, 10 per cent of the land mines, and 3 per cent of the marine mines.

By the end of the war, almost $29 billion worth of products for war had been delivered. This total was approximately 20 per cent of the national output of such products.

1946 Kaiser and Frazer joined the ranks of U. S. passenger car manufacturers in offering new models bearing their names.

A corporation to build Preston Tucker's rear-engine car was organized with $40 million capitalization. The firm leased the Chicago-Dodge plant during the latter part of the year.

Despite a coal strike that impeded automotive produc-

1946—Studebaker pioneered a trend in post-war styling.

1946—The Crosley entered the small car field after World War II.

tion, the one-millionth passenger car assembled since the end of World War II was built in August.

A 12-day celebration in Detroit from May 29 through June 9 marked the Automotive Golden Jubilee.

Radio telephones were used in motor vehicles.

Disabled veterans could obtain cars equipped with special mechanical aids developed by the Society of Automotive Engineers.

Power operated windows were introduced.

Chevrolet Division was one of the first automotive firms to advertise on network television.

The Public Roads Administration removed all restrictions on Federal Aid highway construction not requiring structural steel.

Automobiles of America

Price and wage controls were lifted by the Federal Government on the automotive industry on Nov. 9.
Studebaker offered self-adjusting brakes.
Willys-Overland Motors, Inc., introduced a seven-passenger Jeep all-steel station wagon.

1947 Motor vehicle manufacturers built and purchased a number of new plants. General Motors opened a new assembly plant in Wilmington, Delaware; Studebaker bought a wartime aircraft engine plant at South Bend; and Chevrolet opened new passenger car and truck assembly plants in Flint, Michigan and Van Nuys, California.

1947—The Kaiser was the low-priced car made by Kaiser-Frazer Corp.

1947—A few Tucker "48" pilot models were produced for public displays around the country. The Tucker had a rear engine and a third headlamp which turned with the front wheels.

    Kaiser-Frazer Corporation purchased the automotive assets of the Graham-Paige Motor Corporation.

    Sun visors outside the windshield appeared again as accessories. The trend for such visors had declined during the early thirties.

    Packard produced its one millionth car and offered power-operated windows and seat adjustment.

    Driver education courses were offered in many high schools.

    Tucker Corporations' Torpedo (later called the "48") was unveiled in Chicago.

1948

Because there had not been a National Show since 1940, each automotive firm offered its new models when they were ready.

117

Willys-Overland introduced a six-cylinder Jeep station wagon and a convertible called the Jeepster.

Goodrich introduced tubeless tires.

Under the direction of Charles F. Kettering, General Motors revealed development of a new type of high-compression engine that was designed to use high-octane fuel.

The 100-millionth motor vehicle was produced in the U. S. during August.

Oldsmobile opened a new plant especially tooled to manufacture its new high compression V-8 engines.

Buick introduced Dynaflow transmission, a hydraulic torque converter.

Kaiser-Frazer bought the Willow Run plant near Ypsilanti, Michigan.

Cadillac, Buick and Oldsmobile offered double curved windshields.

The American trucking industry celebrated its 50th anniversary.

Pontiac offered Hydra-Matic drive as optional equipment.

New motor vehicle assembly plants were opened on the East and West Coasts: General Motors at Wilmington, Delaware and Framingham, Massachusetts, Lincoln-Mercury at Los Angeles, and Dodge Division at San Leandro, California.

Great Britain, Canada and the United States signed an agreement for standardization of threads on screws, nuts and bolts. This became known as the A.B.C. thread standard.

Tucker Corporation reported completion of its first assembly line model.

More than 1,000 dual-control cars were loaned by automotive companies to high schools in the U. S. for training student drivers.

1947—Chrysler offered a Town and Country series that combined features of a station wagon and convertible.

1948—Styling and engineering changes in the 1949 model Ford were extensive. It was the first completely new design for Ford since the end of World War II.

119

Automobiles of America

Most 1949 model American-made cars were introduced to the public in the fall.

Three new cars were offered—Playboy, Keller and Davis.

1949—Buick introduced a hardtop convertible which became a popular body style.

1949
General Motors' first show since 1940, "Transportation Unlimited," opened in New York.

Kaiser-Frazer introduced three new body styles—a utility car, a taxicab and a cloth-covered hardtop sports sedan.

Cadillac offered a high compression V-8 engine with hydraulic valve lifters.

Bonded brakes were adopted by Dodge (light trucks), Chevrolet, Chrysler and Crosley.

Oldsmobile introduced its new "88" series with a high compression V-8 engine.

Ford Division was organized to assemble and market Ford cars and trucks.

milestones

Dodge introduced an inexpensive three-passenger roadster, the Wayfarer—the first car of this body style since before World War II.

Buick, Oldsmobile and Cadillac started production of their hardtop (a sedan without center pillars) models, the Riviera, Holiday and Coupe de Ville respectively.

Hupp Corporation announced plans to sell its Detroit plant and apply funds to expansion elsewhere.

Government controls on automobile installment credit (Regulation W) limiting financing to 24 months ended June 30.

De Soto introduced a nine-passenger station wagon.

Willys-Overland introduced a new four-wheel drive all-steel station wagon as part of the Jeep series.

Plymouth introduced the Suburban, a steel station wagon.

Chrysler adopted a new method of starting the engine by using only the ignition key.

1949—Cadillac introduced a high compression V-8 engine with hydraulic valve lifters. The engine was one of the first postwar designs offered to the motoring public.

Kurtis-Kraft, Inc., racing car manufacturer, entered the passenger car field with the announcement of a low-slung convertible sports car.

Steel and coal strikes forced production curtailment at auto plants in the fall.

Crosley introduced a new sports car, the Hotshot.

Ford and Studebaker contracted with Borg-Warner for a new automatic transmission.

Tucker Corporation was ordered by the Federal Court to return its leased Chicago plant to the War Assets Administration.

Nearly all U. S. passenger car manufacturers offered their 1950 models in the fall. Some of the new features included Powerglide automatic transmission on the Chevrolet, Hydra-Matic on some Nash models, and hydraulically-operated valves on the Cadillac, Oldsmobile and Buick.

White Motor Co. introduced several new features for its line of trucks, including a hydraulically-operated tilting cab and Hydro-Torque Drive transmission.

The American Trucking Associations reported that trucks carried about 60 per cent of the total freight tonnage moved in the nation's commerce.

As the year ended, the automotive industry broke its own 20-year-old annual record to hit an all-time high of 6,253,651 units.

1950 Nash-Kelvinator displayed the NXI, a two-passenger experimental car, as part of a survey of public reaction to a new light car. As a result of the findings, the firm introduced the Metropolitan in 1954.

Many of the 1950 cars had reduced prices.

Hardtop models were offered by Chevrolet, Chrysler, Dodge and De Soto.

1950—Nash Rambler with 100-inch wheel-base.

Crosley introduced the Super Sports model, priced to sell for less than $1,000.

At least two new lines of trucks were offered during the year. Dodge introduced a four-ton model, and White offered two new "Super Power" trucks.

Reo started production of the Eager Beaver, a 2½-ton truck, for the U. S. Army.

The three-millionth Oldsmobile was produced in February. In October Oldsmobile discontinued its six-cylinder engine to concentrate output on the Rocket V-8 engine.

Goodrich offered puncture-sealing tubeless tires.

Marmon-Herrington Co., Inc., bought the manufacturing rights to Ford motor coaches.

Nash-Kelvinator introduced the Rambler series, and offered seat belts.

Automobiles of America

Chrysler celebrated its 25th anniversary, and Mack held its golden anniversary in June.

Hostilities in Korea started June 25.

Nearly all automotive companies were awarded military contracts for defense products.

U. S. Department of Defense revealed plans for the reactivation of an Ordnance Tank-Automotive Center in Detroit to expedite mobilization of the automotive and allied industries.

Installment credit was tightened for new and used cars to 15 months with one-third down.

Crosley introduced a farm and road vehicle, the Farm-O-Road, with a 10-to-1 compression ratio engine.

Willys built a small engine for Kaiser-Frazer's Henry J car, which was displayed in September.

Several 1951 models were introduced in the fall. Some of the new features included: V-8 engines and automatic transmissions on Studebaker models; one-piece curved windshields; plastic-insulated ignition system to guard against moisture on the Nash; tinted non-glare glass on the Buick; automatic transmission on Ford (Fordomatic) and Mercury (Merc-O-Matic); crash pads on the Kaiser; and an all-steel station wagon for Chrysler (Town and Country).

Chevrolet produced its 25-millionth vehicle in December.

As the year ended, material shortages resulting from the military build-up caused temporary shutdowns in automotive assembly plants.

1951

Civilian use of nickel, zinc and tin was ordered cut by the Federal government. Automotive companies used new methods and materials in producing car components as a result of the government cutback.

By the first part of the year most automotive companies had already received, or were in the process of negotiating, military contracts for the Korean conflict.

milestones

The National Production Authority halted the shipment of spare tires in new automobiles. Later in the year this ban was lifted.

Several new models were added this year. Ford offered a hardtop model—the Victoria, Lincoln introduced the customized Capri, Plymouth offered the Belvedere hardtop, Kaiser offered four new utility models, Nash added the two-passenger Nash Healey sports car (built by the Donald Healey Co. of England), a hardtop model was added to the Nash Rambler series, Packard added the Mayfair hardtop model to its line of cars, and Oldsmobile introduced the Super 88.

Buick displayed its XP 300 experimental car with a 300 horsepower V-8 supercharged engine. General Motors exhibited the Le Sabre experimental convertible, and Chrysler displayed its K-310 experimental car.

General Motors added 1,000 acres to its Milford Proving Ground to facilitate testing military vehicles.

1951—Increased emphasis was placed on all-steel station wagons by nearly all manufacturers, including Willys.

1951—Oldsmobile introduced the "Super 88" series which featured a new body design combined with a high compression V-8 engine.

Cadillac produced its first T41 Walker Bulldog light tank and Chrysler completed a pilot model of the T43 heavy tank.

Ford offered a six-cylinder engine with overhead valves.

Continental Motors acquired rights to nine gas turbine engines developed by Societé Turbomeca in France.

Buick offered a V-8 engine on some models.

Power steering was offered by Chrysler and Buick.

Oldsmobile offered a watch mounted in the steering wheel.

Sterling Motor Truck Company stockholders approved the sale of its business to the White Motor Company.

Automobile installment credit was extended to 18 months with one-third down payment.

General Motors Truck and Coach Division displayed its new Army 6 × 6 truck, the M135.

The Internal Revenue Act of 1951 increased automotive excise taxes from 5 to 8 per cent on trucks, 7 to 10 per cent

milestones

on passenger cars, and 5 to 8 per cent on automotive parts and accessories.

Willys-Overland Motors, Inc., introduced its first postwar six-cylinder passenger car, the Aero Willys.

Kaiser-Frazer suspended production of the Frazer car.

Sears, Roebuck and Company introduced the new Kaiser-Frazer made Allstate passenger car. The car was displayed in 19 cities in the South and Southwest a week before Christmas.

Michigan State College (later, University) established a driver-training professorship.

The 100,000,000th passenger car built in the U. S. was assembled in December.

1952
The year marked important milestones for two automotive companies. Studebaker celebrated its 100th anniversary and Cadillac marked its golden anniver-

1952—Sears, Roebuck and Co., offered the Allstate. The car, a version of the Henry J made by Kaiser-Frazer, was available with four or six-cylinder engine.

sary. The American Automobile Association (AAA) celebrated its 50th anniversary, and the U. S. Post Office issued a commemorative stamp honoring the 50th anniversary of the trucking industry in the U. S.

Some innovations offered on 1952 models included: Oldsmobile's automatic headlamp dimmer; a suspended brake pedal under the dashboard and ball joint front wheel suspension on the Lincoln; suspended clutch and brake pedals on the Ford; dual range Hydra-Matic on the Pontiac; 12-volt electrical system on the Chrysler Crown Imperial; four way seat adjustment on the Packard; automatic overdrive on the Plymouth; and De Soto offered a V-8 engine.

International Harvester and Reo introduced a liquefied-petroleum gas (LPG) powered line of motor trucks.

GMC offered a 2.5-ton, three-cylinder, diesel truck.

The last nine miles were opened on New Jersey's 118-mile turnpike in January.

Operation of the Detroit Tank Aresenal was transferred to Chrysler Corporation.

General Tire and Rubber bought Crosley Motors in July; production of the Crosley car stopped during the same month.

Dodge and Fisher Body used plastic dies to produce steel stampings for automotive components.

Automotive companies continued to produce military goods for the Korean conflict. In addition to military motor vehicles and tanks, they built aircraft engines, jet and piston type; electronic aircraft gun sights; diesel marine engines; aircraft; and a number of miscellaneous components for weapons.

Hudson introduced a new low-priced car in September, the Jet.

University of Michigan formed a Transportation Institute within the College of Engineering to encourage better understanding of the need for more efficient transportation.

Willys-Overland Motors added the Aero Ace and Aero Lark to its Aero series of passenger cars.
Dearborn Motors Corporation paid $9,250,000 to Harry Ferguson, Inc. in settlement of a judgment which ended the Ford-Ferguson tractor patents litigation.
Buick offered the Skylark deluxe convertible in the $5,000 price bracket.
Lincoln-Mercury Division of Ford Motor Company moved into its new assembly plant at Wayne, Michigan, a Detroit suburb, for production of the division's two cars.
The U. S. Chamber of Commerce estimated that private automobiles carried about 85 per cent of the nation's combined local and long distance traffic.
Chrysler Corp. started construction on its 3,800-acre proving ground at Chelsea, Michigan.

1953 Four significant milestones in the automotive industry were passed during the year. Buick and Ford Motor Company celebrated their golden anniversaries; the Automobile Manufacturers Association, Inc., noted its 40th anniversary; and Plymouth celebrated its 25th year.

Kaiser-Frazer changed its name to Kaiser Motors Corporation. In April, Kaiser purchased Willys-Overland Motors, Inc.

White Motor Company purchased Autocar Company and announced plans for a $2 million Autocar plant at Exton, Pennsylvania.

General Motors dedicated its new 2,280-acre Desert Proving Ground near Phoenix, Arizona.

Six experimental cars were displayed by U. S. auto makers during 1953. Buick had the Wildcat; Lincoln-Mercury displayed its fiberglas body XL-500; Packard unveiled the Balboa; Hudson introduced the Italia; Dodge exhibited the handbuilt Firearrow; and De Soto showed a four-passenger sports car, the Adventurer.

Automobiles of America

Motor vehicles were used in an atomic bomb test in Nevada during March to determine the effects for civilian defense data.

General Motors purchased the outstanding stock in the Euclid Road Machinery Company.

Ford Motor Company purchased a 177-acre site at Mahwah, New Jersey for a Ford Division assembly plant.

1953—Dodge offered a V-8 engine. It was the first year in U. S. automotive history that more eight than six-cylinder engines were produced.

Chevrolet announced plans to add 160,000 square feet to its Cleveland plant.

White sold its Milwaukee plant, formerly owned by the Sterling Motor Truck Company.

1953—First Chevrolet Corvette Shown

Chrysler Corporation purchased the automotive plants and machinery of the Briggs Manufacturing Company.

The Korean truce agreement was signed at Panmunjom, July 26.

A multi-million-dollar fire destroyed the General Motors Transmission plant in Livonia, Michigan on August 12, cutting off production of Hydra-Matic transmissions. Until other facilities could be arranged, Cadillac and Oldsmobile used Dynaflow transmissions and Pontiac adapted Powerglide units as optional equipment. Hydra-Matic production operations were shifted to another plant until General Motors purchased the Willow Run assembly plant from Kaiser Motors for automatic transmission output.

Radio Corporation of America (RCA) announced the development of safety electronic steering and braking controls which would stop or change the course of a car when an obstacle was in the path of the vehicle.

Production started on Chevrolet's plastic laminated fiberglas body sports car, the Corvette.

An American Automobile Association study showed that the average motorist drove 10,000 miles a year and paid about $908 for car maintenance and operation.

Features offered in 1953 included: Air conditioning on a number of makes; automatic transmissions on nearly all cars as optional equipment, and standard equipment in more expensive models; 12-volt electrical system, to replace 6-volt systems; lamps to replace oil pressure and generator gauges in several makes; and tinted, plexiglass roofs on some hardtop models.

Hydra-Matic transmissions became available on GMC trucks.

With the popularity of V-8 engines, the number of eight-cylinder engines exceeded the six-cylinder power plants in new passenger cars for the first time.

1954

Several long-established automotive companies merged. Nash-Kelvinator Corporation and Hudson Motor Car Company combined into American Motors Corporation; Studebaker Corporation and Packard Motor Car Company formed Studebaker-Packard Corporation.

Nearly all automotive companies announced major expansion programs. Research facilities and assembly plants received the largest share of capital expenditures. General Motors announced it would spend over $1 billion in two years; Chrysler worked out a 100-year loan of $250 million with Prudential Insurance Company of America for expansion and modernizations; and Ford invested millions in property and construction for future needs.

The Automotive History Collection of the Detroit Public Library was opened to the public in February. Some of the acquisitions of automobiliana in the Collection included: Charles B. King Collection, Andrew Lee Dyke Collection, and the Nicholas Lazarnick Picture Collection. The Automobile Manufacturers Association, and others, donated funds for the purchase of many important acquisitions in the Automotive History Collection.

milestones

Eight experimental cars were introduced during the year—Dodge's Granada; Packard's fiberglas sports model, the Panther; a gas turbine-powered XP-21 Firebird by General Motors; the Belmont and Explorer by Plymouth; Lincoln-Mercury's Monterey XM-800; the FX-Atmos dream car by Ford; and De Soto's Adventurer II.

Packard adopted tubeless tires as standard equipment in June. By the end of the year, all other U. S. manufacturers offered tubeless tires as original equipment.

The first section of New York State's $962 million Thruway system opened June 24.

A gas turbine engine developed by Chrysler Corporation was installed in a regular production Plymouth passenger car and successfully road tested. The test demonstrated the solution to two major problems in gas turbine engineering—high fuel consumption and exhaust heat—which had previously blocked passenger car application of gas turbine power.

1954—Buick offered the Century series. Power windows and power front seat were standard equipment on the convertible.

Ford introduced the two-passenger Thunderbird in October.

All automotive manufacturing in American Motors was moved to Kenosha, Wisconsin.

Ford Motor Company purchased 4,000 acres of land near Romeo, Michigan for development of a multi-million-dollar proving ground. Chrysler dedicated its new Engineering Proving Ground near Chelsea, Michigan.

Kaiser Motors Corporation transferred Willys body operations from Detroit to Toledo, Ohio.

Improved Sealed Beam headlamps, developed cooperatively through engineering committees of the Automobile Manufacturers Association and lamp manufacturers, were demonstrated. The new headlamps were on all new U. S. passenger cars by the middle of 1955.

West Virginia's new 88-mile turnpike was opened on Nov. 8.

A 22-mile section of the Northern Ohio Turnpike opened to the public on Dec. 1, linking Youngstown, Ohio with the Pennsylvania Turnpike.

Louis Matter of San Diego, California and two friends completed the first non-stop motor trip from Anchorage, Alaska to Mexico City, Mexico a distance of 6,391 miles.

General Motors Corporation produced its 50 millionth car.

President Dwight D. Eisenhower authorized the creation of a permanent President's Action Committee for Highway Safety.

New features offered by car makers during 1954 included panoramic wrap-around windshields; safety padding on dash boards; cowl ventilator air intakes at the bottom of the windshield; automatic transmission selector lever on the dash of Chrysler Corporation cars; dual headlamps and curved glass side windows on the Cadillac-El Camino; V-8 engines for Plymouth and Chevrolet; overhead valves for all

milestones

Ford car and truck engines; and push button control for lubrication of chassis and suspension on the Mercury and the Lincoln.

1955 The automotive industry broke all records in motor vehicle production during 1955. Output totaled 9,204,049 units, including 7,950,377 passenger cars, 1,249,576 trucks and 4,096 motor coaches.

Ford Motor Company announced plans to build a glass manufacturing plant at Nashville, Tennessee and moved assembly operations from Edgewater to Mahwah, New Jersey; Chrysler Corporation bought Universal Products Company, makers of automotive drive shafts and their components; Plymouth opened its new V-8 engine plant in

1954—2-passenger Thunderbird introduced

1955—Packard 400 hardtop featured a "Torsion-Level" ride which dispensed with coil or leaf springs.

Detroit; Chrysler announced plans to construct a large stamping plant at Twinsburg, Ohio; and General Motors automotive divisions added to their plant facilities.

Newcomers to the automotive field were Tri-Car, Inc., with a three-wheeled plastic body model selling for about $1,000, and Dual Motors Corporation of Detroit with a limited production sports car, the Firebomb, with a Ghia-built body from Italy on a U. S. produced chassis.

Kaiser and Willys announced plans to drop passenger car production to concentrate on Jeep vehicles.

Kaiser Motors Corporation was reorganized as Kaiser Industries Corporation, with Willys Motors, Inc., a wholly owned subsidiary.

Slick Airways, Inc., pioneered truck-air-truck shipments with door-to-door freight service with overnight deliveries from coast to coast.

The U. S. Department of Commerce announced plans to conduct a road test near Ottawa, Illinois to determine

milestones

the durability of several methods of highway construction. Cooperating with funds, personnel, and equipment were: Bureau of Public Roads, American Association of State Highway Officials, Department of Defense, Automobile Manufacturers Association, petroleum industry and other allied fields.

Improved Sealed Beam headlamps were installed in all new passenger cars by July.

Ohio's 241-mile turnpike was opened from the Pennsylvania Turnpike to west of Montpelier, Ohio on Oct. 1.

Safety door latches to help prevent doors from being forced open in collisions were made standard equipment on nearly all makes. Vehicle manufacturers also increased emphasis on seat belts.

Michigan was the first state to require a course in driver education before licenses could be issued to youths under 18.

Four-door hardtop models, offered by several manufacturers, became the vogue in body style.

Experimental vehicles displayed during the year were: Chevrolet's Biscayne, the Strato-Star by Pontiac, Oldsmobile's Delta, the Wildcat III from Buick, Cadillac's Eldorado Brougham, the V-6 powered LaSalle II by General Motors, Chrysler Corporation's Flight Sweep I and II along with the Falcon, Ford's plastic Mystere, General Motors' Firebird II gas turbine car, Ford's Futura—a $250,000 laboratory on wheels, and the Universelle truck by General Motors Coach and Truck.

Ford Motor Company's Continental Mark II was introduced at most Lincoln dealerships in October.

Studebaker entered the sports car field with the Hawk in November.

American Motors offered a V-8 engine in the Ambassador line; Packard introduced a V-8 along with torsion bar suspension controlled by a motor; and Chevrolet added the Nomad model at the top of its station wagon line.

Automobiles of America

The American Automobile Association stopped sanction of automobile races.

Cadillac offered a trunk lid lock control operated from the driver's seat.

A push-button, automatic-transmission selector replaced lever controls on the steering columns of 1956 model Chrysler, Imperial, De Soto, Dodge, Plymouth and Packard cars. A record player was also optional on Chrysler Corporation cars. Packard offered electrically-controlled door-latches and a non-slip differential.

The Motor Truck Committee of the Automobile Manufacturers Association reported completion of an auxiliary braking system designed to provide positive emergency stopping for truck-trailer combinations.

1956 Ford Motor Company stock was offered to the public for the first time; more than 10 million shares owned by the Ford Foundation were offered at $64.50 per share. At the first public stockholders' meeting in May, Ford officials announced a $592 million expansion program for 1956.

A new Dual Headlighting System for motor vehicles was announced by the Automobile Manufacturers Association. Scheduled for introduction by the automotive industry for the 1958 models, the system comprised four 5¾-inch Sealed Beam headlamps instead of two 7-inch units. This enabled the headlamps to be aimed for the best individual performance.

Armco Steel Company purchased the grounds and buildings of the American Bantam Company; the remaining assets were bought by Pressed Metals of America, Inc.

Chevrolet entered the heavy duty truck field with a new line of 2½-ton models.

Dual Motors Corp. changed the name of its car from Firebomb to Dual-Ghia.

milestones

General Motors displayed a free-piston engine which burned any type of fuel—from high octane gasoline to whale oil, peanut oil and other vegetable fats.

A 41,000 mile interstate highway system was approved as a result of the Highway Act of 1956. The law committed the federal government to meet 90 per cent of the cost with states and localities supplying the remainder. The highway program was set up on a "pay-as-you-go" basis with the establishment of a Highway Trust Fund supported by highway use taxes to finance the federal share. Federal gasoline and diesel oil taxes were increased one cent on July 1 when the Highway Act became effective.

Mack Truck, Inc., acquired C. D. Beck and Company, Inc., an intercity bus manufacturer in Sidney, Ohio, and the sales, service and manufacturing facilities of Brockway Motor Company, Inc., an early truck manufacturer.

Divco Corporation changed its name to Divco Truck Division of Divco-Wayne Corporation.

1956—A 41,000-mile national network of super highways was started under a $32.4 billion interestate highway program.

Ford Motor Company joined the Automobile Manufacturers Association, Inc.

Production of the Packard car in Detroit stopped at the end of the 1956 model year; all operations were transferred to Studebaker-Packard Corporation's plants in South Bend, Indiana.

The 156-mile Northern Indiana Toll Road was opened Sept. 18. It crossed the state from Gary, at the west edge of Indiana, to the western terminal of the Ohio Turnpike, completing a toll system and enabling motorists to drive from the Chicago area to New York City on super-highways.

Chrysler Corporation's gas turbine powered experimental Plymouth was driven from New York to Los Angeles.

American Motors Corporation developed a 62-horsepower V-4 air-cooled engine that weighed 200 pounds.

The 42nd National Automobile Show, first since 1940, was held in New York's new Coliseum. More than 300,000 square feet of exhibition space on three floors were filled with 1957 car and truck models, and a musical revue was presented on a huge stage. All American passenger cars were displayed along with 11 truck and bus exhibits. It was the first time a National Automobile Show was televised—an estimated 21,600,600 people, in 115 communities across the nation, saw the hour-long network show. The speaker at the industry's traditional banquet was Vice President Richard M. Nixon, who delivered the first major foreign policy address ever made by a vice president of the United States.

New features on the 1957 models displayed at the National Auto Show included: torsion bar suspension on Chrysler Corporation cars; fuel injection was optional on the Rambler, Pontiac and Chevrolet; dual headlamps on some makes; rear facing seats in nine-passenger Plymouth station wagons; 14-inch wheels on three-quarters of the 1957 makes; curved side window glass on the Imperial; retractable rear window controlled from the dash on the Mercury; the Turbo-glide automatic transmission (three turbines and planetary gears with a hill retarder) on the Chevrolet; a metal top retractable convertible was introduced by Ford; six-way power seats were offered by several manufacturers; electric door locks were offered by several luxury lines; a speedometer buzzer which sounded when a pre-set speed was reached; and a non-slip differential was offered by several manufacturers.

1957 Historic and production milestones for the year included Oldsmobile's 60th anniversary, Pontiac's golden anniversary (founded as the Oakland Motor Car Company), International Harvester's 50th anniversary as a truck producer, the Automotive Safety Foundation's 20th anniversary, Plymouth's 10-millionth car, and the three-millionth Mercury.

The Bureau of Public Roads approved 85 miles of the Kansas State Turnpike for inclusion in the Interstate Highway System.

1957—Rambler station wagons featured a roof travel rack.

Automobiles of America

1957—Ford introduced a retractable hardtop convertible.

1957—Plymouth had a low silhouette, and featured a torsion bar front suspension system.

White Motor Company purchased the assets of Reo Motors, Inc., of Lansing, Michigan, a pioneer automotive firm.

A station wagon body was offered on the Packard Clipper —the first of this style for Packard since 1950.

Studebaker offered a low-priced economy model with minimum trim details, the Scotsman.

Mack Trucks, Inc., introduced a 41-passenger cross-country luxury bus.

The board of directors of the Automobile Manufacturers Association, Inc., at its annual June meeting adopted a resolution to exclude speed and racing from automotive advertising and publicity.

Ford production of its two-passenger Thunderbird stopped to prepare for a four-passenger model.

Nash and Hudson names were dropped by American Motors Corporation with the end of the 1957 model. The firm announced its 1958 cars would be part of the Rambler line.

The five-mile Mackinac Bridge, linking the two Michigan peninsulas, opened in November. Before the bridge was built motorists used state-operated ferry boats to cross the Straits of Mackinac.

Chevrolet and General Motors Truck and Coach Division displayed an experimental turbine-powered truck, the Turbo-Titan.

Ford Motor Company developed an aluminum experimental military vehicle with unitized construction. The company also displayed an experimental truck powered by a gas turbine engine.

One new car make and a number of features were offered for the 1958 model year. The Dual Headlamp System (four lamps) was adopted by nearly all makes. Ford Motor Company introduced the Edsel, which had self-adjusting brakes, push button automatic transmission in the center

143

of the steering wheel, a floating drum-type speedometer, and a single air conditioner and heater control. The Lincoln and Continental had unit body construction; an exterior side mirror with adjustment controls inside the car was available on the Lincoln-Continental and Cadillac; and air suspension was optional equipment on the Mercury and all General Motors cars. An off-center rear spring mounting to reduce diving when braking was offered by Studebaker-Packard. Paper air cleaners were used on a number of makes. Aluminum brake drums with cooling fins were offered on the Buick; a double compound windshield extended into the roof line on all Chrysler Corporation cars; and rear coil springs on more than half of the models. Body dip method of prime painting to reduce rust was used on the Rambler, Lincoln and Continental. A removable transistor radio on some General Motors cars was optional equipment, and a device designed to hold a car at a preselected speed for long open country trips was available on Chrysler, Imperial and Cadillac. Hardtop models were added to the Studebaker's President and Commander series; and Chevrolet added the luxury Impala series to its line of cars.

1958 Four automotive milestones were noted during the year. Ford Motor Company produced its 50 millionth motor vehicle; Chrysler Corporation assembled its 25 millionth motor vehicle; General Motors Corporation celebrated its 50th anniversary of incorporation; and Ford Division commenorated the 50th anniversary of the Model T by reassembling a 1909 Model T at the Mahwah, New Jersey plant.

Connecticut's 129-mile turnpike opened to traffic in January, extending from Greenwich to Killingly on the Rhode Island state line.

Additions to the 1958 models included: Mercury's Medalist economy model; American Motor's 100-inch wheelbase

1958—The Thunderbird was restyled with a rear seat and unitized body construction.

Rambler American; and new four-passenger Thunderbird by Ford, with unitized body, in hardtop and convertible body styles.

An additional $1.8 billion was authorized in April to speed up construction on the Interstate Highway System.

Four-Wheel-Drive Auto Company was bought by Paradynamics, Inc., of St. Louis, Missouri.

Ford Motor Company merged three of its car divisions into the Mercury-Edsel-Lincoln (M-E-L) Division.

White Motor Company purchased the Diamond T Motor Car Company. The wholly-owned subsidiary was renamed Diamond T Motor Truck Co.

Studebaker-Packard Corporation announced cessation of the Packard automobile, and concentration on a car with a new smaller wheelbase, the Lark.

Chrysler Corporation purchased 25 per cent of the stock of Simca, a French automotive firm.

Plans for a $17,000 hand-made car to be called the Argonaut were announced by Argonaut Motor Machine Corp., of Cleveland, Ohio.

1958—Chevrolet added the Impala series which featured sculptural styling.

A seven-year study by the University of Michigan to design a secondary school test for prospective students of automotive mechanics was launched by the Automobile Manufacturers Association, Inc. The study was planned to aid in selection and guidance and thus to relieve the shortage of competent mechanics.

The New York Central Railroad started a "piggy-back" service in which loaded semi-trailers were put on flat cars for rail shipment.

Goodyear Tire and Rubber Company introduced a double-chambered captive-air safety tire to avoid complete blow-outs.

At least three full size or scaled-down operating models of antique automobiles were offered for sale.

General Motors engineers demonstrated a car equipped to steer itself over a special road with wire buried in the road surface. Later in the year the firm displayed the Firebird III experimental car with a single-stick control system which eliminated the steering wheel, brake pedal, and accelerator pedal. The car also had a separate power plant for accessories.

Ford Motor Company displayed a three-foot model of a Glideair vehicle which traveled on a thin cushion of air instead of wheels. A scooter version was also displayed.

The Automobile Information Disclosure Act, more commonly known as "the price label law," was passed during the summer to be effective Oct. 1. The new law required every automobile manufacturer to affix a label to the windshield or side window containing the following information: make, model and serial number, final assembly point, name and address of the dealer receiving the car, method of transport from the final assembly point to place of delivery, suggested retail price of the car, factory installed optional accessories, and transportation and delivery charges.

Checker Motors Corporation announced plans to produce the Superba passenger car.

White Motor Company started production of a Fiberglas truck cab.

Highlights and features offered in the fall for the 1959 model year included: swivel front seats as optional equipment on Chrysler Corporation cars; side view mirror controls inside the car on several makes; on Chrysler cars an electronic control which changed the rear view mirror to non-glaring automatically when a headlamp beam hit its surface; Oldsmobile offered a flanged brake drum for faster cooling; the Lark compact car was introduced by Studebaker-Packard; the Galaxie luxury series was added to the Ford line; a town car and limousine were offered in the Continental line; new body finishes that retained a luster for a greater period without waxing became standard on most passenger cars; a trunk lid catch electrically released inside the car by the driver was offered by Ford Motor Company; individually adjustable separate reclining seats were available on the Rambler; Buick renamed its line of cars—Electra (luxury), Invicta (medium) and LeSabre (lowest priced); a seat lock to prevent the back of the right front seat from suddenly moving forward was offered by Buick; and metals on tail pipe and muffler components were plated and made heavier.

1959 During this year Pontiac Motor Division of General Motors produced its seven millionth motor vehicle.

Five experimental vehicles were displayed in 1959: De Soto had a scale model of the Cella I which featured an electrochemical system that converted liquid fuel into electrical energy to power the car; Cadillac showed its Cyclone experimental car equipped with a radar device to warn the driver of objects in the car's path; Ford Motor Company demonstrated the Levacar which floated on a cushion of air above the ground and was propelled by small jets of compressed air; Curtiss-Wright Corporation announced the development of its Air-Car, a 300-horsepower vehicle designed to travel on a cushion of low-pressure, low velocity air at a height of 6 to 12 inches; and Chevrolet displayed a heavy duty Turbo-Titan II dream truck equipped with an experimental gas turbine engine.

Three firms announced plans to manufacture electric vehicles—Nic-L-Silver Battery Company of Santa Ana, California, Stinson Aircraft and Tool Engineering Corporation of San Diego, California, and Cleveland Vehicle Company of Cleveland, Ohio.

National Standard Parts Association and the Motor and Equipment Wholesalers Association merged to form the Automotive Service Industries Association.

Chrysler Corporation announced plans to produce glass at its Detroit-area McGraw plant. The firm also realigned its car sales division by forming the Plymouth-De Soto

1959—The Imperial Southhampton hardtop had a stainless steel roof.

Division: Chrysler-Imperial Division, and the Dodge Division (cars and trucks).

Ford Motor Company established a credit and financing subsidiary, the Ford Motor Credit Company, with the first office in Indianapolis, Indiana.

Glen Alden Corporation sold its Ward LaFrance Truck Corporation division to a group of investors led by Harris J. Klein, a New York attorney. The company was a pioneer in the fire truck field.

The launching of the first mass produced Jupiter ballistic missile, made by Chrysler Corporation in Detroit, was announced by the U. S. Army.

A caravan of 16 motor vehicles with 39 men, women and children, known as the '59ers, drove from Detroit to Alaska's Susitan Valley (90 miles north of Anchorage) to homesteads in the 49th state. Marino Sik of Detroit led the pioneers over the 4,239-mile trip in 25 days.

New truck engine options offered during the year included: a diesel engine by Dodge and a V-6 diesel and V-6 and V-12 gasoline engines on GMC Truck and Coach Division vehicles.

White Motor Company purchased the Montpelier Manufacturing Company of Montpelier, Ohio, producers of small truck bodies.

Two new types of power plants were reported during the year: Curtiss-Wright Corporation and NSU Werke of West Germany announced a rotating internal combustion engine for automotive, aircraft, and marine use—the engine reportedly has only a few moving parts. Williams Research Company of Walled Lake, Michigan, reported the development of a low-cost, lightweight, medium horsepower gas turbine engine using a heat exchange principle.

Willys offered the Maverick Special—a deluxe Jeep station wagon.

Plans for the 43rd National Automobile Show to be held in Detroit's new Cobo Hall in October of 1960, were announced by the Automobile Manufacturers Association, Inc.

Federal tax on gasoline was increased from three to four cents a gallon to keep the Interstate Highway System on a "pay-as-you-go" basis.

A new seven-inch headlamp, with the approximate low beam advantages of the Dual Headlamp System, was offered for vehicles using two, instead of four, headlamps. It was developed by lamp and motor vehicle manufacturers through a committee of the Automobile Manufacturers Association.

Four new makes were offered to the motoring public for 1960. Dodge Division introduced the Dart; Chevrolet offered a light aluminum air-cooled rear engine car—the Corvair; Ford introduced the Falcon economy line; and Plymouth offered its new Valiant.

Highlighted features offered on the 1960 models included: a convertible and four-door station wagon added to the Studebaker-Packard Lark series; electroluminescent dash lighting to reduce eye strain in night driving on Chrysler Corporation cars; an alternator and rectifier a.c. generating system on the Valiant; unit body construction for Plymouth, De Soto, Dodge, Chrysler, Valiant, Corvair and Falcon; folding rear seat for luggage space on the Corvair; vacuum operated remote trunk lock control inside the car on the Oldsmobile; and vacuum safety door locks on most Chrysler cars. Also offered were: torsion bar suspension on Chevrolet trucks; a dual chambered water pump for even distribution on both cylinder banks on the V-8 Pontiac; an automatic control to turn on headlamps when driving at dusk; an air cooled torque converter transmission on the Falcon; and an adjustable mirror on the Buick to reflect the instrument panel for different heights of drivers. Other features were: a side-hinged rear station wagon door on the Rambler; self-adjusting brakes on the Cadillac; an automatic vacuum parking brake release when the transmission is put into drive position on the Cadillac; a sliding metal roof panel on Thunderbird hardtop models; an anti-theft ignition switch with three blade terminals in Ford Motor Company cars; non-round steering wheels by Chrysler; and a four-light emergency flashing system on Chrysler cars.

Ford Motor Company discontinued the Edsel line in November.

A device designed to eliminate substantial portions of smog-producing hydro-carbon emissions from automobiles would be offered on 1961 American cars produced for sale in California, the Automobile Manufacturers Association, Inc., announced on Nov. 30. The device reduced vapors from the engine crankcase by diverting them through the intake manifold.

1960 Five new smaller, or compact automobiles were introduced during the year, bringing to 10 the total of American makes in this class. Lincoln-Mercury offered the Comet (1960 model) in March. The other four

151

makes were 1961 models introduced in the fall—Buick's Special (aluminum V-8 engine), Oldsmobile's F-85 (aluminum V-8 engine), Pontiac's Tempest (front-mounted four-cylinder engine or a V-8 as optional equipment, and a trans-axle in the rear), and Dodge's new Lancer.

Eight automotive companies expanded their operations. American Motors added to its Kenosha and Milwaukee, Wisconsin, plants. Ford Motor Company purchased Sherman Products (manufacturers of Ford tractor accessories), and announced plans for a glass research and development center in Lincoln Park, Michigan. Chrysler Corporation dedicated a new assembly plant near St. Louis, Missouri. General Motors expanded its facilities at Warren, and at Willow Run, Michigan, and at Tarrytown, New York. Mack Trucks, Inc., announced plans to build a new plant at Hagerstown, Maryland. Studebaker-Packard Corporation acquired three firms. White Motor Company bought Oliver Corporation's farm equipment manufacturing business.

Several announcements in the experimental field were reported: General Motors' "electric fence" which would warn the driver if the vehicle was near the pavement edge, and a nuclear-powered combat vehicle for the Defense Department. Chevrolet displayed the XP-700 Corvette experimental car and Plymouth exhibited the NXR experimental sports car; Ford announced a new process for making open hearth steel that would cut production time in half.

Glen Pray of Tulsa, Oklahoma, purchased the assets of the Auburn, Cord and Duesenberg auto plant at Auburn, Indiana, and announced plans to produce parts for the three cars.

Several all-weather radiator coolants were offered by antifreeze makers.

Studies by the Automobile Manufacturers Association, Inc., showed windshield and window areas of 1960 cars

milestones

provided 15 per cent greater vision for the driver compared with 1950 models. The AMA also announced grants totaling $1,706,000 to a number of organizations to promote traffic safety and efficient use of highways.

United States Freight Company offered an intercontinental piggy-back service, combining railroad, steamship and trucking methods of transport of loaded vans.

The U. S. Bureau of Public Roads reported that more than 9,100 miles of the 41,000-mile Interstate Highway System were completed, and that 4,700 additional miles were under construction.

International Harvester Co. reported it would enter the compact car field with the Scout. The new vehicle would have a four-cylinder engine and an integral body.

The National Automobile Show in Detroit's new 10-acre Cobo Hall during October officially opened the 1961 model

1960—National Auto Show, for the first time in Detroit, drew 1,403,872 visitors.

year. Sponsored by the Automobile Manufacturers Association, it was the first national show since 1956 and the first industry-sponsored show to open outside New York City. The show, with its "Wheels of Freedom" theme, set a new international record for attendance at any industrial show—nearly 1.5 million persons. More than 300 cars, trucks and motor coaches were displayed in the 300,000 square foot exhibition space. Suppliers to the automotive industry co-operated with the vehicle manufacturers to put on an "Auto Wonderland" exhibit, a 104,000 square foot display telling how a car is made. The U. S. Post Office issued a special Wheels of Freedom commemorative four-cent stamp in conjunction with the Show's opening day. President Dwight D. Eisenhower was the principal speaker at the industry's traditional banquet.

New features on the 1961 models displayed at the National Auto Show included: an economy line of trucks and station buses by Ford (Econoline) and Chevrolet Corvair; a four-door soft top convertible on the Lincoln-Continental; pre-lubrication on a number of chassis points with a special grease for 30,000 miles on Ford, Mercury and Lincoln-Continental; Cadillac featured a life-time chassis lubrication; Lark offered a sliding soft roof; aluminized mufflers and self-adjusting brakes on the Ford; ceramic-coated muffler and tail pipe on the Rambler; an aluminum six-cylinder Rambler engine; a swing-away steering wheel to assist the driver getting into or out of the Thunderbird; and two-level air conditioning to cool the top level of the car while heating the lower level for dehumidifying on the Cadillac.

Each U. S. automobile company provided embossed pads in the floor pan so dealers could make seat belt installations more easily.

New car warranties were extended by all manufacturers to at least 12 months or 12,000 miles, whichever came first.

1960—One feature of Detroit's Show was carousel of cars circling the great stage.

The Lincoln-Continental warranty was extended to 24 months or 24,000 miles.

Chrysler Corporation announced it would discontinue the De Soto at the end of November.

Two rebate plans were disclosed. Studebaker-Packard offered shareholders a refund of $100 for buying a Studebaker car or truck during a three-month period. American Motors Corporation offered U. S. savings bonds as rebates to purchasers of its cars during a four-month period, providing the firm's car sales rose 10 per cent above the same period in the previous year.

1961

Chevrolet Motor Division produced its 44-millionth vehicle.

Five experimental vehicles were exhibited during the year. Chrysler Corporation displayed its Turboflite and X7, both powered by a gas turbine engine. Ford Motor Company exhibited the two-wheeled gyroscope-controlled Gy-

155

ron. Dodge Division's Fleetwing went on display in New York. Ford Motor Company unveiled a scale model of a 200-passenger Levacar, called the Aerolus. The vehicle slides on a film of air a fraction of an inch above special rail surfaces.

New mid-year models introduced by the industry included: Cadillac Division's Town Sedan in the Calais series; Oldsmobile Division's Starfire sports convertible, a three-seat station wagon in the F-85 series, the F-85 Cutlass and F-85 economy club coupe; Chrysler Corporation's Enforcer, a new model especially equipped for police work, and the Hylander in the Newport series; American Motors' Custom 400 Series in the Rambler American, Classic and Ambassador V-8 lines; Ford Division's Futura in the Falcon line; Dodge Division's 770 Lancer sports coupe; and Buick Division's Skylark, a top-of-the-line model in the Special series.

New models offered in the fall for the 1962 model year included: Chevrolet's new Chevy II series; Mercury's Meteor series; Pontiac's Gran Prix series, Studebaker-Packard's Gran Turismo in the Hawk series; and Chrysler's 300-H, a high performance sports-type car.

Numerous product innovations were introduced with the 1962 models. Dual-brake systems became standard equipment on all 1962 American Motors and Cadillac models. American Motors announced it would offer factory-installed seat belts on all Ramblers for both front and rear seats. American Motors also introduced the E-stick automatic clutch transmission on its Rambler American series. The driver shifts gears manually, but the clutch is automatically engaged and disengaged.

Ford Motor Company introduced a clutch interlock for manual transmissions that prevented shifting into low or reverse by mistake.

Single-leaf rear-spring suspension systems were offered on the Chevy II. Dodge Dart, Phoenix, and Pioneer models

milestones

1961—Restyled Falcon featured a convex-shaped aluminum grille.

1961—The extra space in the passenger compartment and trunk introduced a pleasant luxury to the Dodge Lancer.

adopted dual tail lights as standard equipment. Ford Motor Company offered an engine coolant said to be good for 30,000 miles or two years of driving.

New models and product innovations in the trucking industry included: International Harvester's new line of all-purpose vehicles, including the Scout which can be converted from an enclosed runabout, small pickup or panel truck, to an open model without top, windows or doors. Other models offered were the Travelall, a nine-passenger four-door station wagon, and the Travelette, a four-door, six-passenger pickup truck. General Motors developed the first production models of a new line of inter-city coaches powered by V-8 diesel engines. Willys Motors, Inc., introduced its new Jeep Fleetvan, a half-ton walk-in delivery vehicle.

Studebaker-Packard Corporation announced it would produce a line of medium-duty trucks and truck tractors with diesel engines.

The Detroit Diesel Engine Division of General Motors unveiled a group of 12 engines which can run on a complete range of fuels from gasoline to diesel fuel. In addition, the division developed conversion kits which can change present diesel engines into multi-fuel engines.

Ford Motor Company purchased the Philco Corporation and two Electric Autolite Company plants. Studebaker-Packard purchased Chemical Compounds, Inc., makers of STP, a motor-oil additive, and bought Curtiss-Wright Corporation's South Bend plant. American Motors opened a new engineering and research unit in Kenosha, Wisconsin. Chrysler Corporation combined the marketing operations of its Chrysler-Imperial Division and Plymouth Division into a single Chrysler-Plymouth Division. Oldsmobile Division dedicated a new engineering center.

Most major tire producers developed two-ply tires as a replacement for four-ply on compact cars. Goodyear Tire

milestones

and Rubber Co. announced production of Budene, a new synthetic rubber expected to nearly double the life of tires.

Chrysler Corporation engineers drove a turbine-powered Dodge Dart from New York to Los Angeles for an engineering evaluation run.

Secretary of Commerce Luther H. Hodges announced the official start of the National Driver Register Service. The Service cross-indexes data on motorists in 43 states whose licenses have been revoked on charges of drunken driving or highway-death cases.

1962 General Motors produced its 75,000,000th car, a Bonneville convertible, made by Pontiac Division.

Ford Motor Company became the first automobile manu-

1962—The Studebaker Gran Turismo Hawk incorporated a low silhouette, flat roof line and long tapering hood.

facturer to reach the 30 million mark in production of V-8 engines.

Studebaker dropped the Packard name from its corporate title.

Amber lights for front turn signals were adopted by the entire industry after a recommendation by the AMA Board of Directors. Extensive visibility tests proved that amber signals are seen more readily against glaring reflections than white signals.

Shelby American, Inc., a Los Angeles-based firm, began producing a high-performance sports car called the Cobra. The car was powered by a Ford V-8 engine, the chassis and aluminum body were made in England.

Thirteen mid-year makes were introduced: Buick's new sports models, the Wildcat hardtop and the Skylark convertible; Checker Motors Corporation's new station wagon, the Aerobus, available in 9- or 12-passenger models; Chevrolet's Corvair Monza convertible and Monza Spyder; Dodge's Custom 880; Ford's Galaxy 500XL, Fairlane Sports Coupe and Falcon Sports Futura; Lincoln-Mercury's Villager, a compact station wagon; Oldsmobile's Jetfire sports coupe, the first American production car equipped with a fluid injected turbo-charged V-8 engine; Plymouth's Sports Fury; and Studebaker's new sports coupe, the Avanti.

New models introduced in the fall included: Pontiac's LeMans in the Tempest series; Buick's Riviera; Checker's station wagon, the Texan; Chrysler's two-door hardtop model, the 300-J; and Studebaker's new Lark Standard series, aimed at the fleet buyer.

The tire and rubber industry announced several new developments. A new tire cord made of polyester fiber that combined the best features of nylon and rayon was developed by Goodyear Tire and Rubber Company. A tire introduced by the General Tire and Rubber Company was

milestones

1962—Simulated wood paneling distinguished the styling of the Mercury Comet Villager.

claimed to last 50,000 miles or more. A new chemical bonding agent that solved the problem of ply and tread separation was introduced by U. S. Rubber.

Numerous new features and product innovations were introduced on new model cars. Studebaker's 1963s featured front-wheel disc brakes as an option, and as standard equipment on the Avanti. Self-adjusting brakes were installed on most 1963 models. All models were provided with seat-belt anchors for the front seat. Pontiac offered a fully transistorized ignition system as an option on its 1963 models.

The industry started nationwide installation of positive crankcase ventilating systems on all 1963 model cars and light trucks.

Developments in the gas turbine-engine field continued. To test consumer acceptance, Chrysler Corporation started building 50 turbine-powered passenger cars for distribution to selected motorists in the latter part of 1963. Dodge Truck Division displayed an experimental turbine-powered truck. Ford Motor Company tested an experimental turbine-engine in a 1955 Thunderbird.

New experimental cars exhibited during the year included: Ford's Cougar 406, a sports model featuring electrically operated gull-wing doors; Chevrolet's Cerv-I; Pontiac's Monte Carlo, a two-passenger luxury model featuring magnesium wheels; and American Motors' Metropolitan Royal Runabout.

Continental Motors produced a new multi-fuel engine for the Army, called the Hypercycle LDS-427-2.

Manufacturers offered an expanded selection of mobile homes and campers, a result of the continued rise and popularity of camping as a family recreation. The Champ, a many-purpose camper, was introduced by Studebaker. Special motor-home bodies were available for Chevrolet, Dodge, and Ford truck chassis. Ford Division announced the availability of the Condor, a complete self-contained unit built on a modified Ford truck chassis. Traville Corporation of Detroit produced a self-powered deluxe travel home called the Traville, mounted on a one-ton Chevrolet chassis.

The 44th National Automobile Show was visited by 1,147,742 persons during its nine-day run in Detroit's Cobo Hall.

A scaled-down version of the famed Cord 810, the Sportsman, was announced by Glenn Pray of Oklahoma for limited production.

The International Rectifier Company unveiled a solar energy-propelled Baker electric (1912 vintage) car. The vehicle was outfitted with a roof deck composed of 10,640 individual solar cells.

American Motors opened an Eastern Division Parts Warehouse in Philadelphia and announced a major expan-

milestones

sion program at its Kelvinator plant in Grand Rapids, Michigan. Ford Motor Company completed a major expansion program at its Metuchen, New Jersey, plant. General Motors erected new buildings or additions at its plant in Warren, Michigan, at its Saginaw Steering Gear Division Plant, and at its Cadillac Division Detroit plant. Chrysler Corporation purchased a plant in Warren, Michigan, for the construction of mobile airport lounges. Studebaker Corporation acquired Paxton Products, Inc., a maker of superchargers for automobiles and other vehicles, and also purchased the Franklin Manufacturing Company, a Minneapolis manufacturer of refrigerators and other appliances.

Six new truck models were introduced during the year. General Motors displayed its 6500 series featuring a V-6 gasoline engine. White Motor introduced a new line of trucks, the White 7000 series. International Harvester brought its Loadstar Line, a series of medium and light-heavy duty trucks. Mack Trucks introduced its F series featuring diesel or gasoline engines and four- and six-wheel chassis options. Willys Motors displayed a new series of four-wheel-drive trucks named the Gladiator line.

Studebaker featured a shorter diesel truck tractor in its E-45 line, permitting the tractor to be combined with a 40-foot trailer and still meet the legal length requirements of states.

1963 Studebaker halted production of automobiles in the United States on December 20. While continuing to sell cars in the U. S., the company moved its primary base of automotive manufacturing to Hamilton, Ontario.

The Marmon-Herrington Company, after 31 years in operation, announced it would leave the automotive business.

163

Automobiles of America

1963—An engineering and consumer evaluation program was launched by Chrysler Corporation with its specially designed turbine car.

Kaiser JEEP Corporation, formerly Willys Motors, Inc., moved its headquarters from Toledo, Ohio, to Oakland, California. The Automotive Division of the corporation maintained its executive offices and operations in Toledo.

Two production milestones were established during the year. Ford Motor Company produced its 60-millionth vehicle, and Chevrolet Division produced its 50-millionth vehicle.

New 1963 models introduced included: Chrysler's new luxury model, the New Yorker Salon; Lincoln-Mercury's Comet Sportster and the Marauder in its regular series; and Studebaker's Super-Lark and Super-Hawk.

Checker Motor Corporation revealed technical details of a new Town Custom limousine scheduled for limited production.

Five new 1964 models were introduced in the fall of the year. Chevrolet brought out a new line of cars called the

milestones

Chevelle. Oldsmobile introduced its new Jetstar 88 series and a new sports-type car, the Jetstar I. Studebaker unveiled its new model, the Challenger. Lincoln-Mercury added the Caliente series to its Comet line.

Lincoln-Mercury dropped its Meteor line at the end of the 1963 model run.

Experimental vehicles with internal combustion engines and turbine-power plants were exhibited during the year. Chrysler Corporation introduced a new turbine engine in a specially styled Chrysler turbine car. Ford Motor Company began testing a 300-HP turbine engine in an experimental truck. Pontiac introduced the X-400. Oldsmobile exhibited the J-TR, a four-passenger convertible. Plymouth unveiled its experimental convertible, the Satellite. The Monza GT and Monza SS were exhibited by Chevrolet. Ford Motor Company unveiled the Allegro, Cougar II, and Mustang II.

1963—The highly stylized Buick Riviera was introduced in the fall of 1962 as a two-door hardtop.

Automobiles of America

Lincoln-Mercury introduced the Super Cyclone, Mercury Montego and Super Marauder.

Major construction completed at existing plant sites during the year included: General Motors' expansion and modernization of its Tarrytown, New York, Chevrolet and Fisher Body assembly plants; Ford Motor Company's expansion of its assembly facilities at the Rouge plant in Dearborn, Michigan; and completion of a new final assembly line at American Motors' Kenosha, Wisconsin, assembly plant.

International Harvester acquired an assembly plant in San Leandro, California, from the Kaiser Aluminum & Chemical Corporation, for the production of heavy-duty trucks.

Studebaker Corporation, following a policy of making running rather than annual model changes, began installing seat belts during March. Front-seat belts were installed as standard equipment on all other cars beginning with the 1964 model run. Other innovations developed during the year included: Push-button operated headlights that swing out of the fender's forward edges were offered on the Chevrolet Corvette, and Cadillac Motor Division's Twilight Sentinel, an option that automatically turns headlights on at dusk or off at dawn when the ignition switch is on.

Highlights and features of the trucking industry during 1963 included: The American Association of State Highway Officials recommended that maximum gross weights of truck combinations be increased from 73,280 pounds to between 88,000 and 90,000 pounds, maximum width be increased from 96 to 102 inches and height from $12\frac{1}{2}$ to $13\frac{1}{2}$ feet, and permissible length of single units increased from 35 to 40 feet. International Harvester introduced a new light-duty truck, the model 900, and a new 210 series of heavy-duty trucks. Studebaker's new "Service Champ" was announced as America's first 1/2 and 3/4-ton service truck

milestones

bodies of reinforced fiberglass. Chevrolet Division announced it would start production in late 1963 of a light-duty panel delivery van, the Chevy Van.

Three new mobile homes were introduced during the year. International Harvester unveiled a family camper adaptation of its Scout utility vehicle. Clark Equipment Company introduced the Cortez, a mobile home that provided living and sleeping facilities for four adults. Stewart Coach Industries, of Bristol, Indiana, offered a 17-foot trailer that could also be converted into a home on water.

Goodyear Tire & Rubber Company introduced a premium safety tire featuring an inner "spare" on which a motorist can continue to drive for 100 miles or more after the outer carcass blows.

1964 Four automotive milestones were passed during the year. General Motors Corporation, with its five divisions, produced more than four million vehicles in the 1964 model year, the first time any manufacturer had done so. For the first time new car registrations went over the eight million mark. Dodge Division celebrated its 50th year in the automotive industry. Studebaker Corporation stopped producing engines with the closedown of its South Bend, Indiana, plant. The company began using engines produced by General Motors.

Three new sports-type cars appeared during mid-1964. Ford introduced the Mustang, Chrysler-Plymouth unveiled the Barracuda and American Motors brought out the Marlin.

New models introduced in the fall for the 1965 model run included: Chrysler-Plymouth's 300-L; Dodge's new intermediate Coronet series, and the Dodge Monaco, a top of the line two-door hardtop; Ford's LTD in the Galaxie series; and Buick's Gran Sports models of the Skylark and Riviera series.

167

Fritz Duesenberg, son of one of the brothers who produced Duesenbergs in the 1920s and 1930s, announced that a new firm had been founded in Indianapolis to build modern luxury cars patterned after the famous old Duesenberg.

The selector pattern of automatic transmissions was standardized as Park-Reverse-Neutral-Drive-Low. Manufacturers began switching to anti-glare suede paint for dashboards. They also offered disc brakes on many 1965 models. Ford applied paint primer by a new process called electrocoating on '64 Thunderbirds and Lincolns.

American Motors, Ford and General Motors adopted a two-year or 24,000-mile warranty, whichever came first, on all parts except tires, which are warranted by the tire manufacturer. Chrysler Corporation offered a five-year or 50,000-mile warranty on the engine, transmission, driveline and rear axle.

New plants and expansion programs completed by manufacturers included: General Motors' Fremont, California, assembly plant; Cadillac Division's expansion program at its Detroit facilities, including the dedication of a new engineering center; Ford Motor Company's expansion and conversion of its Nashville, Tennessee, factory to the manufacturing of float glass, and the completion of its new steel making facilities at its Rouge plant in Dearborn, Michigan; and American Motor's new engine and axle plant in Kenosha, Wisconsin.

New developments in the trucking industry included the introduction of Dodge's new Camper Wagon; GMC Truck and Coach Division's Handi-Van, a light duty truck; and Kaiser JEEP Corporation's Tuxedo Park IV, a sporty version of its Jeep Universal. GMC Truck and Bus Division introduced two forged I-Beam axles for front-wheel suspensions of light trucks.

New experimental vehicles exhibited during the year

milestones

1964—The Ford Mustang featured a long hood and short deck with its sports-car styling.

1964—The fast-back styling of the Plymouth Barracuda included a smooth contour line made by the roof, rear window and rear deck.

169

included: Lincoln-Mercury's Park Lane 400, featuring electric blanket-type heating elements installed in the seats; General Motors' Firebird IV, Runabout and GM-X; Chevrolet's Toronado and Chevy II Super Nova. Other vehicles shown included: Buick's Silver Arrow; American Motors' Rambler Tarpon; Dodge's Charger II; and Ford's experimental station wagon, the Aurora.

Developments in the gas turbine field continued as Ford Motor Company introduced a 600 HP truck tractor. General Motors displayed its Turbo Cruiser No. 2, a turbine-powered bus and a turbine-powered freight hauler, called the Bison, designed especially to carry containerized cargo. Chrysler Corporation continued its public testing program of its turbine car.

1965

Passenger-car and commercial-vehicle production in 1965 established all-time records. Automobile production totaled 9,335,277 units, almost 1.4 million above the previous peak established in 1955. Truck and bus production climbed to 1,802,603 units, more than 240 thousand vehicles above the previous high established in 1964.

The United States and Canada agreed to eliminate tariffs on new motor vehicles and original parts for production of new vehicles. The agreement was known as the Automotive Products Trade Act of 1965.

The U. S. motor-vehicle industry granted $10 million to the University of Michigan to establish a highway-research institute and to aid in its support for the first five years. The grant was described by university officials as the largest corporate gift ever received by a university for any purpose.

Chevrolet Division of General Motors became the first producer in the industry to build more than three million cars and trucks in a single year.

A program to establish a nationwide communications network to aid motorists in distress was announced by

1965—Fender skirts and stainless steel on the lower body were two styling highlights of the 1965 Pontiac Bonneville.

the Automobile Manufactuers Association. The system, known as HELP for Highway Emergency Locating Plan, called for the use of Citizens Band two-way radio equipment in private passenger cars. Motorists in need of aid would make their needs known on CB Channel Nine where the message could be picked up by a round-the-clock monitoring station within the 10-to-20-mile range of the equipment.

Experimental vehicles displayed during the year included: American Motors' St. Maritz and the Tahiti; Plymouth's XP-Vip; Lincoln-Mercury's Mercury Astron, Comet Escapade, Comet Cyclone Sportster and Lincoln Continental Coronation Coupe; Dodge's Charger II; Ford's Bordinet Cobra, Mercer Cobra, GT Mark I and the Black Pearl; and Chevrolet's Mako-Shark II and Concours.

Chevrolet Division unveiled its truck of tomorrow with its tractor powered by a 280 HP gas turbine engine.

As part of its truck-turbine program, Ford Motor Company tested its 600 HP turbine truck on a cross country tour. Chrysler Corporation completed its two-year turbine consumer-research testing program.

Rear seat belts became standard equipment on all 1966

models. Dual braking systems were made available on all 1967 U. S.-produced cars. Pontiac introduced an overhead camshaft six-cylinder engine standard on all Tempest, Tempest Custom and LeMans models for 1966. All Ford station wagons featured a dual tailgate that opens either as a tailgate for loading cargo or sideways as a conventional passenger car door.

American Motors Corporation dropped the "Rambler" prefix on its Ambassador line.

The Avanti II, a car similar in design to the Avanti formerly made by Studebaker Corporation, was introduced in August. Made by the Avanti Motor Corporation, South Bend, Indiana, the new Avanti had a fiberglass body and was powered by a Chevrolet engine.

The Cord Automobile Company of Oklahoma began production of the scaled-down model of the classic Cord of the 1930's called the Sportsman.

1965—Dodge's new intermediate Coronet line of cars included the Coronet 440 four-door sedan.

milestones

Chevrolet Division introduced the Sportsvan, a vehicle built with a commercial chassis but including passenger car equipment.

Oldsmobile Division introduced its 1966 Toronado, the first car with front-wheel drive to be built in the United States since 1937. Other new models offered during the fall included: Chrysler-Plymouth Division's Town and Country Station Wagon in the Chrysler Newport series and the Plymouth Vip in the Fury line; American Motors' three new top of the line models, the DPL in the Ambassador line, Rebel in the Classic line and the Rogue in the American line; Ford Motor Company introduced the Bronco, a four-wheeled drive jeep-type vehicle, and added the Fairlane 500/XL and Fairlane GT as new models to its existing line; Chevrolet Division introduced the Caprice, a top of the line model in its Impala series; Lincoln-Mercury Division added the Capri to its Mercury Comet series; Dodge Division introduced its new sports fastback, the Charger; and Shelby American, Inc., introduced the Shelby GT 350, a modified high performance version of the Ford Mustang Fastback.

Highway Products, Inc., of Ohio offered a new line of trucks, called Compac-Vans. Powered by Cummings, Ford, General Motors or Chrysler engines, the units are of an integrated design so that the entire truck including cab, floor, roof and fluted aluminum sides are constructed as a single unit.

Chrysler Corporation announced that it had purchased the Lone Star Boat Company of Plano, Texas.

Major construction of manufacturing facilities completed in 1965 included: Ford Motor Company's Woodhaven, Michigan, stamping plant; Chrysler Corporation's Belvidere, Illinois, assembly plant and its stamping plant in Sterling Township, Michigan. General Motors dedicated its new training center in Detroit.

1966—The Vixen, an American Motors experimental car, featured a landau-type roof with canted vents in the rear.

1966

The year was highlighted by enactment of the National Traffic and Motor Vehicle Safety Act and the Highway Safety Act and establishment of the Department of Transportation.

The National Traffic and Motor Vehicle Safety Act was designed to provide and coordinate a national safety program and establish safety standards for motor vehicles. The Highway Safety Act sought to establish a coordinated national highway safety program through financial assistance to the states to accelerate highway-traffic safety programs. The Department of Transportation was formed to insure that the general welfare and the economic growth and stability of the nation would benefit from policies that would enable fast, safe, efficient and convenient transportation at the lowest cost consistent with other national objectives.

After 64 years as an automobile manufacturer, Studebaker Corporation in Canada terminated car production in March. The first Studebaker, an electric vehicle, was built in 1902. The corporation ended production in the United States in December 1963.

New interest in electric vehicles was aroused as two major motor-vehicle manufacturers outlined their research and testing programs for electric cars. General Motors demonstrated two electric vehicles, a fuel-cell van called the Electrovan and battery-powered Corvair, the Electrovair II. Ford Motor Company announced the development of a new sealed sodium-sulphur battery for electrical vehicles designed to last the life of the vehicle.

1966—The distinctive Oldsmobile Toronado featured front-wheel drive.

Collapsible steering columns were installed on all General Motors, Chrysler Corporation, and American Motors cars. Ford Motor Company offered a newly designed energy-absorbing steering wheel featuring a padded hub. Oldsmobile Division offered as an option an engine preheater designed to keep carburetor inlet temperatures at about 100 degrees, allowing easier cold-weather starting. Optional on 400- and 425-cubic-inch V-8 Oldsmobile engines was an ultra-high-voltage capacitor system. The new system fires fouled plugs to boost their life nearly four times and eliminates engine ignition tuneup for at least 24,000 miles. General Motors, Ford, and American Motors followed Chrysler Corporation in adopting the five-year or 50,000-mile warranty on the engine, transmission, driveline, and rear axle. Chrysler extended its total car warranty to 24 months or 24,000 miles. All 1967 cars had underbodies made of corrosion-resistant galvanized steel for added anti-rust protection.

Two new sports-type cars were introduced during the fall of the year. Lincoln-Mercury Division brought out its Cougar and Chevrolet Division introduced its Camaro. Other new models offered included Chevrolet's Concourse, an addition to the Chevelle series; Dodge's two additions to its Coronet series, the Coronet SE and R/T; Kaiser JEEP Corporation's Super Wagoneer, a luxury station wagon available in 2- or 4-wheel drive; Lincoln-Mercury's new series, the Mercury-Marquis and Mercury Brougham; Cadillac's five-passenger Fleetwood Eldorado; and the Shelby GT 500 by Shelby American, Inc.

Production of the Sportsman, a smaller model of the Classic Cord, terminated in July. Less than 100 of the vehicles had been built when the company was placed in receivership.

Five idea cars were exhibited during the year to test consumer reaction. American Motors displayed Cavalier, Vixen, AMX and AMX II, and Pontiac introduced its Banshee.

White Motor Company developed a heavy-duty truck engine which combines the advantages of both diesel and gasoline in a power plant using regular gasoline and weigh-

milestones

ing 40 per cent less than a diesel engine. Dodge Division offered an automatic dock leveler, a Hi-Lo hydraulic body lift mounted on a Dodge W-500 four wheel drive truck. The unit can be raised from ground level to 48 inches. White Truck's new 4000 and 9000 model series of heavy duty trucks featured fiberglass frame-mounted fenders easily removed for full engine accessibility with a fiberglass integral hood and fender assembly optional. International Harvester exhibited a Scout 800 with Dreamer camper insert and a D-1000 Travelall with compact trailer. Minibus, Inc., began supplying 19–23 passenger miniature buses to metropolitan areas for short-haul downtown service.

White Motor Company announced purchase of Hercules Engine Division of the Hupp Corporation.

New facilities completed during the year included: Chrysler Corporation's truck assembly plant in Fenton, Missouri, and the Huber Avenue Foundry in Detroit; Mack Truck Corporation's Product Development Center in Allentown, Pennsylvania; International Harvester Corporation's Springfield, Ohio, assembly plant; General Motors' new Chevrolet and Fisher Body assembly plants at Lordstown, Ohio, and its Central Foundry Division's new iron foundry at Defiance, Ohio; Ford Motor Company's automotive safety research center in Dearborn, Michigan; and American Motors completion of a major expansion program at its proving ground near Burlington, Wisconsin.

1967 By the beginning of 1967, 57 per cent of the proposed 41,000 mile National System of Interstate and Defense Highways had been opened to traffic. The year was marked by continuing attention to such problems as safety, exhaust emission, mechanic upgrading, and car thefts. Design standards for cars produced in 1968 were announced; manufacturers incorporated over 600 new features into their various models during the year.

Automobiles of America

1967—The five-passenger Fleetwood Eldorado combined front-wheel drive, variable ratio-power steering and automatic level control for luxury driving.

1967—A wide "bumble bee" paint band on the nose helped distinguish Chevrolet's Camaro.

Seven additional states enacted periodic motor vehicle inspection laws, bringing to 26 the number with such laws.

Research on electric vehicles reached new levels with the U. S. Department of Commerce holding a seminar on the subject; eight papers on electrically-powered cars were presented at the annual Society of Automotive Engineers meeting. Ford announced that in conjunction with Ford of Britain it had produced the Comuta, a passenger car driven by electricity. Ford joined with Mobil Oil in a $7 million project to develop emission-free, gas powered vehicles. General Motors showed Electrovair II at the New York International Auto Show and undertook a joint project with the University of Pennsylvania to explore the feasibility of a fleet of small, limited-emission vehicles. Westinghouse unveiled the Markette, a two-passenger electric.

Mid-year model introductions included: Pontiac Firebird; Buick GS40; new sports models for the Jeepster Commando series; the Opel Rallye Kadett, a German-made car sold by Buick dealers; a new, nine passenger, suburban-type station wagon by General Motors Corporation.

The Pontiac Firebird came with a deflated spare tire as standard equipment, along with a charge of Freon gas for inflation.

Under the terms of the United States-Canada Import-Export Free Trade Agreement effected in 1965, 1,162,953 vehicles were exported and imported from the United States and Canada during the three years ending in 1967.

To curb thefts (557,000 reported in 1966), General Motors equipped cars with buzzers that sound when drivers leave their cars while the keys are still in the ignition. Chrysler placed an ignition switch connector in vehicles, making access to the rear of the switch more difficult.

Medium blue was the most popular color with car buyers in 1967; white was their second choice.

Ford established an Industrial and Chemical Products

Division and formed two subsidiaries, Ford of Europe, Inc., and Ford, Philippines, Inc.

General Motors received a federal grant to study ways to perfect a method whereby motorists can find their destination without maps or road signs. The goal is to develop equipment into which a driver could dial his destination at the start of a trip. A device would then pick up the code of the roadside landmarks and transmit instructions to the driver.

A. J. Foyt in a Ford-powered Coyote Special won the Indianapolis "500" at a record average speed of 151.207 m.p.h. after the leading car, a turbine, dropped out with transmission trouble in the 197th lap.

The Cadillac Eldorado, a 1967 model, featured a front wheel drive.

Diamond and Reo, two of the oldest names in truck manufacturing, merged into the Diamond Reo Truck Division, White Motor Corporation.

Lincoln Continental offered dual chamber tires as original equipment. If the outer chamber of the tire went flat, the inner chamber permitted driving until repairs could be made.

Reflective racing stripes along the rocker panels and reflective painted wheels were presented as options for some Ford cars.

The Charles F. Kettering Award was given to Dr. Lawrence F. Hafstad of General Motors for meritorious work in patent, trademark, and copyright research and education.

Almost four out of every 10 cars (38 per cent) produced in 1967 had air conditioning units.

General Motors built its 100 millionth vehicle, a Chevrolet Caprice; Ford its 70 millionth, a Galaxie.

The Glassic, a 1931 Ford "A" replica, and a replica of the Auburn Speedster were placed on the market.

The 1968 autos continued a growing trend toward specialty sports-type cars with a wide range of personal and sports models on all price levels. Plymouth introduced the Road Runner, a new intermediate model; the Javelin was a new American Motors Corporation offering; Ford showed a fastback series called the Torino; and Mercury named a newly styled intermediate series the Montego. Shelby American marketed an all new convertible, the Cobra, with a stylized, padded roll-bar that could double as a ski or surfboard rack.

All makes had exhaust emission control systems as standard equipment. A few lines offered pneumatic load levellers to help maintain normal rear end standing or riding height regardless of load distribution. Disc brakes were more common. A few of the many new safety features on the 68's included seat belts for all passengers, side marker lights, non-reflective windshield surfaces, padded interiors and front seat backs, and no spinner hubs.

The 1968 Fords came with a "controlled crush" front end to lessen impact in case of head-on collisions and new squeeze-type door handles recessed within arm rests.

Concealed windshield wipers were standard on most General Motors cars and ventless side windows on some. A special safety seat for children was offered on General Motors models.

Pontiac's energy-absorbing bumper and an electrical charging system that used integrated micro-circuits were innovations.

Lincoln offered a new option: a transistorized automatic headlight dimmer.

Chrysler and Dodge wagons could be bought with a washer-wiper for the tailgate window.

Oldsmobile featured a horn ring partially imbedded in the inside diameter of the steering wheel.

A buzzer in American Motors Corporation cars warned the driver when he left the lights on.

Automobiles of America

1968

New car registrations in 1968 totaled 9,403,862 units, smashing a record set in 1965. Figures for 1968 showed that for the first time highway travel in the U. S. exceeded one trillion vehicle miles.

Autolite's "Lead Wedge," traveling at a speed of 138.862 m.p.h., set the first official United States Auto Club speed record for battery-powered vehicles.

Dodge introduced a sports-styled pickup truck with bucket seats and a center console.

The United States Post Office Department reported that it would buy more than 24,000 quarter-ton trucks to help some city carriers substitute wheels for feet.

Many Formula I racing cars started using air foils, a high-mounted horizontal wing installed at the rear of the car to provide additional down thrust.

Warranties on '69 models were set at 12 months/12,000 miles for the full car, five years/50,000 miles on the drive train components. Coverage was restricted to first and second owners.

Mercury and Chrysler adopted a wood-like paneling applique on some hardtops and convertibles, the first time such an option was ever offered for other than station wagons.

A new official United States presidential limousine, a glass-roofed Lincoln Continental, was put into service.

International Harvester introduced a prototype gas turbine engine on the Turbostar, and a new hinged and spring-mounted car on another line. The cab had a separate frame hinged at front and supported by a coil spring at the rear.

Two new mid-year models, American Motors' fastback two-seat AMX sports coupe and the Lincoln Continental Mark III, were placed on the market.

General Motors dedicated a new safety laboratory and a 67-acre vehicle dynamics test area at its Milford Proving Grounds.

Checker Motors Corporation offered diesel-powered

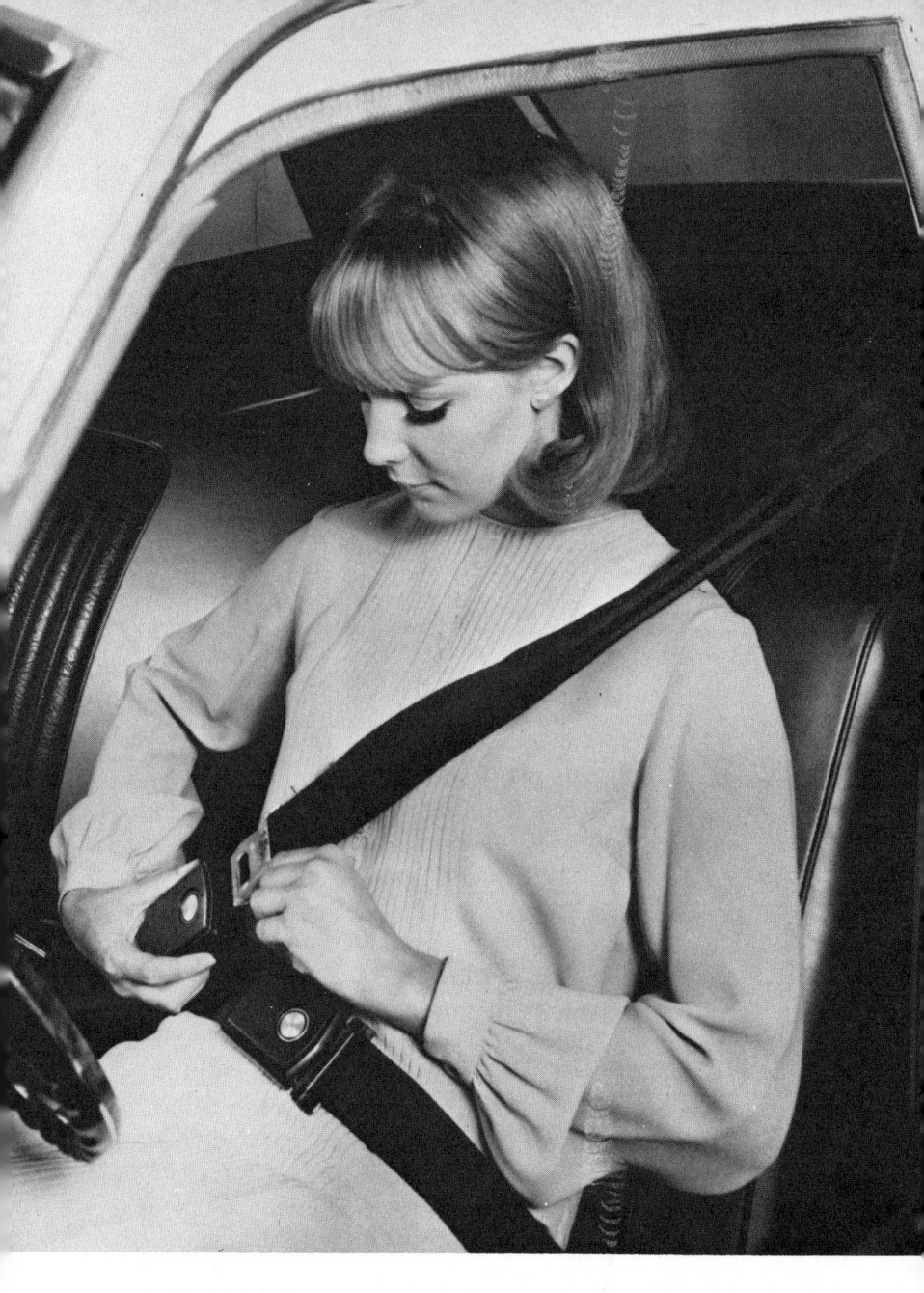

1968—Shoulder harnesses were required equipment on all cars sold after Jan. 1, 1968.

1968—The sporty fastback Cyclone, introduced by Mercury, included energy-absorbing steering columns and steering wheels as safety features.

models on taxicabs and passenger cars, becoming the only United States manufacturer with such an option.

The Amitron, an electric compact powered by lithium-nickel fluoride batteries, was shown. The vehicle was developed by American Motors Corporation in conjunction with Gulton Industries.

Rowan Controller Corporation presented an electric car at the New York International Auto Show. Chevrolet's Astra II and Ford's Mach II, both mid-engine prototype cars, were exhibited at the same show.

Ford expanded its training program for mechanics, graduating 1,200 in 1968 vs. 840 in 1967. General Motors instituted Project Transition to help men soon to be separated from the armed forces to learn automotive repair skills.

Experimental activity during 1968 included: General Motors' and Chrysler's building of cars with fluidic controls in which air was used instead of mechanical or electrical devices to activate various accessories; Lincoln-Mercury and Plymouth experimented with a periscope-like device to

milestones

aid rear and side vision; automotive safety engineers experimented with gas bags that would inflate instantly in case of an accident to cushion the occupants of the car.

Pontiac introduced the "Mini-Pump," an emergency air pump to inflate tires, driven by the car's engine.

Chrysler Corporation's 20th annual Trouble Shooting Contest was held on the front stretch of the Indianapolis Speedway. More than 200 teen-agers competed to discover and correct "bugs" planted in 1968 Plymouths.

Michigan International Speedway held its first race. The M.I.S. is a $6 million race course near Detroit designed for high speed racing cars of all types. It was estimated that paid attendance at all auto race events in the United States would exceed 60 million in 1968.

A 12-cent postage stamp commemorating the 105th birthday of Henry Ford was issued.

The highest price—$45,000—ever paid at public auction for an antique car was brought by a 1913 Mercer Raceabout. This eclipsed the previous high of $31,000, paid in 1967 for a 1913 Stanley Mountain Wagon.

It became illegal, according to federal regulations, to mail master keys which would operate ignition switches, door locks and trunk locks of two or more vehicles.

Several new models were included in the 1969 line-up of new cars: the Pontiac Grand Prix "J," a hardtop coupe boasting the longest hood in the industry, and the Mercury Marauder, a sports-type hardtop.

Among the new features were a skid-control braking system actuated by a miniature computer as an option on the Ford Thunderbird and the Lincoln Continental, safety door beams to protect passengers against side impacts on most General Motors cars, and special energy absorbing frames with an S-shaped front section to help absorb front end collisions on the large Ford line and Mercurys.

Other developments on the '69's: Pontiac Grand Prix,

radio antenna imbedded in the windshield; a sealed cooling system on the Cadillac; and Chevrolet's Liquid Tire Chain, a device to spray blended resins on tires to give increased traction on ice or snow.

Dodge offered an auxiliary light, called Super-Lite, which filled in the gap between bright and dim lights. The Chevrolet Corvette came with headlamp washers. Chrysler's station wagons featured air spoilers on their roofs to help keep the rear windows clear.

American Motors Corporation adopted translucent battery cases for see-through fluid level checking and made fiberglass, bias-belted tires standard on the AMX line. Locking steering columns appeared on General Motors cars as an anti-theft measure.

The U. S. motor vehicle industry reached a historic milestone in January 1968 when the 250 millionth vehicle was produced.

1969

Nearly 106 million drivers' licenses were in force at the beginning of 1969, representing a 12 million increase over a 5-year period.

Plans for United States-built compacts and sub-compacts were readied as final tabulations of new car sales for 1968 revealed that imports had claimed nearly one million sales for the year. The Ford Maverick, a small 103″ w.b. model priced to sell under $2000, was a new compact offering; American Motors followed with a 179″ over-all length economy compact called the Hornet.

Mid-year introductions brought these new models to the market: American Motors Corporation's SC/Rambler, a custom-built car in the high performance category; a four-wheel-drive utility vehicle called the Blazer by Chevrolet; a new high performance Pontiac Firebird with an air foil spanning the rear deck; a new Mercury performance model, the Cyclone Spoiler; International's restyled compact rec-

milestones

reational vehicle, the Aristocrat, with a convertible top in a vinyl-coated fabric; and the Dodge Charger Daytona, featuring concealed headlights, rear stabilizer, and a 375 h.p. engine.

General Motors Parts Division was established as a separate division of General Motors. GMC Truck and Coach Division added Cummins diesel engines to its line of heavy-duty truck engines.

Mobil Oil announced the discontinuance of its annual Economy Run.

Pontiac's 13 millionth car and International Harvester's one millionth tractor were produced.

General Motors fitted their vehicles with "tell-tale" odometers designed to provide visual evidence if someone turns back mileage readings. Five experimental special purpose vehicles for limited urban use were demonstrated as part of the General Motors "Progress of Power" show: two

1969—The Chevrolet Blazer, a new four-wheel drive entry in the sports-utility field, offered an optional hard-top.

1969—The Ford Maverick, with a 103-inch wheelbase and a suggested retail price of $1,995, challenged the U. S. imported car market.

were gasoline powered; one, electric, another, gasoline-electric; and the fifth was a hybrid gasoline-electric with front-wheel drive.

A total of 540,000 truck camper pick-ups were on the road as the booming recreational-vehicle market reached new heights. Ford introduced a new recreational vehicle, the Minihome, a complete home on wheels, on its Econoline van.

In mid-year car makers switched to bias-belted tires on about two-thirds of new car production. Remaining cars were fitted with bias-belted tires at the beginning of the 1970 model year.

A U. S. Senate staff report prepared for the Commerce Committee urged the government to start developing steam powered cars to help combat air pollution.

The Post Office Department awarded a contract to Electric Fuel Propulsion, Inc., of Ferndale, Mich., to build four experimental electric vehicles for test and evaluation.

The government issued advance notice of a proposed rule that would require the installation of inflatable air bags in the dashboard of vehicles for passenger protection. Some of the safety features incorporated into the 1970 autos were bigger and brighter turn signals, lighting systems with four front lamps operating at night, side impact bars, concealed headlights that open in three seconds, and bias-belted tires.

The Tire Industry Safety Council was formed by U. S. tire manufacturers in response to growing public interest in tires and tire safety.

American Motors Corporation launched a major expansion program which will increase its styling, engineering research and planning facilities in Detroit by more than 50%.

A copy of the Stutz Bearcat will be produced, it was announced by the Stutz Motor Car Co. of America.

The federal Truth in Lending Law went into effect, requiring auto dealers selling on installment plans to state the cost, terms and conditions of credit in a uniform way so that prospective purchasers can compare credit terms.

Aerocar III, a flying automobile produced by Aerocar, Inc., in Longview, Wash., was shown.

Representatives of the major independent auto service associations agreed to form a National Certification Board to certify automotive mechanics and paint and body men.

Ford expanded by 10-fold its Project Transition training program, which prepares men nearing the end of their military service to become auto mechanics, after a successful pilot project.

Ford changed to a simplified, 12-month warranty with its 1970 models. The warranty had no limitation on mileage or number of owners. It also eliminated all requirements for validation of maintenance.

All the car makers presented auto theft protection in their cars in the form of steering column locks.

A move toward body-on-frame construction, as opposed to unitized body construction, was followed by some manufacturers. Other trends in the 1970 models were seen in such features as concealed radio antennas and windshield wipers, increased use of plastic grilles, front seat back locks that automatically unlatch when a door is opened, tamper-proof odometers, electronic skid control brake systems, electrically heated rear glass defrosters, and disc brakes as standard equipment on more models than before.

General Motors offered, as an option on many cars, a fingertip wiper control system whereby wipers and washers can be operated from the turn signal lever. Cadillac offered a new luxury option for production cars—an electrically operated sunroof. Pontiac installed plastic gas tanks on some of its station wagons. The Monte Carlo, a prestige-type specialty car from Chevrolet, came with a hood that measured six feet from grille to windshield wiper, the longest hood in Chevrolet history. GMC added the Jimmy, a multipurpose sport and utility vehicle with a removeable fiberglass top, to its 1970 truck line.

Mercurys featured a freon-filled shock absorber and some Ford Motor Co. cars adopted a ventilation system which brings fresh air in through the cowl area and exhausts it through the door pillar.

Chrysler offered a headlamp delay system, as optional equipment on Plymouth, Dodge, and Chrysler, which gives the driver the choice of leaving his headlights on for approximately 90 seconds after turning off the headlight and ignition switch. Plymouth Barracudas and Dodge Challengers had a new roll-over structure set under the roof panel as a safety feature.

American Motors' cars displayed a new type windshield with a chemically treated inner pane which granulates into tiny blunt-edged particles upon impact, reducing the possibility of facial lacerations. The inner pane also stretches on impact to provide a cushioning effect. Some AMC cars offered an optional low fuel warning light.

Hood scoops, air spoilers in the rear, and racing stripes continued to identify many of the performance cars which offered a myriad of special equipment for the auto enthusiast.

U. S. car makers produced a total of 351 models for 1970.

milestones

1970

A general business recession coupled with a 67-day strike by the U.A.W. against GM dropped new car sales by 2.1 million units in 1970. U.S. automakers also found themselves fighting to keep their leadership in a global automotive battle. Japanese manufacturers, especially, were challenging the older makers in Europe and the U.S.

By April the first of a new generation of American subcompacts reached the market. AMC's Gremlin, a 161" slantback with a counterbalanced rear window lift gate was introduced first. It came with a 6-cylinder engine and had a fold-down rear seat for additional carrying space.

AMC's Gremlin was the first American subcompact to reach the market.

Two more subcompacts were brought out in September: Ford's Pinto and Chevrolet's Vega. The 96" w.b. Vega was built on a highly automated and computerized assembly line. It featured an innovative 4-cylinder sleeveless aluminum en-

191

gine, front disc brakes, electric fuel pump and bolt-on fenders and front panels.

Ford installed a 4-cylinder, 75 h.p. German-made motor in the Pinto. The latter weighed 2000 pounds and had a rack and pinion steering system. Its short 20″ steering column came only to the dash; from there on in place of a column, there was a thick stranded cable.

Late in the year Chrysler entered the small car market with imported autos carrying the corporation's nameplates: Dodge Colt, made in Japan, and Plymouth Cricket from England. However, America's new small cars failed to displace the well-entrenched imports; by the end of 1970 imports had claimed a record 14.6 per cent of U.S. car sales.

Refineries started to turn out lead-free gasoline and most 1971 engines were designed to burn unleaded or low-pollutant fuels.

A car for moon exploration, the Lunar Rover vehicle, was unveiled. NASA's moon-rover was a 400-pound, electrically-powered car guided by a pistol-grip type control.

A Soviet delegation visited Ford company facilities in the U.S. in connection with the Russians' proposal to have Ford construct a truck plant in Eastern Europe; the bid was later turned down.

GMC announced that it would build a new medium-duty truck plant adjacent to its Pontiac factories. This was the biggest expansion in the division's history.

The government awarded contracts for development of experimental safety vehicles to Fairchild-Hiller Corp., American Machine and Foundry Co., and GM. Requirements called for vehicles in which passengers could survive a 50 m.p.h. crash into a rigid barrier.

GM signed a 5-year $50 million license agreement with Curtiss-Wright Corp. for rights to develop a Wankel rotary engine.

Chrysler offered a block heater as an option on its cars

1970—The sporty Scout SR-2, from I.H.C., came with an optional convertible Safari top and a flame-red body.

built in the U.S. and Canada.

All companies marketed emission control kits for their older models.

International Harvester produced a new air suspension system for its trucks. It also showed the first production version of a hydraulic brake anti-skid system for light trucks.

The AMA launched a new study to isolate, identify, and analyze various types of traffic noises. The $150,000 project would be conducted by acoustical experts.

AMC's stockholders approved the merger of Kaiser Jeep with their corporation. This ended Kaiser Corporation's vehicle venture dating back to 1946 when it had built its first car.

Gary Gabelich set a new world land-speed record. His Blue Flame, a rocket car running on liquefied natural gas, averaged 622 m.p.h. For the first time, the Indianapolis "500" purse exceeded $1 million.

The introduction of a series of 22 big diesel-engined trucks put Chevrolet in the big truck market. Mack trucks installed aluminum bumpers as standard equipment, a first for any U.S. vehicle maker.

193

More 4-cylinder new cars were sold than ones with 6-cylinder engines for the first time since Model "T" days.

Leonard Woodcock became president of the U.A.W. upon the death of Walter Reuther. Reuther, who was killed in a plane crash, had been president of the giant union since 1946.

Among milestone production records for the year were: Chevrolet's 70-millionth vehicle, Pontiac's 14-millionth and IHC's 5-millionth.

Mid-year introductions saw several new models: Lincoln-Mercury's small European-made Capri; Chrysler's 300-H, continuing the company's performance-oriented letter series; the GSX sports coupe from Buick with front and rear spoilers; the Dodge Challenger T/A featuring three 2-barrel carburetors and side exhaust.

The Federal Aid Highway Act of 1970 provided for future use of Highway Trust money for highway safety programs.

The drunk driver was the subject of a safety campaign sponsored by the National Safety Council. The Council noted that in 1969 drunk drivers were responsible for 25,000 traffic deaths and 800,000 accidents.

Emission control requirements caused a general lowering of horsepower in 1971 models. Other features of note: a steel guard beam in the doors of more cars; a maintenance-free sealed battery on certain GM cars; the Imperial's four-wheel, anti-skid braking system; a tailgate wiper-washer on Ford station wagons and, on some GM wagons, a disappearing tailgate with the glass sliding up into the roof and the gate into the underbody; "ventilating rotor" front power-disc-brakes on AMC cars; Buick's anti-wheel-spin system using a computer to prevent wheel spin on slippery surfaces; a Chrysler headlamp washer system for concealed headlamps and, on some Ford lines, automatic temperature-control air conditioning.

milestones

1971

Much of the auto industry's research and development effort in 1971 was devoted to meeting government regulations in safety and emission-control areas. There was also a rising tide of consumerism with the industry facing critics in Congress and elsewhere.

Auto-makers tested more than 1600 catalysts in their attempts to build a catalytic converter which would meet U.S. projected exhaust-emission standards.

As a running model change, Chrysler made automatic transmission, power steering and power disc brakes standard on all Chrysler cars.

The City of New York ordered a turbine vehicle and the GSA announced that its fleet of cars operating on liquified natural gas had reached 850. In the Los Angeles area more than 5,000 fleet vehicles were converted to burn natural gas and propane.

Mack Trucks cancelled plans to build a huge truck plant in the Soviet Union.

The AMA presented $1 million to the Highway Safety Research Institute at the University of Michigan for support of its programs.

1971—Chevrolet's entry in the small-car field, the Vega, had a fold-down rear seat for extra cargo space.

One of the casualities of the 1971 car year was the high performance, or "muscle" car, reflecting the increased insurance rates placed on it, a consumer trend towards less expensive cars and the clean air crusade.

The Automotive Information Council comprising 45 trade associations plus many individual corporate members from the vehicle service industry was formed; its purpose, to make the public aware of the industry's positive accomplishments.

Mazda dealers in the U.S. marketed a Japanese-made car with a Wankel rotary engine.

Dodge and AMC signed non-dealer shops to handle service work on their products.

Ford, ordered to divest itself of the assets of the Autolite Co., changed the name for its replacement parts to Motorcraft.

Domestic and foreign auto companies conducted 235 safety defect-recall campaigns involving around 9.4 million vehicles.

The cost of operating a car was 15.5 cents per mile based on 10,000 miles of travel per year, according to AAA estimates.

AMC inaugurated a liberalized warranty with its 1972 models. The company's Buyer Protection Plan included cost-free repair of any car for a 12,000-mile or 12-month period and free use of a late model loaner for owners whose cars had to be left overnight for repairs.

Ralph Nader, whose 1965 book "Unsafe at any Speed" became a rallying point for consumers, published a book, *What to Do with Your Bad Car: An Action Manual for Lemon Owners.*

A new safety standard designed to prevent the threat of death or injury from power-operated windows went into effect.

The Federal Highway Administration approved standardization of color combinations for highway signs and the use of symbols instead of words to give information and warning to drivers.

Thirty cars from Harrah's Automobile Collection in Reno, Nevada, were sent on a tour of Japan. The star of the tour was a Bugatti Royale coupe valued at more than $250,000. Studded tires were causing extensive damage to highways, according to several states considering legislation banning tires with studs.

The 75th anniversary of the auto industry was celebrated with a ceremony at Greenfield Village.

Truck sales in 1971 topped the 2-million mark for the first time ever. Light truck design reflected the growing trend toward increased use of trucks for personal transportation. Options such as AM-FM radios, plush carpeting, inflatable shock absorbers, automatic transmissions, and stylish colors were common.

In mid-year Lincoln-Mercury dealers introduced the De-Tomaso Pantera, a mid-engine sports car; Dodge brought out the Demon Sizzler, a compact with a slant six engine, and Pontiac showed its new compact, a 111″ w.b. model called Ventura II.

Chrysler discontinued importation of the French-made Simca, citing expenditures that would be required to have the car meet emission requirements.

Under a new regulation, the FTC called for documentation of claims made by some car-makers in their advertisements.

GM purchased a share of Isuzu Motors in Japan and Chrysler Corp. bought into Mitsubishi Motors Corp., also in Japan.

AM General, a subsidiary of American Motors Corp., announced plans to build a diesel transit bus.

As sales of off-the-road recreational vehicles—snowmobiles, all-terrain vehicles, dune buggies, and trail bikes—zoomed, more states began registration requirements and enacted safety and usage regulations.

Richard Petty became the first racing driver to win more than $1 million in prize money. A new world speed record for electric cars was set by the Silver Eagle at the Bonneville Salt Flats; its speed, 146 m.p.h.

Ford signed an agreement with the government to build

1971—Plymouth Sport Fury featured an optional power sunroof, which was opened by a switch near the rear view mirror.

an experimental safety vehicle for $1.00.

The 1972 models showed more emphasis on engineering, safety, and emission control than on styling. Manufacturers switched from reporting gross-horsepower ratings for their engines (output under laboratory conditions without accessories) to net horsepower. The latter represents the actual use of the engine on the car. Heavier and more massive bumpers were installed on most cars with increased clearance between the bumper and the body metal. Pontiac and Chrysler Corp. cars offered solid-state ignition systems which eliminate points and condensers; Lincoln featured a radiator with a 3-quart plastic reservoir to take an overflow for recycling later. The AMC's Hornet Sportabout could be bought with an exclusive interior trim design by Gucci, and Buick offered a manually operated sun roof.

Following President Nixon's announcement of a 90-day wage-price freeze, termination of the excise tax on automobiles, and a hike in import car tariffs, the industry recorded its first one million-unit sales month in history.

milestones

1972
Starting in January, a buzzer and light system to remind passengers to hook up their seat belts became mandatory.

A growing popularity of the sunroof option as an answer to the convertible (sales of convertibles had declined to 1.02 per cent of the market in 1971) was seen. All makers offered a sliding roof in either a manually- or power-operated version.

Mack Trucks approved a $1-million contribution to establish an American truck historical museum in Allentown, Pa.

The beginning of a new subcompact era in the light truck field was noted: Chevrolet started importing and selling a small pickup from Japan, the LUV; a subcompact pickup named the Courier, also from Japan, was marketed by Ford.

1973—Made in Japan, the Courier was Ford's compact import in the light truck field.

Chevrolet discontinued its 38-year sponsorship of the All American Soap Box Derby, a racing event for youngsters.

Automakers devoted considerable attention to the Wankel rotary engine. GM announced plans to install a Wankel engine on one of their small-car lines in the near future.

President Nixon, on a visit to Russia, presented a new Cadillac Eldorado to the Communist party secretary.

The Automobile Manufacturers Association (which had started life as the Automobile Board of Trade in New York in 1911, becoming the National Automobile Chamber of Commerce in 1913 and the AMA in 1934) changed its name to the Motor Vehicle Manufacturers Association. The MVMA stated that the new name would more accurately reflect the make-up of the association.

A new control system whereby large power-shift transmissions can be fully automatic, was shown by Detroit Diesel. The development made automatic shifting for off-highway vehicles practicable.

Electronic digital clocks were made standard on the Imperial and optional on Chrysler New Yorkers and Newports.

Allstate Insurance Co. took delivery of 200 Mercurys with air bags as part of Ford's pilot project of equipping about 1000 production cars with a bag-belt system.

Ford signed an agreement with a Dutch firm for the development of a Stirling engine. The Stirling, invented by a Scottish clergyman over 150 years ago, is an external combustion engine using hydrogen which is alternately heated and cooled to drive its pistons.

Chrysler, which had tested a fleet of turbine cars in the early '60's, received a contract to develop a turbo-car low in emissions and fuel consumption.

One hundred and fifty snowmobiles were fitted with rotary engines as part of field test.

Prestolite introduced a maintenance-free battery which eliminates the need to add water during the battery's normal life.

General Motors tested an experimental "on board" diagnostic system that monitors brakes, shock absorbers and steering

milestones

to warn drivers of existing or impending failures.

Plymouth added a station wagon to its Cricket line in mid-year, Ford offered a seat belt engine-interlock system on 1000 of its '72-1/2 Pintos, and the Jeep Renegade with many Custom appearance and performance accessories as standard equipment was introduced by AMC.

Auto thefts declined 7 per cent, reflecting the rising effectiveness of anti-theft devices the makers were installing.

A new 5-ton armor-plated Lincoln Continental limousine with bullet-proof glass and a hydraulic bubbletop was delivered to the White House.

The Automotive Organization Team (formerly The Automotive Old Timers) announced that an Automotive Hall of Fame would be built at the Northwood Institute campus in Midland, Michigan.

At the first United States International Transportation Ex-

1972—The Lincoln Continental Town Car's features included power "mini-vent" windows and a set of silver finished monograms for mounting on the car doors.

Automobiles of America

hibit ("Transpo '72") in Washington, D.C., the automakers showed their products and concepts for the future. Included were steam- and turbine- powered cars, safety vehicles and mass transportation systems.

An electronic-ignition option became available for Dodge light trucks and vans.

Fiberglass radial tires were marketed.

Eaton Corp. conducted what was believed to be the first test of air bags with humans as passengers.

GM announced plans to build a full scale permanent cold-weather test facility in Canada and an automotive wind tunnel in the U.S. to test full-sized cars.

All the '73's were equipped with front bumpers which would withstand a 5 m.p.h. barrier crash in front and a 2-1/2 m.p.h. crash in the rear. Reappearing on some of the 1973 cars as options were side-vent windows—a feature which had begun to disappear a few years earlier after decades of being standard on all cars. GM introduced a body style called a colonnade hardtop, with a thick center pillar and convertible-type door with no frame around the side glass. Ford and Chrysler offered anti-theft devices which activate the horns and lights if forced entry of the passenger compartment or trunk is attempted.

Oldsmobile introduced a new 197.5" compact called the Omega. Chrysler made its electronic ignition standard on all engines. Ford featured forged aluminum wheels as options on several of its smaller cars and for Cougar buyers, an AM/FM radio stereo tape player in one single unit. AMC's new Hornet Hatchback model came with a large rear opening which combines the rear window and trunk in a single unit. Swiveled swing-out bucket seats were options on Chevrolet Monte Carlo and Chevelle coupes.

1973 American Motors signed a licensing agreement with Curtiss-Wright Corp. to manufacture and sell Wankel rotary engines.

1972—The self-powered motor home represented one of the fastest-growing segments of the recreational vehicle industry.

The recreational vehicle market continued to grow and automakers became more closely involved. General Motors entered the field with a front-wheel-drive motor home carrying the GM name; Ford dealers began selling American Road camper bodies designed by Ford; IHC produced a rear-engine chassis specifically designed for motor homes.

Safety regulations required that as of January 1 all cars have side beams in their doors.

Two Mercedes-Benz cars which had been custom built for Adolph Hitler were sold for a record-breaking price at public auction in Arizona; one brought $153,000; the other, $93,000.

AMC's compact Hornet Sportabout offered a straw-colored, textured, 3-dimensional vinyl reproduction of woven cane fiberglass.

American truck-makers looked to developing countries as a huge new market for easily assembled, low-priced utility vehicles; Ford showed its Fiera, made in the Philippines; GM, the Harimau, assembled in Malaysia; IHC, the WUT (World

Utility Vehicle), made from components produced in Europe.

The new federal ban on odometer rollbacks also required that all sellers of motor vehicles—new and used car dealers and individuals—must disclose to the buyer, in writing, the number of miles the vehicle had travelled.

GM placed 1000 air-bag-equipped Impalas in service throughout the country and tested another 500 within its own organization.

Ford helped in the development of a fire-fighting pumper vehicle powered by a gas turbine.

Wide stripe whitewall tires showed signs of making a comeback.

Worldwide increases in fuel consumption raised fears of an energy crisis, and gasoline shortages developed in some areas of the U.S.

The first foreign experimental safety vehicle, a Fiat, was delivered to the U.S. government for testing.

International Harvester-Europe was organized as an IHC subsidiary.

GM tested a drunk driver device which requires drivers to pass a test by controlling the movement of a needle on an instrument panel dial before the car can start.

Among mid-year model offerings were: Buick's $2605 compact, the Apollo; Lincoln-Mercury's imported Pantera L, a 44″-high, 2-seat sports car; Dodge's Dart Sport Rallye featuring a small V-8 engine with 4-speed manual transmission.

The Indy "500" race, delayed several days because of rain and marred by fiery crashes, was stopped after 332-1/2 miles.

Chrysler celebrated the 25th anniversary of its Plymouth Trouble Shooting Contest.

Sales of subcompacts and compacts set new records as the large and intermediates' share of the market declined.

Ferris State College granted its first baccalaureate degrees to students enrolled in an automotive and heavy technology program.

milestones

Chrysler tested a new air conditioning system using air instead of Freon gas as a coolant and several automakers experimented with a new paint process involving the use of dry powder paint as a replacement for the present solvent-based liquid paint.

A completely sealed kingpin was installed on some of its lines by I.H.C.

By government edict, all 1974 model cars were equipped with seat belt interlock-ignition systems that required the driver and front seat passenger to fasten combination lap-shoulder belts before the car could be started and with energy absorbing rear bumpers capable of protecting the car from a 5 m.p.h. impact.

Ford announced America's first mass-produced metric system automobile engine. The 2.3 liter motor became standard on the 1974 Mustang II, a small, sporty and luxurious model with bucket seats, tachometer and cut pile carpeting. The Cougar XR-7, a two-door hardtop with standard power disc brakes in front was a new addition to Mercury's line. All Chevrolets were equipped with front disc brake wear sensors.

1974—Ford's Mustang II is 19 inches shorter than the 1973 Mustang and seven inches shorter than the original Mustang, 1964 (see p. 169).

Automobiles of America

The Caprice Classic coupe and the Impala Custom coupe continued GM's new Colonnade-type roof design with Chevelles featuring opera windows. Corvette celebrated its 20th anniversary. Four-wheel power disc brakes and a gauge to tell the level of the windshield wiper fluid were standard on '74 Imperials. To supplement the electronic ignition systems on all Chrysler Corporation cars, Dodge added an electronic gauge alert option which indicates low fuel level and low electrical system voltage. AMC's 1974 line featured free-standing front and rear bumpers. The company introduced a sporty Matador coupe with a 114" w.b., a long tapering hood and sloping rear deck. A trim and upholstery option, created by Oleg Cassini, was available on the new Matador. Jeep's Cherokee, a two-door sports utility vehicle, was also new for 1974.

pioneers

In the 19th century, the nearest thing to a practical form of personalized transportation was the horse and buggy. But there were men in America who envisioned something better. It was the imagination, resourcefulness and determination of men such as these that brought to America four million miles of modern roads and streets traveled by more than 100 million cars, trucks and buses.

APPERSON, Edgar

1870•1959 On July 4, 1894, drove his first car, manufactured on assignment for Elwood Haynes, with whom he and his brother Elmer later formed Haynes-Apperson Auto Company . . . after dissolution of Haynes-Apperson, Edgar and his brother formed Apperson Brothers Motor Car Company to manufacture the Apperson *Jack Rabbit* . . . following his brother's death, Edgar sold to a syndicate in 1924 . . . in 1946 made the initial member of industry's "Hall of Fame."

APPERSON, Elmer

1861•1920 Collaborated with brother Edgar on the manufacture of Elwood Haynes' first car . . . partner in both the Haynes-Apperson and the Apperson Brothers Motor Car

Company . . . died while watching auto race at Los Angeles Speedway.

AUSTIN, Walter S.

1866•1965 Along with his father, built the Austin Highway King in a little shop in Grand Rapids, Michigan, 1901–1918 . . . the Austin was a luxury car with some models costing $6,000 and up . . . his major contributions include inventions covering the four-speed planetary transmission with steering post shift, double cantilever springs, and two-speed axle.

BENDIX, Vincent

1883•1945 In 1907 organized an auto firm, and sold some 7,000 Bendix motor buggies before the company failed . . . developed the starter drive which bears his name, first selling it to the Eclipse Machine Company in 1913 . . . became a leader in the aircraft field, and sponsor of the Bendix-Transcontinental Air Races.

BRISCOE, Benjamin

1869•1945 Founded the Briscoe Manufacturing Company in 1887 . . . in 1903 joined with Jonathan Maxwell to form the Maxwell-Briscoe Motor Company . . . in 1910 organized the United States Motor Company, a short-lived (1912) aggregation of some 130 separate firms . . . left United States Motor Company in 1912, and in 1913 organized the Briscoe Motor Company and the Argo Motor Company to manufacture cyclecars.

pioneers

BRISCOE, Frank

1875•1954 Founder and president of Brush Runabout Company... also connected with brother Benjamin with Briscoe Manufacturing Company.... other endeavors included interests in Maxwell-Briscoe, United States Motor Company, and Briscoe Motor Company.

BUICK, David Dunbar

1855•1929 Instrumental in devising a technique for applying enamel to cast iron... using the money he received from his plumbing ventures, Buick in 1902 founded the Buick Manufacturing Company to work on a valve-in-head engine... having perfected the engine, he organized Buick Motor Car Company in 1903 with the backing of the Briscoe brothers... the company was unsuccessful, and on Nov. 1, 1904, William Durant bought the controlling interest.

CHADWICK, Lee S.

1875•1958 Engineering genius who held close to 200 patents, many in automotive field... built his first two cars in 1899 while superintendent of the Boston Ball Bearing Company... when company was sold in 1900, became general superintendent of the Searchmont Motor Company... built the Chadwick, 1903-1911... first car to use a supercharger, 1906... in racing competition, one of the fastest cars of its day... credited with developing a carburetor employing a variable gasoline flow for different throttle openings... president of Perfection Stove Company, 1923-1952.

CHALMERS, Hugh

1873•1932 Worked for National Cash Register from the time he was 14, rose to vice president before he was 30 . . . in 1907 bought the Thomas half of the Thomas-Detroit Company . . . by 1909 had complete control of Chalmers-Detroit, then renamed the Chalmers Motor Company . . . Chalmers backed Harry W. Ford's Saxon Motor Company in 1913 in a spectacular, though eventually unsuccessful, attempt to challenge the Model T . . . became chairman of the board of Chalmers when it was leased to Maxwell in 1917, a position he held until his retirement in 1922.

CHAPIN, Roy D.

1880•1936 First worked for Ransom E. Olds as a photographer and gear filer . . . while still in Olds' employ, drove a 1901 curved-dash model to New York for the second annual National Auto Show . . . left Olds in 1906 to organize, along with Howard E. Coffin, Thomas-Detroit Company later Chalmers-Detroit Company . . . in 1909, again with H. E. Coffin, Chapin with the backing of J. L. Hudson left Chalmers-Detroit to organize and head Hudson Motor Car Company . . . backed movement for good roads as chairman of numerous highway institutions . . . served as Secretary of Commerce under President Herbert Hoover in 1932.

CHEVROLET, Louis

1878•1941 Came to the United States from Switzerland in 1900 to sell a wine pump which he had invented . . . drove with brothers Gaston and Arthur . . . raced against Barney Oldfield . . . his racing style attracted William C. Durant, who engaged Chevrolet as team driver for Buick . . . designed the first models of the Chevrolet for the Chevrolet Motor Car Company in 1911 . . . president of Frontenac Motor Company, which, in addition to race cars, made a racing conversion for the Model T Ford.

CHRISTIE, John W.

1886•1944 First builder of a successful front wheel drive automobile . . . Christie racers, competing on tracks in the United States and abroad from 1904 to 1910, proved soundness of Christie's engineering concepts . . . manufacturered fire engine tractors, 1912-1916 . . . developed an armored tank in the 1930's capable of cross-country speeds of 50 m.p.h. . . . tested and liked by United States military but rejected by War Department . . . Christie's designs were sold abroad . . . British and Russians promptly began manufacturing Christie tanks in large numbers.

CHRYSLER, Walter P.

1875•1940 Left his job as works manager for American Locomotive in 1911 to join Buick Motor Company . . . when he left General Motors for Willys in 1920, Chrysler was president of Buick and first vice president of General Motors . . . at Willys Chrysler was executive vice-president engaged primarily in saving the company from bankruptcy . . . almost simultaneously, he was attempting to salvage the foundering Maxwell-Chalmers Company . . . by 1922 Willys was back on its feet, and Chrysler turned his full attention to the Maxwell-Chalmers situation . . . in 1924 he brought Maxwell-Chalmers out of the woods with the introduction at the National Automobile Show of the new Chrysler models . . . shortly thereafter, Chase Securities Corporation agreed to lend Maxwell $50 million, and the

corporation that was to become Chrysler was on its way
... the years following 1924 brought continuing success to
the Chrysler Corporation.

CLIFTON, Colonel Charles

1853•1928 In 1897 left Ball, Lewis and Yates Coal Mining Company to become secretary and treasurer for George N. Pierce Company . . . remained treasurer after a 1909 reorganization which saw the formation of Pierce-Arrow Motor Car Company . . . in 1916, Colonel Clifton became president of Pierce-Arrow, and in 1919 was named chairman of its board of directors . . . apart from his duties with Pierce-Arrow, Colonel Clifton served as president of National Automobile Chamber of Commerce from its birth in 1913 until March 2, 1927, when he resigned his active post to serve in an honorary capacity.

CUMMINS, Clessie L.

1888•1968 Developed first high-speed light-weight diesel engine . . . founder of the Cummins Engine Company . . . credited with revolutionizing the highway transportation industry by adapting the sometime cumbersome marine diesel engine to truck use . . . demonstrated the automotive capabilities of the diesel by installing a four-cylinder marine diesel engine in a Packard automobile chassis in 1929 and driving it from Indianapolis to New York . . . in 1931 one of Cummins' diesel-powered trucks was driven from New York to Los Angeles . . . Cummins retired as president and board chairman of Cummins Diesel in 1956.

DOBLE, Abner

1890•1961 Built his first steam car at the age of 16, and in his spare time as a student at MIT he designed and built several more . . . in 1914 he drove a prototype model to Detroit where he found recognition and backing . . . four years later 80 Doble Detroit Steam cars had been built . . . in 1920 he founded Doble Steam Motors in the San Francisco area . . . much of Doble's fame came as a result of the prominence of his clientele . . . Hollywood stars and starlets of the day along with royalty from Europe and Asia absorbed much of his modest production . . . in later years Doble spent much of his time abroad working as a steam power consultant to locomotive manufacturers and other firms . . . he returned to the U.S. in 1950 . . . ill health forced him into retirement in the early 1950's.

DODGE BROTHERS, John and Horace

John 1864•1920, Horace 1868•1920 After working as machinists for several companies, the brothers developed a ball bearing bicycle and organized Evans and Dodge Bicycle Company to manufacture it . . . after numerous financial transactions, their company was absorbed by a Canadian firm and the Dodges went to Detroit to open a machine shop . . . in 1901 and 1902 they made transmissions for the Olds Motor Works . . . in 1903 Henry Ford offered each of the brothers 50 shares of stock in his new company, provided they would manufacture engines for him . . . although criticized by friends for doing so, the Dodges accepted Ford's terms, becoming the owners of one-tenth of the newly formed Ford Motor Company . . . in 1919 they received $25,000,000 for their original $20,000 investment . . . the Dodge Brothers left Ford to found their own company, Dodge Brothers, Inc., and manufactured their Dodge Brothers car.

DORRIS, George P.

1874•1968 With the help of his brother, Dorris built his first car in Nashville, Tennessee, in 1897 . . . helped found the St. Louis Motor Carriage Company in St. Louis, Missouri, in 1898 . . . when firm moved to Peoria, Illinois, in 1906, Dorris established the Dorris Motor Car Company in St. Louis . . . Dorris cars were always of advanced design, some with overhead valve engines and custom bodies . . . the company also made a line of trucks and buses . . . production of all vehicles stopped in 1926.

DUESENBERG, Frederick Samuel

1877•1932 By 1902 Duesenberg's racing experience had won him a position as test driver for the Rambler Company . . . in 1904 he designed his own car, a racer, which was manufactured by the Mason Auto Company until 1910 . . . about that time, Duesenberg designed his famous horizontal valve engines and introduced them to the racing world . . . in 1913 the Duesenberg Motor Company was organized, producing a multitude of engines for the war effort . . . following the war, Fred and brother August organized Duesenberg Brothers Incorporated to manufacture the racing machines which in 1919 captured all the world's records up to 300 miles in every class from 161 to 450 cubic inches . . . although E. L. Cord bought control of his company in 1927, Duesenberg remained active in racing until his death, the result of a driving accident.

DURANT, William Crapo

1860•1947 At 25, Durant teamed with Dallas Dort to form the Durant-Dort Carriage Company, manufacturers of two-wheeled carts . . . in 1904 Durant bought out and reorganized Buick Motor Car Company . . . after a 1908 attempt to merge Buick, Maxwell-Briscoe, Ford, and Reo proved unsuccessful, Durant on Sept. 16, 1908, launched the General Motors Co. . . . in the next two years, Durant bought in quick succession Cadillac, Olds, Oakland, Carter, Elmore, Ewing, Welch and several other lesser auto producers . . . financial difficulties forced Durant out of General Motors in 1910, but by 1915, after his spectacular success with Chevrolet, "Fabulous Billy" was back to take over the corporation he had founded . . . Durant remained at the head of GM until 1920, when a depression saw the corporation's stock tumble from $400 to $12 a share despite his attempts to turn the tide . . . 1920 saw a management reorganization at General Motors leaving Durant on his own to start over again . . . and start he did, participating in a series of enterprises ranging from Durant, Dort, and Star cars to Flint cars and finally Mason trucks . . . the 1929 depression, however, all but ended Durant's financial undertakings, and he lived in comparative obscurity until his death.

DURYEA, Charles E.

1861•1939 Started in the bicycle business . . . by 1891 had secured financial backing for a carriage-engine combination of his own design . . . September 22, 1893, was recorded in the Springfield "Evening Union" as the official debut of the first Duryea car, whose creation is still lost in controversy between Charles E. and brother J. Frank . . . after proving the vehicle's reliability in numerous races, the brothers went into business as the Duryea Motor Wagon Company in 1896 . . . two years later both Duryeas left the company, and Charles E. organized the Duryea Power Company of Reading, Pennsylvania, which manufactured a three-cylinder car until 1914 . . . after 1914 Duryea devoted much of his time to the writing of textbooks about the automobile.

DURYEA, J. Frank

1870•1967 Shares credit with his brother Charles for designing and building America's first marketable gasoline-powered automobile . . . the Duryea brothers road tested their first car in Springfield, Massachusetts, in 1893 . . . in 1895 James drove a Duryea Motor Wagon to victory in the first American automobile race . . . averaged 7½ m.p.h. over a snow-covered course between Chicago and Evanston, Illinois . . . James subsequently manufactured the Stevens-Duryea from 1901 to 1915, when he sold his stock in the company and retired.

DYKE, Andrew L.

1876•1959 Organized first automobile parts and supply business in America in St. Louis, Missouri, in 1899 . . . Dyke developed and manufactured (1900) what is regarded as first American float-feed carburetor . . . published *Dr. Dyke's Anatomy of the Automobile*, one of America's first how-to-do-it books for owner-mechanics (1904) . . . from 1910 to 1952, edited and published the highly respected *Dyke's Automobile and Gasoline Engine Encyclopedia* . . . Dyke established or became active in many early car producing firms: St. Louis, Dyke-Britton, D.L.G., Dorris . . . from 1899 to 1904 Dyke sold kits from which buyers could assemble their own cars . . . conducted one of America's first correspondence schools for auto mechanics.

EARL, Harley J.

1893•1969 Like many other auto pioneers, Earl received his training in a carriage shop . . . in the late teens and early

1920's was director of Don Lee Corp., a California firm which specialized in building custom-bodies cars for Hollywood stars and other celebrities . . . Cadillac retained Earl to design the original La Salle and redesign Cadillac line . . . became director of GM's art and color section in 1927 and from 1940 until 1958, vice president in charge of styling staff . . . Earl's influence was important in transforming the high, box-shaped cars of the 1920's to today's sleek automobile . . . credited with many styling innovations including: Built-in luggage compartment and elimination of running boards and outside spare tire, non-glare windshields, hardtop body style, curved glass rear windows, panoramic windshields and fiberglass bodies.

ERSKINE, Albert Russel

1871•1933 Became treasurer of Studebaker in 1910 . . . became first vice president in 1913, and president in 1915 . . . in 1928, as president, Erskine witnessed the greatest sales in the company's history up to that time . . . in that same year, he negotiated the Pierce-Arrow-Studebaker merger.

FISHER BROTHERS, Frederic J., Charles T., Alfred J., Lawrence P., Howard A., William A., Edward F.

Frederic **1878•1941**, Howard **1902•1942**, Charles **1880•1963**, Alfred **1892•1963**, Lawrence **1888•1961**, William **1886•1969**, Edward **1892•1972**. With skills acquired from their father, a master carriage maker, and $50,000 in capital, Frederic and Charles established the Fisher Body Company in 1908, and in succeeding years Lawrence, Alfred and Howard were brought into the business . . . Frederic and Charles realized that motoring would remain a seasonal activity until motorists could be protected from the elements . . . they began campaigning for closed bodies, and in 1910 their efforts were rewarded when 150 closed bodies were ordered by the Cadillac Motor Company . . . in December of that year the Fisher Closed Body Company was formed . . . in 1916 the two companies were merged into the Fisher Body Corporation . . . the brothers sold their corporation to General Motors, their biggest customer, in 1926 for an estimated $208 million of General Motors stock . . . the brothers became key General Motors officials, helping to run the firm's newly acquired Fisher Body Division . . . Lawrence became president of the Cadillac Motor Car Company one of General Motors' biggest divisions . . . Frederic and Charles, both GM vice-presidents, retired in 1934 to devote their time to personal business interests and philanthropic organizations . . . William served as president of Fisher Body Corp., vice president and director of GM and as a bank executive and director . . . Edward, last of the brothers to die, had been a GM executive, vice president and general manager of Fisher Body, president of Gar Wood Industries . . . he was an active supporter of boys' clubs.

FLANDERS, Walter E.

1871•1923 One of the auto industry's first mass-production experts . . . in 1907 Flanders headed an Ohio firm which secured a contract for 1,000 Ford crankshafts . . . in 1908 firm produced 10,000 units for Ford . . . Ford was so impressed that he hired Flanders as production manager . . . left Ford in 1909 to found the E.M.F. Co., whose cars were distributed by Studebaker . . . served for a short time as vice president and general manager of Studebaker . . . left Studebaker in 1911 and started the Flanders Manufacturing Company and subsequently the United States Motor Company . . . latter included Maxwell, Stoddard-Dayton, Brush, Alden Sampson truck and component manufacturers . . . eventually Maxwell and another Flanders-based company, Chalmers, formed the nucelus of Chrysler Corporation.

FORD, Henry

1863●1947 As a youngster Ford showed his mechanical aptitude by constructing a steam engine when he was 15, and became an expert watch repairman before he was twenty . . . his first car, built while he was an engineer with the Edison Illuminating Company, made its first successful run in 1896 . . . in 1899 he resigned from Edison to become chief engineer for the Detroit Automobile Company, remaining with them until 1902 . . . in that year, Ford left Detroit Automobile (later reorganized as the Henry Ford Company, and finally the Cadillac Automobile Company) because of policy differences . . . six months later he organized Ford Motor Company . . . a proponent of light, serviceable cars, Ford on Oct. 1, 1908, introduced the Model T and produced in the 19 years that followed over 15 million "Tin Lizzies" . . . 1927 marked the end of "T" production, followed by the Model A . . . Ford established a $5 minimum wage in 1914, increasing it to $6 in 1922, introduced the eight hour day and profit-sharing in 1914, and adopted a 40-hour week in 1926 . . . Mr. Ford played an active role in the management of the Ford Motor Company until 1945, when his grandson, Henry Ford II, was named president of the company.

FRANKLIN, Herbert H.

1867●1956 Started out as a reporter on the weekly Coxsackie, New York, *Herald* and eventually became owner of the paper . . . sold it in 1893 to form the H. H. Franklin Manufacturing Company, which pioneered in die casting

. . . in 1902 placed the Franklin air-cooled car on the market . . . it pioneered in many progressive and innovative design features . . . under Franklin's guidance the firm's production climbed from 12 the first year to 11,000 in 1923, and nearly 15,000 by 1930.

FRAZER, Joseph W.

1894•1973 A Yale graduate, Frazer apprenticed as a mechanic at Packard . . . in 1919 joined export division of GM and became assistant treasurer of GMAC where he participated in the evolution of auto installment financing . . . sales manager of Pierce-Arrow Finance Co. in 1923 and in 1939, president of Willys-Overland . . . during World War II Willys was active in development and building of the Jeep . . . co-founded, with Henry Kaiser, Kaiser-Frazer Corp. in 1946 . . . in 1949 Frazer resigned as president of the corporation and served as vice chairman until 1954.

GLIDDEN, Charles Jasper

1857•1927 In 1900 Glidden retired from active business life, having accumulated a comfortable fortune during his association with the Bell Telephone Company . . . in 1903 he made a motor tour of the major countries of Europe, followed a year later by an auto journey around the world, the first of its kind . . . during the latter trip, Glidden conceived the idea of organizing a series of motor tours around the United States to promote the infant auto industry . . . the first Glidden Trophy was awarded to Percy Pierce in 1905, the last to a team of Metz cars in 1913 . . . while in existence the Glidden Tour was conducted annually (with the exception of 1912) and served to capture the imagination of its spectators, while at the same time stimulating their interest in the burgeoning auto industry . . . in his later years he devoted much of his time to promoting interest in aviation.

GRAHAM BROTHERS, Ray A., Robert C., Joseph B.

Ray 1887•1932, Robert 1885•1967, Joseph 1883•1971. Along with brothers Robert C. and Joseph C., began in the glass manufacturing business, using machines invented by Joseph . . . while managing the family's farm properties, Ray became interested in the possibilities of light weight trucks and invented a rear axle to be used under a Ford chassis . . . after their glass company merged with the Owens Bottle Company, Joseph and Robert joined Ray to form the Graham Brothers Truck Company, builders of truck bodies . . . in 1921 the brothers made an agreement with Dodge allowing them to build a truck carrying the Graham nameplate, but using Dodge engines and transmissions . . . to keep the arrangement permanent, Dodge bought majority interest in Graham Brothers six months after the original agreement, and the Grahams became officials of Dodge Brothers . . . their association with Dodge was brief, lasting only until 1927 when they left to buy and reorganize Paige-Detroit, forming the Graham-Paige Motors Corporation.

HAYNES, Elwood G.

1857•1925 Haynes' car, among the first built in the United States, was constructed with the aid of the Apperson Brothers and successfully tested in 1894 . . . four years later he started Haynes Automobile Company; initially successful, it went out of business in 1925 . . . aside from his manufacturing endeavors, Haynes was a prominent metallurgist, pioneering in the use of aluminum in motor cars as well as in developing several important structural alloys.

JEFFERY, Thomas B.

1845•1910 Came to the United States in 1863, and in 1879 began to manufacture bicycles under the trademark "Rambler" . . . Jeffery, who invented the clincher tire in 1881, began experimenting with motor vehicles as early as 1897, but it wasn't until 1900 that he successfully produced one . . . in that year, he sold his bicycle business, and purchased a factory in which he began to manufacture G & J cars (later known as Rambler cars) in 1902 . . . Jeffery remained president of Thomas B. Jeffery Company, later the Nash Motors Company, until his death.

JORDAN, Edward "Ned"

1882●1958 Entered the auto industry as advertising manager for the Thomas B. Jeffery Company . . . Jordan remained with the Jeffery Company until 1916, when he organized his own company—the Jordan Motor Car Company . . . although production was low—Jordan refused to build more than 5,000 "Playboys" in any single year—the company always showed a profit, largely as a result of its advertising program . . . instituted by Jordan himself it was the first to stress the esthetic value of the car and make an appeal to the prospective buyer's sense of adventure and glamor . . . the company prospered until the 1929 market crash . . . after the depression, Jordan worked as an advertising consultant, and in 1950 began writing a weekly column in the Automotive News.

JOY, Henry Bourne

1864●1936 Served as president of the Fort Street Depot Company from 1896 to 1907 . . . while with Fort Street Depot, Joy became interested in W. D. Packard's auto company, initially as an investor, eventually becoming president of Packard in 1901 . . . while with Packard, he also championed the movement for good roads as president of the Lincoln

pioneers

Highway Association . . . Joy remained president of Packard until 1916, at which time he became chairman of the board . . . ill health forced him to retire several years before his death.

KELSEY, Cadwallader W.

1880•1970 Built an experimental car in 1897 and a year later, in collaboration with I. S. Tilney, set up the Auto-Tri Manufacturing Co. to produce 3-wheeled automobiles . . . the prototype of the Auto-Tri is now in the Smithsonian Institute . . . from 1905 to 1909 sales manager for the Maxwell car . . . in 1909 was responsible for sending the first woman driver coast-to-coast in a car, a Maxwell . . . produced the Motorette car in Hartford, Conn. from 1910-1912 and the Kelsey auto in Belleville, N.J. from 1921-1924 . . . president of Rototiller, Inc., 1938-1960 . . . just prior to his death, Kelsey was active in developing a flying automobile, the Skycar.

KETTERING, Charles F.

1876•1958 Began his career as an engineer for National Cash Register . . . after working at NCR for five years, left to organize Delco Laboratories for the purpose of developing an ignition system . . . one of his first customers was Henry Leland, president of Cadillac, who, after ordering 8,000 ignition systems, later called upon Kettering to perfect the electric self-starter that appeared on the 1911 Cadillac . . . in 1916 he sold his interest in Delco to the United Motors Corporation . . . in 1920, "Boss Ket" became the head of the General Motors research laboratories, contributing toward the development of such things as quick-drying paint and Ethyl gasoline . . . Kettering went into a purely nominal retirement in 1947, remaining with General Motors as a director and research consultant until his death in Dayton, Ohio.

KING, Charles Brady

1868•1957 Like Ford, King first became interested in self-propelled vehicles upon seeing one at the 1893 Columbian Exposition, where he had gone to exhibit some of his own inventions . . . preceding the 1896 debut of his first practical vehicle, King, in 1895, had organized American Motor League, a pioneer association to promote better roads . . . King also designed the 1902 "Silent Northern," a vehicle which featured three-point suspension and an integral engine-transmission assembly . . . he organized the King Motor Car Company in 1910, and in 1916 turned his efforts to the design of aircraft engines.

KNUDSEN, William S.

1879•1948 Joined the Ford Motor Company in 1912 as manager of the company's 27 plants . . . during World War I, Knudsen was in charge of manufacturing Eagle boats for the Navy . . . before leaving Ford in 1921 he had installed assembly plants in several foreign countries . . . resigned from Ford to become general manager of Ireland and Matthews Manufacturing Company, but in less than a year he was called to Chevrolet Motor Company . . . two years later he became president and general manager of Chevrolet, as well as vice president of General Motors . . . under Knudsen's guidance, Chevrolet in 1928 switched from a four to a six-cylinder engine, and within a year had produced well over a million of the new models . . . after becoming president of General Motors in 1937, Knudsen in 1940 resigned his office to take a position on the National Defense Advisory Commission . . . during the war he served with several government agencies, usually acting as a co-ordinator and general "trouble shooter" . . . so thorough was his work that in 1944, Knudsen, then a three star general, received the Army's Distinguished Service Medal.

LELAND, Henry M.

1843●1932 Spent his younger years working in the factories of several well-known firearms manufacturers learning first-hand the technique of parts interchangeability, a method he employed so successfully in the auto industry . . . after a series of ventures that ran from inventing the mechanical hair clipper to manufacturing engines, Leland in 1902 reorganized the Henry Ford Company, which became the Cadillac Motor Car Company . . . while with Cadillac, Leland was responsible for the company's introduction of such innovations as standardized parts, electric starting, and automatic ignition advance . . . Leland left Cadillac in 1917, and some years later organized the Lincoln Motor Car Company, which was purchased by Ford in 1922.

MACAULEY, Alvan

1872●1952 Began his career as a patent attorney, holding various positions with National Cash Register and American Arithmometer, predecessor of Burroughs Corporation . . . Macauley joined Packard as general manager in 1910 . . . three years later he was made vice president, and in 1916 became president of Packard . . . under Macauley's guidance, Packard, as well as becoming a leading auto producer, specialized in the development of engines, contributing such things as the Liberty engine of World War I, the first engine specifically designed for a tank, the first production diesel aircraft engine . . . Macauley, a director of the National Automobile Chamber of Commerce from 1913, became its president in 1928, an office he held until 1946 . . . he was made chairman of the board of Packard in 1939, serving in that capacity until retiring in 1948.

MARMON, Howard C.

1876•1943 Worked as an associate with his father in a flour mill machinery business that was eventually absorbed in the auto industry . . . became vice president in charge of engineering at the Marmon Motor Company in 1902 . . . designed the Marmon automobile as well as the 1911 Indianapolis Race winning Marmon "Wasp" . . . invented the duplex down draft manifold and pioneered in the use of weight saving aluminum in V-16 engines . . . served as president of the Society of Automobile Engineers during the years 1913–1914, and in 1931 was awarded a medal for the outstanding automotive design of the year, the Marmon Sixteen . . . developed the Liberty engine during World War I . . . selected as the only American honorary member of the British Society of Automotive Engineers.

MASON, George Walter

1891•1954 Entered the auto industry in 1913 with Studebaker . . . a year later, he joined Dodge, leaving in 1915 to become purchasing agent for the American Auto Trimming Company . . . during World War I Mason acted as a co-ordinator for the Army Ordnance Department . . . in 1919 accepted a position with Irving National Bank in New York . . . in 1921 Mason returned to the auto industry, taking a position with Maxwell-Chalmers Corporation, then being reorganized by Walter P. Chrysler . . . a year later he was named general works manager, holding that position until leaving Chrysler to become vice president of Copeland Products, Incorporated, in 1926 . . . although elected president of Copeland in 1927, Mason in 1928 left to become president of Kelvinator Corporation . . . in 1936, an offer of the presidency of Nash Motors ultimately resulted in the formation of the Nash-Kelvinator Corporation with Mason as president and Charles W. Nash board chairman . . . with Nash's death in 1948, Mason, at that time president of the Automobile Manufacturers Association, also became board chairman of N-K . . . when the Nash-Kelvinator-Hudson Motor Car Company merger in 1954 was completed, Mason became president and chairman of the newly formed American Motors Corporation.

MATHESON BROTHERS, Charles W. and Frank

Charles 1876•1940, Frank 1872•1967 They built the Matheson between 1903 and 1913 . . . in 1921, after spending a year as New York sales representative for Dodge Brothers, Charles became vice president of that company . . . three years later he became vice president and sales director for General Motors' Oakland Motor Car Company . . . after resigning his post with General Motors, Charles assumed a similar position with Kelvinator . . . In 1928 he moved on to Chrysler Corporation, becoming vice president in charge of sales . . . ten years later he left Chrysler to become president and general manager of Reo Motor Car Company, a position Charles Matheson held until his death.

MAXWELL, Jonathan Dixon

1864•1928 Like many other automobile manufacturers, Maxwell got his start in the bicycle business, operating a repair shop with Elmer Apperson . . . he assisted Elmer Apperson and Elwood Haynes in building the latter's first car . . . in 1903 Maxwell teamed with Benjamin Briscoe to organize the Maxwell-Briscoe Company, producers of a $500 two-cylinder runabout . . . aside from his manufacturing accomplishments, Maxwell was an inventor of note, assisting in the design of the Oldsmobile and Northern automobiles and inventing the thermo-siphon cooling system . . . he served as vice president of the United States Motor Company before retiring from the auto industry in 1913.

METZ, Charles

1864•1937 Organized the Waltham Manufacturing Company to build bicycles . . . later associated with the Orient Oil Bicycle and the Orient Buckboard companies . . . in 1909 Metz purchased the Waltham factory, and began to manufacture the low priced Metz "22" . . . a team of three of his cars won the 1913 Glidden Tour with a perfect score . . . throughout his association with the auto industry, Metz championed the movement toward smaller, lower-priced cars, at one time going so far as to devise a plan for shipping component parts to dealers for assembly . . . Metz Company was dissolved in 1922, at which time Mr. Metz retired from the industry.

MILES, Samuel A.

1862•1932 Dean of American automobile shows . . . born in England . . . came to America and edited cycling publications, promoted bicycle shows, and helped found *Motor Age* magazine . . . staged the first Chicago auto show in 1901 . . . soon became manager of the New York and Chicago shows . . . general manager of the N.A.A.M. in 1903 . . . served about a year (1913–14) as first manager of the N.A.C.C. . . . then devoted himself exclusively to the shows until his death.

pioneers

MOTT, Charles S.

1875•1973 As widely known for his philanthropies as for his auto pioneer work and role in helping to build GM, Mott was one of the wealthiest men in America and gave huge sums of money to the city of Flint and, through the Mott Foundation, to other projects . . . after serving in the Spanish American War, Mott joined his father in a firm making bicycle wheels . . . the company, Weston-Mott, turned to making auto axles and wheels . . . in 1905 moved from Utica, N.Y. to Flint at the invitation of Durant . . . after Weston-Mott was acquired for GM stock in 1908, Mott continued as manager . . . from 1916 to 1937 he was a GM vice president . . . instrumental in such developments as the change in Duco paint, use of ethyl gasoline, retention of Chevrolet in the GM family and promotion of Pontiac as a new car line . . . known as the "Dean of GM Directors," having served on the board from 1913 until his death.

NASH, Charles W.

1864•1948 Started his career working in the Durant-Dort carriage works, where he developed the straight-line conveyor-belt system, a standard item in today's auto assembly plants . . . when Durant left the wagon business to start Buick, Nash went along with him and in 1910 became president of that company . . . Buick so prospered under Nash's leadership that in 1912 he was made president of General Motors, a position he held until 1916 . . . in that year Nash purchased the Thomas B. Jeffery Company and in 1917 began to manufacture Nash cars . . . Nash remained president of the Nash Motor Company until 1930 when he became chairman of the board . . . shortly thereafter, merger negotiations with the Kelvinator Corporation were completed, and the Nash-Kelvinator Corporation was

229

formed with George Mason as president and Charles W. Nash as chairman of the board.

OLDS, Ransom E.

1864•1950 After successful experiments with steam vehicles as early as 1886, Olds completed his first gasoline powered vehicle in 1894 . . . encouraged by the interest shown in his vehicle, Olds organized Olds Motor Vehicle Company in 1897 . . . this first endeavor was not successful; the company was reorganized in 1899 as the Olds Motor Works . . . in 1901 Olds developed his famous "curved dash runabout" priced at $650, making it the first really low-priced car . . . after a 1901 fire destroyed the Detroit plant, the company moved to its Lansing location . . . two years later Olds sold his interest in the Olds Motor Works, later Olds Division of General Motors, and organized the Reo Motor Car Company . . . seemingly not content with founding an industry, Olds continued his experiments with the internal combustion engine, contributing, among other things, the first practical power mower.

PACKARD, James Ward

1863•1928 Organized the Packard Electric Company in 1890 . . . by 1893 Packard had drawn the plans for his first auto, but financial difficulties delayed its production until 1899 . . . after experiments with the initial car proved successful, Packard in 1900 organized New York and Ohio Automobile Co. . . . with increased capital, the company moved to Detroit in 1903 and became Packard Motor Company . . . Mr. Packard, prior to this time president, became chairman of the board, a post which he held until retiring in 1915.

pioneers

PAIGE, Fred O.

1864•1935 Organized Paige-Detroit Motor Company in 1909 to produce two-cycle automobiles . . . Paige was president of the company until 1910, at which time Harry Jewett assumed control . . . in 1927 the Graham Brothers acquired control of Jewett's interests, and the company became Graham-Paige.

PIERCE, George N.

1846•1910 Father of the Pierce-Arrow car and one of the founders of Pierce-Arrow Motor Company . . . began career in 1872 as a member of a firm producing birdcages and iceboxes . . . in the 1880's the company began manufacturing bicycles and tricycles . . . the first little Pierce motorette was the outcome of experimenting Pierce had started in the 1890's . . . president and director of Pierce at the time of his retirement in 1908.

POPE, Albert Augustus

1843•1909 After serving in the Civil War, Pope organized in 1879 a company to manufacture bicycles, a venture which was to earn for him the title "the founder of American bicycle industries" . . . following his highly successful bicycle ventures, Pope began to manufacture electric runabouts through the Columbia Electric Company in 1896 . . . within a few years, he controlled the Pope-Toledo, Pope-Harford, and Pope-Waverly Companies . . . however, with auto success on one hand, Pope faced a crisis on the other in the form of a decline of his bicycle business, eventually forcing the Pope Manufacturing Company into receivership.

PORTER, Finley R.

1872•1964 Chief engineer of the Mercer Company, 1910–1915, and designer of the Mercer Raceabout . . . Porter left school at the age of 11 and took correspondence courses in mechanical engineering . . . became head of his own company at Port Jefferson, Long Island, where the manufacture of F.R.P. autos started in 1914 . . . only a few made . . . however, F.R.P. designs later formed the basis for one of America's most powerful and expensive cars of its period, the Porter, 1920–1922 . . . chief engineer of Curtiss Air Craft Corporation, Engine Division, 1919 . . . consulting engineer with Bendix Corporation during World War II.

REEVES, Alfred P.

1875•1962 Began as a bicycle writer in Brooklyn . . . managed bicycle races, later auto races . . . when popularity of the bicycle declined, Reeves became one of country's first automotive editors, starting in 1902 with the *New York Evening Mail* . . . his managerial talents were widely recognized throughout the industry . . . in 1906 selected to manage the A.M.C.M.A. . . . in 1909, the A.L.A.M. . . . appointed general manager of the N.A.C.C. in 1914 . . . name of association changed to A.M.A. in 1934, and six years later its headquarters were moved to Detroit . . . Reeves continued as advisory vice president and manager of the New York office . . . instrumental in forming A.M.A.'s patent cross-licensing agreement . . . known as "Mr. Auto Show" for having had a part in producing every National Auto Show from 1900 to 1940.

RICKENBACKER, Edward V. (Capt.)

1890•1973 Quit school at 12 to help support his mother and 4 younger sisters and brothers . . . worked for companies

pioneers

producing Frayer-Miller and Firestone-Columbus cars . . . in 1910 started a colorful racing career and by 1915 won the AAA Championship . . . Rickenbacker was America's leading combat flyer during WWI . . . among the many American and foreign decorations he received was the Congressional Medal of Honor . . . 1921-1926 joined Walter E. Flanders, Barney F. Everitt, and Harry L. Cunningham to help run company which built the Rickenbacker car . . . nameplate of this car was the famed "Hat-in-the-Ring" insignia of Rickenbacker's wartime squadron . . . purchased Indianapolis Speedway in 1928 . . . served as president until 1945 . . . bought Eastern Airlines in 1938 and was president and chief executive until 1959 . . . served as chairman of the board of directors for Eastern through 1963.

RIKER, Andrew L.

1868●1930 Built an electric tricycle in 1884 at the age of 16 . . . after graduation from Columbia Law School formed his own company which began producing a full line of electric passenger and commercial vehicles in New Jersey in 1899 . . . deserted the electric field in 1902 and joined Locomobile to help design their first gasoline car . . . until about 1920 vice president and chief engineer of Locomobile . . . Riker helped organize S.A.E. . . . served as its first president . . . chairman of the Mechanical Branch of the Association of Licensed Automobile Manufacturers.

SELDEN, George Baldwin

1846●1932 A veteran of the Civil War, he became a patent attorney in 1871 . . . having a keen interest in mechanics, Selden unsuccessfully experimented with engines of his own design during the years 1873-1875 . . . by 1876, he was working on the design for a self-propelled vehicle using an engine operating on the Brayton cycle . . . Selden had developed a three-cylinder-Brayton type engine by 1877, and proceeded to design the road locomotive disclosed in his patent application of May 8, 1879 . . . although never successful in obtaining the funds to build the proposed machine, Selden was granted his patent—No. 549,160 "Road Machine" Nov. 5, 1895 . . . on Nov. 4, 1899, he sold the patent on a royalty basis to W. C. Whitney of Columbia Electric who successfully brought suit against a number of automobile manufacturers before the now historic appeal judgment Jan. 11, 1911 (Electric Vehicle Company vs. C. A. Buerr) wherein the patent was held valid but not infringed by virtue of the fact that all manufacturers were using Otto, not Brayton, type engines . . . Selden unsuccessfully entered other auto firms before his death.

SLOAN, Alfred P., Jr.

1875•1966 President of General Motors from 1923 to 1936 . . . started as a draftsman with Hyatt Roller Bearing in 1895 . . . soon headed company and in 1916 at Durant's urging merged a group of accessories companies, including Hyatt, to form United Motors Corporation . . . latter corporation soon became part of General Motors . . . Sloan's administrative genius welded the loosely-knit General Motors units into world's largest, most profitable auto making concern . . . stepped down as board chairman of General Motors in 1956 . . . devoted full time to various philanthropies . . . Sloan established Sloan Foundation in 1934 . . . later, the Sloan-Kettering Institute for Cancer Research.

SORENSEN, Charles E.

1881•1968 Vice president and director of Ford Motor Company . . . Henry Ford's close associate and consultant

pioneers

. . . born in Denmark and came to America at age of four . . . joined Ford in 1905 as a patternmaker and soon demonstrated a genius for production . . . helped develop the conveyor systems, assembly lines, and other innovations, which established Ford as a front-runner in industrial mass-production . . . credited with basic design of many Ford facilities throughout the world, including the Willow Run plant, which produced bombers during World War II . . . left Ford in 1944 and served a year as president of Willys-Overland, Inc.

STANLEY BROTHERS, Francis E. and Freelan O.

Francis **1849●1918**, Freelan **1849●1940** In 1893, the twin brothers invented the Stanley dry plate process which revolutionized photography . . . they were co-designers of the Stanley Steamer—1897—and the world-record-holding steamer of 1906 (Ormond Beach, 127.66 m.p.h.) . . . as owners of the Stanley Motor Company they directed the business until retiring in 1917.

STUDEBAKER, John Mohler

1833●1917 In 1858 bought brother Henry's share of the Studebaker Brothers (Wagon) Company which then became C. (for brother Clem) and J. M. Studebaker Company . . . the company entered the auto industry as a body maker in 1899 . . . in 1902 produced its first vehicle, an electric car . . . in 1908 Studebaker contracted to market the entire output of the E-M-F Company . . . in 1911 the two firms merged to form the Studebaker Corporation, which produced the first car with a Studebaker name plate in 1912 . . . John M. Studebaker served as chairman of the corporation until his death.

235

STUTZ, Harry C.

1871•1930 After winning recognition among the early auto manufacturers with the invention of an improved rear axle, Stutz became successively sales manager for the Schebler Carburetor Company, engineer for the Marion Motor Car Company, and designer of the famous "American Underslung" for the American Motor Car Company . . . in 1910 he entered into the Stutz Motor Parts Company and in 1911 organized the Ideal Motor Company to manufacture Stutz cars . . . two years later the companies merged to form the Stutz Motor Car Company with Stutz as president . . . although he sold his interest in Stutz Motor Car Company in 1919, Harry Stutz later joined Henry Campbell, his partner in the Stutz Motor Parts Company, in the H.C.S. Motor Car Company, again as president . . . Stutz remained president of H.C.S. until his retirement.

THOMAS, Edwin Ross

1850•1936 Started the E. R. Thomas Motor Company of Buffalo in 1900 . . . the company was quite successful, and Thomas remained its president until his decision to retire in 1911, when he sold his holding to the United States Motor Company . . . although successful as an auto maker, Thomas probably gained his greatest fame as the designer-builder of the "Thomas Flyer," winner of the 1908 New York to Paris (via California, Siberia and Europe) Race . . . despite the fact that he officially retired in 1911, Thomas was active in numerous enterprises until his death.

VANDERBILT, William K., Jr.

1878•1944 Heir to vast wealth who did much to help the automotive industry in its formative years . . . originated (1904) and sponsored the Vanderbilt Cup Races in an effort

pioneers

to bring to America the motoring impetus spawned by the Gordon Bennett Cup Races in Europe . . . a racing driver of highest ability . . . established several world's road and straight-away records in the 1902-1904 period . . . Vanderbilt's personal records and his cup races did much to inspire American manufacturers to build cars which could and did successfully challenge European dominance.

WHITE BROTHERS, Windsor T., Rollin H., Walter C.

Windsor 1866•1958, Rollin 1872•1962, Walter 1876•1929 The brothers began their careers working for the White Sewing Machine Company, owned by their father . . . Rollin and Windsor did experimental work on steam engines and produced the first steam powered White automobile in 1900 . . . in 1901 Walter was sent to London to demonstrate the car and establish a niche in the European market . . . he returned to the United States in 1904 and continued to demonstrate the company's vehicles in races and hill climbs . . . in 1906 the White Company was organized, with Windsor as president, to handle the automotive line . . . the brothers introduced their first gasoline car in 1909, and in 1910, their first gasoline powered truck . . . in 1915 the White Motor Company was formed with Windsor as president . . . Rollin left the company in 1914, founded the Cleveland Plow Company and manufactured tractors . . . he re-entered the automotive industry in 1923 producing the Rollin car until 1925 . . . in 1921 Walter assumed the presidency of the White Motor Company as Windsor was made Chairman of the Board.

WILLS, Childe Harold

1878•1940 Spent the years 1900-1903 working for the Boyer Machine Company and nights as a draftsman for Henry

237

Ford's new organization . . . when the Ford Motor Company was formed, Wills was made production manager and chief engineer . . . he gained fame from his development of the use of vanadium steel for commercial purposes, and is credited with introducing molybdenum steel in auto construction . . . in 1919 Wills, by then a millionaire, left Ford, and in 1920 organized his own company, Wills-St. Claire . . . never particularly successful, the company went out of business in 1927 . . . in 1933, Wills became chief metallurgist for Chrysler, a position he held until his death.

WILLYS, John North

1873●1933 In 1906 he organized the American Motor Car Sales Company to sell the entire output of the Overland Company . . . during panic of 1907 he acquired the manufacturing facilities of the Pope-Toledo Company in an effort to revive the sinking Overland concern . . . the company was moved to Toledo with Willys as president and in 1908 the production of Willys-Overland totaled 4,000 units . . . by 1915 Willys-Overland production reached 94,500, second only to Ford . . . after a post-war bankruptcy threat was averted by Walter P. Chrysler, the company prospered, and in 1929 John N. Willys sold his holdings for $21 million . . . hard times after the market crash prompted Willys to return to the company in 1932, but his attempts to save it from bankruptcy were unsuccessful, and Willys-Overland went into receivership in 1933 . . . in 1953 the firm became part of Kaiser Industries Corporation.

WINTON, Alexander

1860●1932 Started the Winton Bicycle Company in 1890, ten years after his arrival in the United States . . . in 1896 Winton built his first car, which he sold to a Pennsylvania

pioneers

engineer the following year . . . he organized the Winton Motor Carriage Company in 1897 . . . by 1905 he had produced an eight-cylinder motor vehicle, presumably one of the first . . . other contributions to the industry include the development of a practical storage battery, design of a successful speed governor, and four years before his death, perfection of a light, oil burning aircraft engine . . . he remained president of the Winton Motor Car Company until it suspended production in 1924 . . . organized the Winton Engine Company which made marine, rail and industrial diesel engines—the latter firm was purchased by General Motors in 1930 and became the Cleveland Diesel Division.

roll call

More than 3,000 makes of cars and trucks have been produced by some 1,500 manufacturers in the United States since the dawn of the auto age. Some were trial models, some were produced for one year only, others have a longer story. Listed below are the names of the more than 3,000 makes that can be documented, with known years of production. The fact that more than one manufacturer may have used a specific name at the same time or at different times is not indicated. Model names, such as Corvair (Chevrolet) and Valiant (Chrysler), are not listed. A final dash (—) means to date.

Abbott, 1909–18
Abbott-Cleveland, 1917
Abbott-Detroit, 1909
Abbott-Downing, 1919
A.B.C., 1906–11, 1922, 1939
A.B.C. Steamer, 1901
Abenaque, 1900
Abendroth & Root, 1907–13
Able, 1916
Abresch-Cramer, 1910–11
Acadia, 1904
Acason, 1915–26
Ace, 1919–22
Ace Truck, 1919–23
A.C.F., 1926
Acme, 1902–1910
Acorn, 1910
Acorn Truck, 1925
Adams, 1906–7, 1911–12, 1924
Adams-Farwell, 1903–13
Adelphia, 1921
Adette, 1947
Admiral, 1914
Adria, 1921
Adrian, 1902–3
Advance, 1910
A.E.C., 1914–16
Aero, 1921

Aerocar, 1905-8, 1948, 1950
Aero-Type, 1921
Aetna, 1915, 1922
Ahrens-Fox, 1911-33
A.I.C., 1913
Airphibian, 1946, 1952
Airscoot, 1947
Airway, 1948-49
Ajax, 1901-3, 1914, 1920-21, 1925-26
Ajax Electric, 1901-3
Akron, 1901, 1912-13
Alamobile, 1902
Aland, 1917
Albany, 1907-8
Alco, 1905-14
Alco Truck, 1910-14
Aldo, 1910
Aldrich, 1897-98
Alena, 1922
Algonquin, 1913
All American, 1919, 1923
Allegheny, 1908
Allen, 1914-22
Allen & Clark, 1908-9
Allen Cyclecar, 1914
Allen-Kingston, 1907-10
Allfour, 1919
Allis-Chalmers, 1914-17
Allith, 1908
All Power, 1917-21
Allstate, 1951-53
Alma, 1913
Alpena, 1911-13
Alsace, 1919-20
Alstel, 1915-17
Alter, 1915-17
Altha Electric, 1900-1

Altham, 1896-1901
Altman, 1898
Alxo, 1905
Amalgamated, 1905
Ambassador, 1921-25, 1966—
Amco, 1917-21
America, 1911
American, 1900-3
American Austin, 1930-37
American Auto, 1904
American Auto Vehicle, 1907
American Bantam, 1937-41
American Beauty, 1915-16, 1920-21
American Berliet, 1905-7
American Coulthard, 1905-7
American Electric, 1899-1900
American Fiat, 1915
American Gas, 1895
American Knight, 1919
American LaFrance Truck, 1910
American Mercedes, 1905-7
American Mors, 1906-9
American Motor, 1902-3, 1905-6
American Motors, 1970—
American Motor Truck, 1906-11
American Napier, 1904
American Populaire, 1904
American Power Carriage, 1900
American Simplex, 1905-10
American Six, 1916-17
American Southern, 1921
American Steam, 1922-23
American Steamer, 1900

roll call

American Tri-Car, 1912
American Underslung, 1906–14
American Voiturette, 1899
Americar, 1940–42
Ames, 1898, 1910–16
Amesbury, 1898
Amos, 1913
Amoskeag Fire Engine, 1867–1906
Amplex, 1910–15
Ams-Sterling, 1917
AMX, 1968—
Anchor, 1909–11
Anderson, 1908, 1916–25
Anderson Electric, 1907–19
Andover, 1914–17
Andrews, 1895
Anhut, 1910–11
Ann Arbor, 1909–11
Annhauser-Busch Truck, 1905
Ansted, 1927
Anthony, 1897
Apex, 1920–22
Apollo, 1906–7
Appel, 1909
Apperson, 1902–25
Apple, 1909, 1915–16
Appleton, 1922
Arbenz, 1911–18
Arcadia, 1911
Ardsley, 1905–6
Argo-Borland Electric, 1914
Argo-Case, 1905
Argo Electric, 1911–16
Argo Gas, 1914
Argonne Four, 1919–20
Ariel, 1905–7

Ariston, 1906
Armleder, 1914
Arnold Electric, 1895
Arrow, 1907, 1914
Artzberger, 1904
Asardo, 1962
Aster, 1906–7
Astor, 1925
Astra, 1920
Atco, 1920–22
Atlantic, 1915
Atlas, 1904–13
Atlas Truck, 1918
Atterbury Truck, 1915
Auburn, 1903–36, 1968—
Auburn Motor Buggy, 1908
Auglaize Truck, 1912
Aultman, 1901
Aurora, 1906–8
Austin, 1901–20, 1930
Austin Steamer, 1894
Auto-Acetylene, 1899
Auto-Bug, 1910
Autobuggy, 1906
Autocar, 1897–1912
Autocar Truck, 1908
Autocycle, 1907, 1913
Auto Dynamic, 1901
Auto Fore Car, 1900
Auto-Go, 1900
Autohorse, 1917–21
Auto-King, 1900
Automatic, 1906, 1921–25
Automobile Forecarriage, 1900
Automobile Voiturette, 1900
Automotor, 1901–4
Auto Motor, 1912

243

Automobiles of America

Auto Red Bug, 1924
Auto-Tricar, 1914
Autotwo, 1900
Auto Vehicle, 1903
Available Truck, 1910
Avanti, 1962—
Average Man's Runabout, 1906
Avery, 1921
Avery Tractor, 1942
Avery Truck, 1912-16

Babcock, 1910-12, 1914
Babcock Electric, 1906-12
Bachelle Electric, 1901
Backhus, 1925
Bacon, 1901-3
Badger, 1910-12
Bailey, 1907-10
Bailey-Electric, 1907-15
Bailey-Klapp, 1915
Bailey-Perking, 1907
Baker-Bell, 1913-14
Baker & Elberg Electric, 1894
Baker Electric, 1899-1915
Baker R & L Electric, 1915-20
Baker-Steam, 1917
Baker Steamer, 1921-23
Balboa, 1924
Baldner, 1902-6
Baldwin, 1900-1
Ball, 1902
Ballard, 1894
Baltimore, 1900
Balzer, 1894
Banker, 1905
Banker Bros., 1896
Banker Electric, 1905

Banner, 1910-11, 1915
Bantam, 1914
Barbarino, 1923
Barby, 1910
Barker, 1912
Barley, 1905-24
Barlow, 1924
Barlow Steamer, 1922
Barnes, 1905, 1912
Barnhart, 1905
Barrett & Perret Electric, 1895
Barrows Electric, 1897
Barrows Motor Vehicle, 1897
Bartholomew, 1901-20
Bartlett, 1921
Barver, 1925
Bateman, 1917
Bates, 1903-5
Bauer, 1914, 1925
Bauroth, 1899
Bayard, 1903
Bay State, 1906-7, 1922-23
B.D.A.C., 1904
Beacon, 1933
Beacon Flyer, 1908
Beardsley, 1901-2
Beardsley Electric, 1914-17
Beau-Chamberlain, 1901
Beaver, 1913-23
Beck, 1921
Bedelia, 1909
Beebe, 1906-7
Beech Creek, 1915-19
Beggs, 1918-23
B.E.L., 1921-23
Belden, 1907-10
Bell, 1907, 1911-23
Bellefontaine, 1908-17

roll call

Belmont, 1908, 1910, 1912, 1916
Bemmel & Burnham, 1908
Bender Special, 1918
Bendix, 1907-9
Benham, 1914
Ben-Hur, 1917
Benner, 1908-9
Benson, 1901
Benton, 1913
Benton Harbor Motor Carriage, 1896
Berg, 1902-7
Bergdoll, 1910-13
Berg Electric, 1921
Berkley, 1907
Berkshire, 1905-12
Berliet, 1905
Bertolet, 1908-12
Berwick Electric, 1904, 1926
Bessemer Truck, 1922
Best, 1900
Bethlehem, 1906-8, 1917
Bethlen, 1909
Betz, 1919
Beverly, 1905-7
Bewis, 1915
Bewman, 1912
Beyster-Detroit, 1910-11
B.F., 1912
Bi-Autogo, 1913
Bicar, 1912
Biddle, 1915-20
Biddle-Crane, 1922-23
Biddle-Murray, 1906-8
Biederman Truck, 1921
Billy Four, 1910
Bimel, 1911, 1915-17

Binney-Burnham, 1902
Birch, 1917-24
Bird, 1896-97
Birmingham, 1921-22
Birnel, 1911
Black, 1891, 1907-10
Black Crow, 1907, 1909
Black Diamond, 1904-5
Blackhawk, 1903, 1929-31
Blackstone, 1916
Blair, 1911
Blaisdell, 1903
Blakeslee Electric, 1906
Blemline, 1898
Bliss, 1906
B.L.M., 1906-7
B.L.M.C., 1907-9
Block Bros., 1905
Blomstrom, 1904-6
Blood, 1905
Blue Streak, 1908
Bluffelimber, 1901
Blumberg, 1918
Board, 1912
Bobbi-Car, 1947
Boggs, 1903
Boisselot, 1901
Bollee, 1908
Bollstrom, 1920
Bolte, 1901
Bonner, 1908
Booth, 1896
Borbein, 1904-8
Borland Electric, 1913
Borland-Grannis, 1912-16
Boss, 1903-9
Boston, 1900
Boston & Amesbury, 1902

245

Automobiles of America

Boston Electric, 1907
Boston-Haynes Apperson, 1898
Boston High Wheel, 1908
Bour-Davis, 1915–23
Bourne, 1917
Bowling Green, 1912
Bowman, 1921
Boyd, 1911
Bradfield, 1929
Bradford, 1920
Bradley, 1920
Bramwell, 1902–3
Bramwell-Robinson, 1899
Brasie Cyclecar, 1914
Brasie Truck, 1915–16
Brazier, 1902–4
Brecht, 1901–2
Breer Steam Car, 1900
Breese & Lawrence, 1905
Bremac, 1923
Brennan, 1908
Brew-Hatcher, 1904–5
Brewster, 1934–36
Brewster-Knight, 1916–25
Bridgeport, 1922
Briggs, 1933
Briggs-Detroiter, 1910–18
Briggs & Stratton, 1922
Brighton, 1896, 1914
Brightwood, 1912
Brintel, 1912
Briscoe, 1914–22
Bristol, 1902–3, 1908
Broc Electric, 1909–16
Brock, 1920–21
Brockville-Atlas, 1911
Brockway Truck, 1912

Brodesser Truck, 1909
Brogan, 1946
Brook, 1920–21
Brooks, 1908
Brooks Steamer, 1924
Brothers, 1908
Brown, 1899–1900, 1909, 1912, 1914, 1916, 1922
Brown-Burtt, 1904
Brownell, 1910
Brownie, 1915
Browniekar, 1908–9
Brown Steamer, 1888
Brown's Touring Cart, 1898
Brunn, 1906–10
Brunner Truck, 1910
Brunswick, 1916
Brush Runabout, 1906–12
Brush Truck, 1907
Bryan Steam, 1918
Buck, 1925
Buckeye, 1905–17
Buckeye Gas Buggy, 1895
Buckles, 1914
Buckmobile, 1903–4
Buddie, 1921
Buddy, 1925
Buffalo, 1900–2, 1907, 1912–15
Buffalo Electric, 1900–12
Buffington, 1900
Buffman, 1900
Buffum, 1900–6
Bug, 1914
Buggyaut, 1909
Buggycar, 1907–10
Bugmobile, 1907–9
Buick, 1903—

246

roll call

Bull Dog, 1924
Bundy Steam Wagon, 1895
Burdick, 1909-11
Burford, 1916
Burg, 1910-15
Burns, 1908-12
Burroughs, 1914
Burrows, 1915
Burtt, 1917-23
Bus, 1917
Bush, 1917-23
Bushbury, 1897
Bushnell, 1912
Busser, 1915
Butler, 1908, 1914
Buzmobile, 1917
Byrider, 1908-9
Byron, 1912
B.Z.T., 1915

C.A.C., 1912-16
Cadillac, 1902—
California, 1912
California Cyclecar, 1914
Californian, 1920
Call, 1911
Calorie, 1904
Calvert, 1927
Cameron, 1907-20
Campbell, 1917-19
Canada, 1911
Canadian, 1921
Canda, 1900-1
Cannon, 1904
Canton, 1906
Cantono Electric, 1905-7
Capital, 1902
Capitol, 1912, 1920

Carbon, 1902
Car Deluxe, 1907
Cardway, 1923
Carhart Steamer, 1872
Carhartt, 1911-16
Carlson, 1904-10
Carnation, 1913-15
Carnegie, 1915-16
Carpenter Electric, 1895
Carrison, 1908
Carroll, 1912-13
Carroll Six, 1920-21
Carter, 1907-12, 1916
Cartercar, 1908-15
Cartermobile, 1924
Carthage, 1924
Casco, 1926
Case, 1910, 1920
Casey, 1914
Cass, 1915
Cato, 1907
Cavac, 1910
Cavalier, 1913, 1927
Caward-Dart, 1924
Cawley, 1917
C.B., 1917
Ceco, 1914
Celt, 1927
Centaur, 1902-3
Central, 1905
Central Steam, 1905-6
Century, 1900-4, 1927
Century Electric, 1901, 1912-16
Century Steam, 1901
C-F, 1907-8
C.G.V., 1903
Chadwick, 1906-16

247

Automobiles of America

Chalfant, 1906-12
Chalmers, 1910-23
Chalmers-Detroit, 1908-10
Champion, 1902, 1909, 1915, 1921-25
Champion Electric, 1899
Chandler, 1913-28
Chapman, 1899-1901
Charter Car, 1904
Charter Oak, 1917
Chase, 1907
Chatham, 1907
Checker Cab, 1921—
Chelsea, 1901-4, 1915
Chevrolet, 1909, 1911—
Chevrolet Truck, 1918—
Chicago, 1899-1910, 1917
Chicago Commercial, 1905-7
Chicago Electric, 1912-14
Chicago Motor Buggy, 1908
Chicago Steamer, 1905
Chief, 1908-9, 1947
Christie, 1904-10
Christman, 1901-2
Chrysler, 1924—
Church, 1901-3, 1910-11, 1914
Church Electric, 1912-13
Churchfield, 1911-15
Cincinnati, 1903
Cino, 1909-13
Circa-Hermann, 1914
Cla-Holme, 1923
Clapps Motor Carriage, 1898
Clark, 1898-1903
Clarke Carter, 1909-13
Clark Electric, 1912
Clark-Hatfield, 1908-9
Clarkmobile, 1903-7

Clarkspeed, 1926
Clark Steamer, 1901
Classic, 1917-21
Clear & Dunham, 1905
Cleburne, 1912
Clegg Steamer, 1885
Clendon, 1908
Clermont, 1903
Clermont Steamer, 1922
Cletrac Truck, 1922
Cleveland, 1902-9, 1919-25
Cleveland Cycle Car, 1913
Cleveland Electric, 1900
Climax, 1907
Climber, 1919-23
Clinton, 1923
Cloughley, 1902-3
Club Car, 1911
Clyde, 1919
Clydesdale Truck, 1914
Clymer, 1908
Coates-Goshen, 1908-11
Coats Steam, 1922-23
Coey, 1911
Coey Flyer, 1913
Coggswell, 1912
Colburn, 1907-11
Colby, 1911-14
Cole, 1909-25
Coleman Truck, 1928
Collier, 1917
Collinet, 1922
Collins, 1920-21
Collins Electric, 1901
Colly, 1901
Colonial, 1921-22
Colonial Electric, 1912-13, 1917-18

248

roll call

Colt, 1908
Colt Truck, 1908
Columbia, 1899–1907, 1916–24
Columbia Cyclecar, 1914
Columbia Electric, 1895, 1899–1904, 1906–18
Columbia Gas, 1900
Columbia Knight, 1911
Columbia Motor Carriage, 1897
Columbian, 1914–17
Columbia & Riker, 1901
Columbia Steamer, 1900
Columbia Taxicab, 1915
Columbia Truck, 1916–20
Columbia Wagonette, 1901
Columbus, 1902–4
Columbus Electric, 1905–14
Comet, 1907, 1916–36, 1946
Comet Cyclecar, 1914
Comet Electric, 1921
Commander, 1921–22
Commer, 1912
Commerce, 1916
Commercial, 1902–9, 1927
Commodore, 1921–22
Commonwealth, 1903, 1917–21
Compound, 1904
Concord, 1916
Condor Truck, 1929
Conestoga, 1918
Conklin Electric, 1895
Connersville, 1914
Conover, 1907–8
Conrad, 1900–3
Consolidated, 1903–6, 1916

Continental, 1907–9, 1912, 1914–15, 1933–34
Continental Mark II, 1955–57
Cook, 1921
Copley, Minor, 1907
Coppock, 1907–12
Corbett, 1907
Corbin, 1903–12
Corbitt, 1911–14
Cord, 1929–32, 1935–37, 1965–66
Corinthian, 1922–23
Corl, 1911
Corliss, 1917
Cornelian, 1913
Correja, 1908–14
Cort, 1914
Cortland, 1911, 1916–24
Corweg, 1947
Corwin, 1905–7
Cory, 1907
Cosmopolitan, 1897–1910
Co-Tay, 1920
Cotta, 1901
Country Club, 1904
Couple-Gear, 1905
Courier, 1904, 1909–12, 1922–23
Covel Electric, 1912
Covert Motorette, 1902–7
Covic, 1930
Coyote, 1909
C.P., 1908
C.P. Truck, 1909–14
Craig-Hunt, 1920
Craig-Toledo, 1906–7
Crane, 1912–15
Crane & Breed, 1912

249

Crane-Simplex, 1915–17, 1923–24
Crawford, 1905–30
Crescent, 1900–18, 1923
Cresson, 1915
Crestmobile, 1901–5
Cricket, 1914
Criterion, 1912
Croce, 1914
Crock, 1909
Croesus Jr., 1906
Crofton Bug, 1959
Crompton, 1903
Crosley, 1939–52
Cross Steam Carriage, 1897
Crouch, 1900
Crow, 1910–22
Crowdus, 1901
Crow-Elkhart, 1911
Crown, 1908–10, 1914
Crown-Magnetic, 1920
Crowther-Duryea, 1915–18
Croxton, 1911–15
Croxton-Keeton, 1909–10
Crusader, 1923
Crusier, 1918–19
Cucmobile, 1907
Cull, 1901
Culver, 1905, 1916
Cummins, 1930
Cunningham, 1909–33, 1951
Cunningham Steamer, 1901
Curran, 1928
Curtis, 1921–22
Curtis Steamer, 1866
Curtis Truck, 1915–16
Custer, 1921
Cutting, 1909–13

Cuyahoga Electric, 1909
C.V.I., 1907–8
Cyclecar, 1914
Cycleplane, 1914–15
Cyclomobile, 1920

D.A.C., 1923
Dagmar, 1922–27
Daimler, 1900–7
Dain, 1912
Daley Steam Wagon, 1893
Dalton, 1911
Daniels, 1912, 1915–23
Danielson, 1914
Dan Patch, 1911
Darby, 1909–10
Darling, 1901, 1917
Darrin, 1946
Darrow, 1903
Dart, 1911
Dart Cyclecar, 1914
Dartmobile, 1922
Dart Truck, 1916
Davenport, 1902
Davids, 1902
DaVinci Pup, 1925
Davis, 1909, 1911–28, 1947–50
Davis Cycle Car, 1913
Dawson, 1904
Day, 1911–14
Day Elder Truck, 1919
Dayton, 1904–14
Day Utility, 1914–16
Deal, 1908–11
Dearborn, 1910–11, 1919
Decatur, 1912
Decauville, 1909–12
Decker, 1902–3

roll call

Decross, 1914
De Dion Bouton, 1888-1904
De Dion Motorette, 1900
Deemotor, 1923
Deemster, 1923
Deere, 1916
Deere-Clark, 1906-7
Deering, 1918
Deering Magnetic, 1918
Defiance, 1919
DeKalb Jr., 1916
Delage, 1922
De LaVergne Motor Drag, 1896
Delia Truck, 1916
Delling Steam Car, 1924-29
Del Mar, 1949
Delmore, 1923
Delta, 1916
Deltal, 1914
DeLuxe, 1906-9
DeLuxe Electric, 1905
DeMars, 1905
DeMartini, 1919
DeMot, 1910-11
DeMotte, 1904
Denby, 1922
Deneen, 1917
Denegre, 1920
Dependable, 1919
Derain, 1911
Derby, 1924
Desberon, 1901
DeSchaum, 1908-10
Desert Flyer, 1908
DeShaw, 1910
De Soto, 1913-14, 1928-60
De Tamble, 1909, 1912

Detroit, 1904-7, 1916
Detroit-Chatham, 1912
Detroit-Dearborn, 1909
Detroit Electric, 1907-39
Detroiter, 1912
Detroit Speedster, 1914
Detroit Steamer, 1918
DeVaux, 1931-32
Dewabout, 1899
Dey, 1895
Dial, 1923
Diamond, 1907
Diamond-Arrow, 1907
Diamond T., 1905-11
Diamond T. Truck, 1911—
Diana, 1925-28
Dickson Steamer Truck, 1865
Dictator, 1913
Diebel, 1900-1
Diehl, 1923
Differential, 1921, 1932
Dile, 1914-16
Dillon Steam, 1920
Direct Drive, 1917
Disbrow, 1917-18
Dispatch, 1911-19
Divco Truck, 1927
Dixie, 1912, 1917
Dixie Flyer, 1916-24
Dixie Tourist, 1908-10
Dixon, 1922
D.L.G., 1907-8
Doane Truck, 1929
Doble-Detroit, 1919
Doble Steam Car, 1918-32
Dodge, 1914—
Dodge-Graham, 1929
Dodgeson Eight, 1926

251

Automobiles of America

Dodo, 1909, 1912–13
Dolly Madison, 1915
Dolson, 1904–7
D'Olt, 1921–26
Dorris, 1905–25
Dorris Truck, 1919
Dort, 1915–24
Double Drive, 1920
Douglas, 1918–19
Dover, 1929
Dowagiac, 1908
Downing, 1914–17
Downing-Detroit, 1913
Doyle, 1900
Dragon, 1906–8, 1921
Drake, 1921
Drednot, 1913
Drexel, 1916–17
Driggs, 1921–23
Driggs-Seabury, 1915
Drummond, 1916
Dudgeon Steam, 1853, 1866–67
Dudley Electric, 1915
Dudly, 1914–15
Duer, 1907–10, 1925
Duesenberg, 1920–37
Dunmore, 1917–18
Dunn, 1914–17
Duplex, 1908–9
duPont, 1919–32
Duquesne, 1903–6, 1912
Durable Dayton, 1916
Durant, 1921–31
Durocar, 1907
Duryea, 1893–97, 1907–12
Duryea-Gem, 1917
Duryea Lightcar, 1915

Dusseau, 1912
Duty, 1920
Duyo, 1914
D. & V., 1903
Dyke, 1902–4
Dymaxion, 1933–35

Eagle, 1906–7, 1909, 1924
Eagle Cyclecar, 1914–15
Eagle-Macomber, 1917
Eagle Rotary, 1917–18
Earl, 1907–8, 1921–23
Eastern, 1910
Eastern Dairies, 1925
Eastman, 1899–1902
Easton, 1907–13
Eaton, 1898
Eck, 1903
Eckhardt & Souter, 1903
Eclipse, 1901–2, 1908
Economy, 1906, 1908–11, 1917–22
Economycar, 1914
Eddy, 1902
Edmond, 1900
Edsel, 1957–59
Edwards-Knight, 1912–14
E.H.V., 1903–6
Eichstaedt, 1902
E.I.M., 1916
Eisenhuth, 1896
Eisenhuth-Compound, 1903
Elbert, 1915–16
Elbert Cyclecar, 1914–15
Elcar, 1915–31
Elcar-Lever, 1930
Elco, 1915
Elcurto, 1921

252

roll call

Eldredge, 1903
Eldridge Truck, 1913
Electra, 1913
Electric Vehicle, 1897
Electric Wagon, 1897
Electrobat, 1895
Electrocar, 1922
Electronomic, 1901
Electruck, 1924
Elgin, 1916-24
Elinore, 1903
Elite, 1906, 1909
Elite Steamer, 1901
Elk, 1913
Elkhart, 1908-16, 1922
Elliot, 1897, 1902
Ellis, 1901
Ellsworth, 1908, 1917
Elmira, 1920
Elmore, 1901-12
Elston, 1895
Elvick, 1895
Elwell-Parker, 1909
Elysee, 1926
Emancipator, 1909
Emblem, 1910
Embree-McLean, 1910
Emerson, 1907
E.M.F., 1908-12
Emmerson & Fisher Motor Wagon, 1896
Empire, 1898, 1910-19
Empire State, 1901
Empress, 1906
E.M.S., 1908
Endurance-Steam, 1922-23
Enger, 1909
Enger-Everitt, 1906-17

Englehardt, 1901
Engler, 1914
Enkel Truck, 1915
Entz, 1914
Epperson, 1912
Erbes, 1915-16
Erie, 1897, 1916-20
Erie & Sturgis, 1897
Ernst, 1896
Erskine, 1926-30
Erving, 1911-13
Ess Eff, 1912
Essex, 1906-8, 1919-32
Essex Steam Car, 1901
Etnyre, 1910-11
Euclid, 1903-4, 1907
Eugol, 1921
Eureka, 1907-9
Evans, 1904, 1912, 1914
Evansville, 1907-11, 1914-17
Everitt, 1909, 1911
Everybody's, 1908-9
Ewing, 1908-10
Excelsior, 1910

Facto, 1921-26
Fageol, 1916
Fageolbus, 1916
Fairbanks-Morse, 1909
Fairmount, 1906-7
F.A.L., 1909-14
Falcar, 1909, 1922
Falcon, 1908, 1914, 1922, 1938-43
Falcon Cycle Car, 1913-14
Falcon-Knight, 1926-29
Famous, 1908-9, 1917
Fanning, 1899-1903

253

Fargo, 1913
Fargo Truck, 1929—
Farmack, 1915-16
Farmer, 1907
Farmobile, 1908
Farner, 1922
Fast, 1904
Fauber Auto Cycle Car, 1914
Fawick, 1910
Fay, 1912
Federal, 1907-9
Federal Steamer, 1905
Federal Truck, 1910
Fee, 1908-9
Fenton, 1914
Fergus, 1917, 1920-21
Ferris, 1920-22
Fey, 1898-1905
Fiat, 1915
Fidelity, 1909
Field Steam, 1887
Fifth Avenue Coach, 1924
Finch, 1902
Findley, 1910, 1912
Firestone-Columbus, 1907-15
Fischer, 1902-04, 1914
Fish, 1908
Fisher, 1924
Fisher Steamer Truck, 1865
Flagler, 1914
Flanders, 1910
Flanders Electric, 1911, 1915-16
Fleetruck, 1926-27
Flexbi, 1904
Flexible, 1932
Flint, 1902-4, 1910-12, 1923
Flyer, 1913, 1933

Flying Auto, 1947, 1950
Fool-Proof, 1912
Foos, 1913
Ford, 1896, 1903—
Fordmobile, 1903
Forest, 1902
Forest City, 1906-9
Forster Six, 1920
Fort Wayne, 1911
Foster Steam, 1900-3
Fostoria, 1906-7, 1916
Fournier, 1902
Four Traction, 1907-9
Four Wheel Drive, 1902-7
Four-Wheel Drive Truck, 1912—
Fox, 1921-23
Frankfort, 1922
Franklin, 1902-34
Franklin Truck, 1907
Frantz, 1900-2
Frayer, 1904
Frayer-Miller, 1904-8
Frazer, 1946-51
Fredonia, 1902-4
Fredrickson, 1914
Freeman, 1901, 1931
Freemont, 1923
Freighter, 1917
French, 1913
Friedberg, 1908
Friedman, 1900-3
Friend, 1920-23
Frisbee, 1921
Fritchle Electric, 1907-22
Front-Away, 1917
Front Drive, 1921
Frontenac, 1908, 1917-22

roll call

Frontmobile, 1917–19
F.R.P., 1914–16
F.S., 1912
Fuller, 1908–11
Fulton, 1908–9, 1917
F.W.D. Car, 1910
F.W.D. Truck, 1910

Gabriel, 1912
Gadabout, 1914–16
Gaeth, 1898, 1902–10
Gale, 1904–10
Galt, 1914
Gardner, 1919–31
Garford, 1907–8
Garford Truck, 1902
Garoscope, 1917
Gary, 1915
Gary Truck, 1917
Gas-Au-Lec, 1905–6
Gas Engine, 1905–6
Gasmobile, 1900–2
Gasoline Motor Carriage, 1897
Gatts Horseless Carriage, 1905
Gawley, 1895
Gay, 1915
Gaylord, 1911–14
Gearless, 1907–9, 1921–23
Gearless Steamer, 1919–22
Gem, 1917–18
General, 1903–4, 1912
General Cab, 1929
General Electric, 1898–1901
General Vehicle, 1906–19
Genesee, 1911–12
Geneva, 1901–3, 1911, 1917

Gerlinger, 1917
German-American, 1902
Geronimo, 1918–21
Gersix, 1915
Ghent, 1917–18
Giant Truck, 1915
Gibbs, 1903–5
Gibson, 1899
Gifford-Pettit, 1907–8
Gillette, 1916
G.J.G., 1909–15
Glassic, 1931
Gleason, 1910–15
Glide, 1901–20
Globe, 1917, 1921
Glover, 1911, 1921
G.M.C. Truck, 1912–
Golden Eagle, 1906
Golden Gate, 1895
Golden State, 1902, 1928
Golden State, 1928
Golden West, 1919
Goodspeed, 1922
Goodwin, 1923
Gopher, 1911
Gotfredson Truck, 1921
Gove, 1921
Grabowsky, 1908–13
Graham, 1930–41
Graham Electric, 1903
Graham-Fox, 1903
Graham Motorette, 1903–5
Graham-Paige, 1928–30
Gramm, 1901
Gramm-Bernstein, 1912
Gramm-Logan, 1908–10
Gramm Truck, 1911
Grand, 1912

255

Grand Rapids, 1913
Granite Falls, 1912
Grant, 1913-22
Grant-Ferris, 1901
Grass-Premier, 1923
Graves-Condon, 1899
Gray, 1916, 1922-26
Gray-Dort, 1917-24
Great, 1903
Great-Arrow, 1903
Great Eagle, 1911
Great Smith, 1907-12
Great Southern, 1911-14
Great Western, 1908-16
Greeley, 1903
Green Bay Steamer, 1877
Greenleaf, 1902
Greenville, 1925
Gregory, 1948
Gregory Front Drive, 1922
Grensfelder, 1901
Greuter, 1899
Greyhound, 1921-23, 1929
Gride, 1903
Grinnell, 1910-15
Griswold, 1907-8
Grout, 1898-1914
Grout-Steamer, 1906
Guilder Truck, 1922
Gurley, 1901
Guy-Vaughan, 1912
G.W.W., 1919
Gyroscope, 1908

Haase, 1903-4
Hackett, 1915-20
Hackley, 1905-6
Hahn Truck, 1914

H.A.L., 1916-18
Hale, 1917
Hal-Fur, 1919-31
Hall, 1903-4, 1915, 1917
Halladay, 1907-15, 1919-20
Hall Gasoline Trap, 1895
Halsey, 1901-9
Halton, 1901
Hambrick, 1908
Hamely, 1903
Hamilton, 1917-22
Hamlin-Holmes, 1921
Hammer, 1905-6
Hammer-Sommer, 1903-4
Handley, 1923
Handley-Knight, 1921-23
Hanger, 1915
Hannay Truck, 1917
Hanover, 1921-23
Hansen, 1902
Hansen-Whitman, 1907
Hanson, 1918-23
Harberer, 1910-13
Harder, 1911
Harding, 1911
Hardinge, 1903
Hardy, 1903
Hare, 1918
Harper, 1907
Harrie, 1925
Harrigan, 1922
Harris, 1893, 1898
Harrisburg, 1922
Harrison, 1906-7, 1912
Harris Six, 1923
Harroun, 1916-21
Hart-Kraft, 1908
Hartley, 1898

roll call

Hartman, 1898
Harvard, 1915-22
Harvey, 1914
Hasbrouck, 1899-1901
Haseltine, 1916
Hassler, 1917
Hatfield, 1906-8, 1916-24
Hathaway, 1924
Haupt, 1909
Haven, 1917
Havers, 1911-14
Haviland, 1895
Havoc, 1914
Hawk, 1914
Hawkeye, 1917, 1923
Hawkins, 1915
Hawley, 1907
Hay-Berg, 1907-8
Haydock, 1907-10
Hayes-Anderson, 1928
Haynes, 1894-1924
Haynes-Apperson, 1895
Hayward, 1913
Hazard, 1914
H.C.S., 1920-26
Healey, 1951
Healy Electric, 1911
Hebb, 1918
Heifner, 1921
Heilman, 1908
Heine-Velox, 1906-8, 1921
Heinzelman, 1908
Hendel, 1904
Henderson, 1912-14
Hendrickson Truck, 1916
Henley, 1899
Hennegin, 1908-9
Henney Hearse, 1922

Henrietta, 1901
Henry, 1911-12
Henry J, 1950-54
Henrylee, 1912
Hercules, 1907, 1914
Hercules Electric, 1902
Herff-Brooks, 1914-16
Herreshoff, 1909-15
Herreshoff-Detroit, 1914
Herschmann, 1904
Hershell-Spillman, 1901, 1904-7
Hertel, 1895-1901
Hertz, 1926
Heseltine, 1917
Hess Steam, 1902
Hewitt, 1905-13
Hewitt-Lindstrom, 1900
Heymann, 1898
H & F, 1911
Hickenhull, 1904
Hicks, 1900
Hidley, 1901
Higdon & Higdon Horseless Carriage, 1896
Highlander, 1922
Highway Knight, 1920
Higrade, 1919
Hill, 1907-8
Hillsdale, 1908
Hill's Locomotor, 1895
Hilton, 1908
Hinde & Dauch, 1906-8
Hines, 1908
Hinkel, 1925
Hobbie, 1909-10
Hodge Steamer Fire Engine, 1840

257

Hodgson, 1902
Hoffman, 1931
Hoffman Gas, 1901
Hoffman Steam, 1902-4
Holden, 1915
Holland Steam, 1905
Holley, 1899-1904
Hollier, 1916-20
Holly, 1910-17
Holmes, 1908, 1918-22
Holmes Gastricycle, 1895
Holsman, 1902-10
Hol-Tan, 1906
Holton, 1921
Holtzer-Cabot, 1895
Holyoke, 1903
Holyoke-Steam, 1899-1903
Homer, 1908
Homer Laughlin, 1916-18
Hoosier Scout, 1914
Hoover, 1917
Hopkins, 1902
Hoppenstand, 1948
Horner, 1917
Horsey Horseless Carriage, 1899
Hoskins, 1921
Houghton, 1916
Houghton Steamer, 1900-1
Houk, 1917
Houpt, 1909
Houpt-Rockwell, 1910
House, 1920
House-Steamer, 1901
Howard, 1901, 1903-6, 1913-17
Howard Gasoline Wagon, 1895

Howe, 1907
Howey, 1907
H.R.L., 1921
Huber, 1894
Hudson, 1909-57
Hudson Steam, 1904
Hudson Steam Car, 1901
Huebner, 1914
Huffman, 1920-26
Hughes, 1899
Hug Truck, 1922-24
Hunt, 1905
Hunter, 1921
Huntington, 1907
Huntington-Buckboard, 1889
Hupmobile, 1908-41
Hupp-Yeats, 1911-19
Hurlburt, 1912-25
Huron, 1921
Hurryton, 1922
Huselton, 1914
Hustler Power Car, 1911
Hydro-Car, 1901
Hydromotor, 1917
Hylander, 1922

Ideal, 1902-9, 1912, 1914
Ideal Electric, 1910-11
I.H.C., 1907-11
Illinois Electric, 1901, 1909-14
Imp, 1913-14
Imperial, 1900, 1903-5, 1907-8, 1912-16, 1926—
Independence, 1912
Independent, 1911, 1915-16, 1920, 1927
Indian, 1922

roll call

Indiana, 1910, 1921
Indianapolis, 1899
Indiana Truck, 1909
Ingersoll-Rand, 1921
Ingram-Hatch, 1917-18
Inland, 1920
Innes, 1921
International, 1948
International Auto Wagon, 1900
International Harvester, 1907—
International Harvester Auto Buggy, 1907-12
International Truck, 1901
Inter-State, 1908-19
Interurban Electric, 1905
Intrepid, 1903-4
Iowa, 1908-9, 1919
Iroquois Buffalo, 1906-8
Iroquois Seneca, 1905-8
Irvin, 1902
Iverson, 1908
Izzer, 1910

Jackson, 1899, 1902-23
Jacks Runabout, 1900
Jacquet Flyer, 1921
James, 1911
Janney, 1906-7
Jarvis-Huntington, 1912
Jarvis Truck, 1903
Jaxon, 1903
Jay, 1907-9
Jay-Eye-See, 1921
Jeannin, 1908-9
Jeep, 1941—
Jeffery, 1902-16

Jem Special, 1922
Jenkins, 1901, 1907-15
Jersey City, 1919
Jetmobile, 1952
Jewel, 1911
Jewell, 1906-9
Jewett, 1906, 1922-27
J.I.C., *see* Jay-Eye-See
Joerns, 1911
Johnson, 1905-13
Johnson Steamer, 1901
Joliet, 1912
Joly & Lambert, 1916
Jones, 1916-20
Jones-Corbin, 1902-7
Jones Steam Car, 1898
Jonz, 1909-12
Jordan, 1916-30
J.P.L., 1914
Juergens, 1908
Jules, 1911
Julian, 1925
Julian-Brown, 1925
Jumbo, 1918
Junior, 1925
Juno Truck, 1911
Junz, 1902
Juvenile, 1906-7

Kadix, 1913
Kaiser, 1946-55
Kaiser Darrin, 1952-54
Kalamazoo, 1914, 1922
Kane-Pennington, 1894
Kankakee, 1919
Kansas City, 1905-7
Karavan Truck, 1920-22
Karbach, 1908-9

259

Automobiles of America

Kardell, 1918
Kato, 1907
Kauffman, 1909-10
Kavan, 1905
Kaws, 1922
K-D, 1913-14
Kearns, 1908-17
Keasler, 1922
Keene, 1900-2
Keeton, 1908
Keldon, 1920
Keller, 1947-49
Keller Cyclecar, 1915
Keller-Kar, 1914
Kelley-Springfield, 1918
Kellogg, 1903
Kelly, 1911
Kelsey, 1902, 1922-24
Kelsey Friction, 1921-24
Kelsey Motorette, 1910-13
Kelsey & Tilney, 1899
Kendle, 1912
Kenilworth, 1923
Kenmore, 1909-12
Kennedy, 1898, 1911
Kensington, 1899-1903
Kensington Steam, 1908
Kent, 1916-17
Kent's Pacemaker, 1900
Kentucky, 1915-24
Kenworth Truck, 1923
Kenworthy, 1920-22
Kermet, 1900
Kermoth, 1908
Kerns, 1914
Kerosene Surrey, 1900
Kessler, 1921
Kess-Line, 1922

Keystone, 1900, 1909-10, 1918-19
Keystone-Motorette, 1896
Keystone Steamer, 1909
Kiblinger, 1907-9
Kidder, 1901
Kidney, 1910
Kimball, 1922
Kimball Electric, 1912
King, 1896, 1909, 1911-24
King Midget, 1945-49
King-Remick, 1906
Kingston, 1907-8
King Zeitler, 1919
Kinnear, 1913
Kinney, 1922
Kirk, 1903-5
Kirkham, 1906
Kirksell, 1907
Kissel, 1906-31
Kleiber, 1925-30
Kleiber Truck, 1914-37
Klemm, 1917
Kline, 1909-23
Kline-Kar, 1916
Kling, 1907
Klink, 1907-9
Klock, 1900
Klondike, 1918
K & M, 1908
Knickerbocker, 1901, 1912
Knight & Kilbourne, 1906-9
Knight Special, 1917
Know, 1900
Knox, 1900-15, 1922
Knox-Landsen, 1904
Knox Truck, 1904-7
Knudson, 1899

roll call

K.O., 1921
Kobusch, 1906
Koehler, 1910-12, 1919
Komet, 1911
Konigslow, 1901-4
Kopp, 1911
Koppin, 1914
Kosmos, 1909
Kraft Steam, 1901
Kramer, 1915
Krastin, 1902-3
Krebs, 1913
Krebs Truck, 1922
Kreuger, 1904
K-R-I-T, 1909-15
Kron, 1915
Krueger, 1904-6
Kuhn, 1918
Kunz, 1902-5
Kurtis, 1954
Kurtis-Kraft, 1949-55
Kurtz, 1921-26

Laconia, 1900
Lad's Car, 1914
LaFayette, 1920-24, 1934-39
La France, 1910
La France-Republic, 1925
La Marne, 1920-21
La Marne Jr., 1919
Lambert, 1891, 1903-17
Lamphen, 1904
Lampher, 1909
Lamson, 1917
Lancamobile, 1899
Lancaster, 1900-1
Lancer, 1960—

Landover, 1917-18
Landshaft, 1913
Lane, 1920
Lane Steamer, 1899-1911
Langan, 1898
Langer, 1896
Lange Truck, 1921
Lansden, 1904-10
La Petite, 1905-6
Larchmont, 1900
Larre-Bee-Deyo, 1920
Larsen, 1908
Larson, 1910
La Salle, 1927-40
La Salle Niagara, 1906
Lasky, 1916
Laughlin, 1916-18
Laurel, 1916-21
Lauth-Juergens, 1907-9
Lavigne, 1914
Law, 1902, 1912
Lawson, 1900
Lawter, 1909
L.C.E. 1914
L & E, 1922
Leach, 1899
Leach-Biltwell, 1920-23
Leader, 1911
Lear, 1903-9
Lebanon, 1906-7
Lebgett, 1903
Lee Diamond, 1911
Lehigh, 1926
Lehr, 1908
LeJeal, 1902
Le Moon Truck, 1917
Lenawee, 1903-4
Lende, 1908-9

Lengert, 1896
Lennon, 1909
Lenot, 1912-22
Lenox, 1911
Lenox Electric, 1908
Leon Mendel, 1890
Leon Rubay, 1923
Leslie, 1918
Lesperance, 1911
Lethbridge, 1907
Lever, 1930
Lewis, 1898, 1901, 1913-16
Lewis Airmobile, 1937
Lexington, 1909-26
Liberty, 1916-23, 1926
Liberty-Brush, 1912
Light, 1914
Lima, 1915
Limited, 1911
Lincoln, 1908, 1910-11, 1914, 1920—
Lincoln Continental, 1939-48, 1957—
Lincoln Truck, 1917
Lincoln Zephyr, 1935-42
Lindsay, 1908
Lindsley, 1908
Linn, 1929
Linscott, 1916
Lion, 1910-12
Lippard, 1912
Little, 1911-14, 1921
Little Giant Truck, 1910
Littlemac, 1930
L.M.C., 1919
Locke Steamer, 1902
Locomobile, 1899-1930
Locomobile Steamer, 1899

Logan, 1905-8, 1914
Lomax, 1913
Lombard, 1921
London, 1922
Lone Star, 1920-23
Long, 1875, 1923
Long Distance, 1900
Longest, 1912
Loomis, 1896-1904
Lord, 1913-14
Lord Baltimore, 1912-13
Lorraine, 1907-8, 1920-21
Los Angeles, 1913
Louisiana, 1900
Lowell, 1917
Lowell-American, 1908-9
Loyal, 1920
Lozier, 1904-17
Lozier Steamer, 1900-1, 1912
L.P.C., 1914-16
Luck Utility, 1913
Ludlow, 1915
Luedinghaus-Espenschied, 1919
Luitwieler, 1909
Lulu, 1914
Lutz, 1917
Luverne, 1906-17
Luxor Cab, 1920-26
Lyman, 1904, 1909
Lyman & Burnham, 1903-4
Lyon, 1911
Lyons-Atlas, 1914-15
Lyons-Knight, 1914

Maccar, 1914
McCarron, 1929
McCormick, 1899

roll call

McCrea, 1906–8
McCue, 1909–10
McCullough, 1899
McCurdy, 1922
MacDonald, 1920–23
MacDonald Steamer, 1923
McFarlan, 1910–28
McGee Steamer, 1937
McGill, 1922
McIntyre, 1909–15
Mack, 1900—
McKay Steam, 1900
Mackenzie, 1914
Mackle-Thompson, 1903
Mack Truck, 1905
McLaughlin, 1911, 1916
McLean, 1910
McNabb, 1910
MacNaughton, 1907
Macomber, 1913
Macon, 1917
Macy-Roger, 1895
Madison, 1915–21
Magic, 1922
Magnolia, 1903
Mahoning, 1904–5
Maibohm, 1916–22
Maine, 1915–18
Mais, 1911
Maja, 1908
Majestic, 1913, 1917–18, 1925
Malcolm, 1915
Malcolm-Jones, 1914
Malcomson, 1906
Malden Steam, 1902
Malvern, 1905
Manexall, 1921
Manhattan, 1907, 1921
Manistee, 1912
Manlius, 1910
Manly, 1919
Mann, 1895
Mansfield, 1919
Mansur, 1914
Maplebay, 1908
Maple-Leaf, 1921
Marathon, 1908–15
Marble-Swift, 1903–5
Marion, 1901, 1903–15
Marion-Handley, 1916
Marion-Overland, 1910
Maritime, 1913
Mark-Electric, 1897
Marlan, 1920
Marlboro, 1900
Marlin, 1964–67
Marmon, 1903–33
Marmon-Herrington, 1931–64
Marmon & Nordyke, 1902
Marquette, 1912, 1929–30
Marr, 1903–4
Marron, 1903
Marsh, 1898–99, 1905, 1920–23
Marshall, 1919–21
Martin, 1910, 1920, 1926, 1931, 1954
Martin-Wasp, 1919–24
Marvel, 1907
Marwin Truck, 1918
Maryland, 1908–10
Maryland Electric, 1914
Mascotte, 1911
Mason, 1906–15, 1922
Mason Steamer, 1898
Massachusetts, 1901

Massillon, 1909
Master, 1918
Mather, 1901
Matheson, 1903-13
Mathews, 1907
Mathewson, 1904
Mathis, 1930-31
Matilda, 1894
Maumee, 1906
Maxen, 1913
Maxfer, 1919
Maxim, 1912, 1920, 1928
Maxim-Goodridge, 1908
Maxim Motortricycle, 1895
Maxwell, 1904-25
May, 1912
Mayer, 1899, 1913
Mayfair, 1925
Maytag, 1911
M.B., 1910
Mead, 1912
Mearo, 1909
Mecca, 1915
Mechaley, 1903
Mechanics, 1925
Med-Bow, 1907-8
Medcraft, 1907-8
Media, 1900, 1907
Meech-Stoddard, 1924
Meiselbach, 1904-9
Melbourne, 1904
Mel Special, 1923
Menard, 1921
Menges, 1908
Menominee, 1911-36
Mercedes, 1902
Mercer, 1909-25, 1931
Merchant, 1914

Merciless, 1906
Mercu, 1909-29
Mercury, 1904, 1910, 1914-18, 1922, 1930, 1938—
Merit, 1920-23
Merkel, 1905-6
Merz, 1914
Messerer, 1901
Metcar, 1901
Meteor, 1902-3, 1908-9, 1914, 1921
Metropol, 1914-15
Metropolitan, 1917, 1922-23
Metz, 1909-21
Metzcar, 1909-12
Metzger, 1909
Meyer, 1922
Michelet, 1921
Michigan, 1903-7, 1910-13
Michigan Hearse, 1914
Michigan Steamer, 1908-9
Middleby, 1908-12
Midgley, 1905
Midland, 1908-13
Midwest Tractor, 1918
Mier, 1908-10
Mieusset, 1907
Mighty Michigan, 1913
Milac, 1916
Milburn Electric, 1915-24
Miller, 1903, 1907-8, 1912-13, 1921
Miller Special, 1907-8
Mills, 1876
Mills Milwaukee, 1900
Milwaukee, 1925
Milwaukee Steam, 1900-2
Minneapolis, 1919

roll call

Mino, 1914
Mission, 1914
Mitchell, 1903-23
Mobile, 1902
Mobile Steamer, 1899-1903
Mobilette, 1913-15
Mock, 1906
Model, 1903-9
Modern, 1907-10, 1912
Modoc, 1911
Moehn, 1895
Moeller, 1911
Mogul, 1912
Mohawk, 1903-4, 1914
Mohler, 1901-5
Mohler & DeGress, 1901-5
Moligan, 1920
Moline, 1904-17, 1920
Moline-Knight, 1913, 1918
Moller Cab, 1920
Monarch, 1903-9, 1914-16
Moncrief, 1901
Mondex-Magic, 1914
Monitor, 1910, 1915
Monroe, 1915-22
Monsen, 1908-9
Moody, 1900
Mooers, 1900
Moon, 1905-31
Moore, 1902-3, 1906-7, 1916-20
Moorespring Vehicle, 1890
Moorespring Vehicle Steam, 1888
Mora, 1906-11
Moreland Truck, 1911
Morgan, 1897, 1908-9
Morlock, 1903

Mor-Power, 1921
Morris-London, 1920-23
Morrison Electric, 1891
Morris Salom Electrobat, 1895-97
Morrissey, 1925
Mors, 1901, 1906
Morse, 1904, 1909, 1915-16
Morse Cyclecar, 1914-15
Morse Steam Car, 1904-6
Mort, 1925
Motor Buggy, 1908-10
Motorcar, 1906-8
Motorette, 1906, 1910-11, 1946
Motor Truck, 1902
Mountain Road, 1917
Mt. Pleasant, 1914-16
Mover, 1902
Moyea, 1903-4
Moyer, 1912-15
M.P.C., 1925
M & P. Electric, 1912-13
M.P.M., 1915
Mueller, 1896
Mueller-Benz, 1895
Mueller-Trap, 1901
Mulford, 1909
Multiplex, 1913
Muncie, 1903, 1906
Munsing, 1908, 1913
Munson, 1900
Muntz Jet, 1951
Murdaugh, 1900
Murray, 1901, 1916-20
Murray-Max Six, 1921-26
Muskegon, 1918
Mustang, 1948

Mutual, 1914-19
Myer B. & F., 1912
Myers, 1904

Nadig, 1889
Nance, 1911-12
Napier, 1904-12
Napoleon, 1916-18
Narragansett, 1915
Nash, 1917-57
Nash Healey, 1951-54
Natco, 1912
National, 1900-24
National Electric, 1900
National Sextet, 1920
Nebraska, 1926
Neilson, 1907
Nelson, 1905, 1917-20
Nelson-Brennen-Peterson, 1914-15
Nelson & Le Moon, 1915-20
Netco Truck, 1916
Neustadt, 1912
Neustadt-Perry, 1903
Nevada, 1908
Nevada Truck, 1913-15
Nevin, 1927
Newark, 1912
Newcomb, 1921
New England Truck, 1914
New Era, 1902, 1916
New Haven, 1899, 1911
New Home, 1901
New Orleans, 1920
New Perry, 1903
Newport, 1916
New Way, 1907
New York, 1900, 1907, 1926

Niagara, 1903, 1915
Nichols-Shepard, 1912
Niles, 1916, 1921
Noble Truck, 1917-31
Noel, 1913
Nolan, 1924
Noma, 1919-23
Nonpareil, 1913
Northern, 1903-8
Northway, 1921
Norton, 1901-2
Norwalk, 1912-22
Novara, 1917
Nucar, 1929
Nyberg, 1912-14

Oakland, 1907-31
Oakman, 1898-1900
Obertine, 1915
O.B. Truck, 1928
O'Connell, 1928
Odelot, 1916
Offenhauser, 1934
Ogden Truck, 1918
Ogren, 1907, 1915-20
Ohio, 1909-18
Ohio Electric, 1900-15
Ohio Falls, 1911-15
Okay, 1907
Okey, 1903-8
O.K. Truck, 1917, 1925
Oldfield, 1917
Old Hickory, 1915
Old Reliable, 1912, 1926
Oldsmobile, 1896—
Olds Steam Car, 1896
Oliver, 1911, 1935
Olympian, 1917-20

roll call

Olympic, 1913, 1922
Omaha, 1912-13
Omar, 1908-10
Omort, 1926-34
Oneida Truck, 1917
Only, 1909-11
Only Car, 1911-15
Oregon, 1916
Orient, 1900
Orient-Auto-Go, 1900
Oriole, 1927
Orion, 1900
Orleans, 1920
Orlo, 1904
Ormond, 1904
Orson, 1911
Oscar-lear, 1905
Oshkosh, 1926
Oshkosh Steamer, 1877
Oshkosh Truck, 1917
Otto, 1909
Ottokar, 1903-4
Otto-Mobile, 1911-12
Overholt Steam, 1912
Overland, 1903, 1906-09
Overman, 1899-1902
Owatonna, 1903
O-We-Go, 1914
Owen, 1899, 1910
Owen Magnetic, 1915-20
Owen-Schoenieck, 1915
Owen-Thomas, 1908
Owosso, 1911
Oxford, 1905-6

Pacific, 1914
Pacific Special, 1911
Packard, 1899-1958
Packers, 1911
Packet, 1915, 1917
Page, 1907-9, 1923
Page-Toledo, 1910
Paige, 1910
Paige-Detroit, 1909-28
Pak-Age-Car, 1925
Palace, 1912
Palmer, 1906, 1912
Palmer-Moore, 1905
Palmer-Singer, 1907-14
Pan, 1917-22
Pan-American, 1902-4, 1917-21
Panda, 1954
Panhard Truck, 1917-18
Panther, 1908
Paragon, 1906, 1917, 1922
Paramount Cab, 1924
Parenth, 1921
Parenti, 1920-21
Parker, 1919, 1922
Parkin, 1903-9
Parry, 1911
Parsons, 1906
Partin, 1913
Partin-Palmer, 1913-17
Pasco, 1908
Pastora, 1913
Paterson, 1908-24
Pathfinder, 1911-18
Patrician, 1917
Patriot, 1922
Patterson-Greenfield, 1916
Pawtucket, 1901-2
Payne-Modern, 1906
Peabody, 1907
Peck, 1897

267

Peerless, 1900-32
Peerless Steam, 1902-9
Peet, 1923-26
Peets, 1908
Pelletier, 1906
Penford, 1924
Peninsular, 1915
Penn, 1911-13
Pennant, 1923
Pennington, 1890, 1894
Pennsy, 1917-18
Pennsylvania, 1907-13, 1916-17
Penn-Unit, 1911
People's, 1901
Perego-Clarkston Truck, 1920
Perfection, 1906-8
Perfex, 1912
Perry, 1895
Peru, 1938
P.E.T., 1913
Peter Pan, 1907, 1914
Peters, 1921-24
Peters-Walton, 1914
Petrel, 1908-12
Phelps, 1902-5
Phianna, 1917-20
Philadelphia, 1924
Philion, 1892
Phipps, 1911-12
Phipps-Johnston, 1909
Phoenix, 1900
Pickard, 1908-12
Pickwick, 1930
Piedmont, 1908, 1918-20
Pierce, 1903
Pierce-Arrow, 1901-38
Pierce Motorette, 1901

Pierce-Racine, 1903-11
Pierce-Stanhope, 1903
Piggins, 1909-10, 1912
Pilgrim, 1916-18
Pilliod, 1916
Pilot, 1911-23
Pioneer, 1909-11, 1914-15, 1917, 1920
Pirate, 1907
Pirsch, 1910
Piscorski, 1901
Pitcher, 1920
Pittsburgh, 1896-99, 1905-11
Pittsburgh Electric, 1905-11
Pittsburgher, 1919
Pittsfield, 1907
Planche, 1906
Plass Motor Sleigh, 1895
Playboy, 1946-49
Plymouth, 1910, 1928—
Plymouth Truck, 1908
P.M.C. Buggyabout, 1908
Pneumobile, 1914-15
Pokorney, 1904-5
Polo, 1927
Pomeroy, 1902
Ponder, 1916, 1922
Pontiac, 1906-9, 1926—
Pope, 1895-99
Pope Columbia, 1897
Pope-Hartford, 1897-1914
Pope Motor, 1903-8
Pope-Robinson, 1902-4
Pope-Toledo, 1901-9
Pope-Tribune, 1902-9
Pope-Waverly, 1903-8
Poppy Car, 1917
Porter, 1900, 1920-22

roll call

Port Huron, 1918
Portland, 1914
Poss, 1912
Postal, 1907-8
Powell, 1912
Powercar, 1909-11
Poyer, 1913
Practical, 1906-9
Prado, 1921
Pratt, 1911-16
Praul, 1895
Preferred, 1920
Premier, 1903-26
Premocar, 1920
Prescott, 1901-5
Preston, 1921-23
Price, 1908
Pridemore, 1914
Primo, 1906, 1911
Prince, 1902
Princess, 1905, 1914-18
Princeton, 1923
Progress, 1912
Prospect, 1902
Prudence, 1912
Publix, 1947-48
Pullman, 1907-8
Pungs-Finch, 1904-10
Pup, 1948
Puritan, 1917
Puritan Steam, 1902
Pyramid, 1902

Quakertown, 1915
Queen, 1902-6
Quick, 1899
Quinlan, 1904
Quinsler, 1904

R.A.C., 1911-12
Racine, 1895
Rae, 1909
Rae Electric, 1898
Railsbach, 1914
Rainier, 1905-11
Ralco, 1904
Raleigh, 1920
Rambler, 1900, 1902-13, 1957-69
Randall, 1903-6
Randall Steamer, 1902-3
Randolph Steam, 1908-10
Ranger, 1907, 1910-11, 1921-22
Ranier, 1911
Rapid Truck, 1902-13
Rassel, 1911
Rassler, 1907
Rauch & Lang Electric, 1905-24, 1927-30
Rayfield, 1911-15
R.C.H., 1911-14
Read, 1913-14
Reading, 1912-18
Reading Steamer, 1960
Real, 1915
Rebel, 1968—
Reber, 1902-3
Red Arrow, 1915-16
Red Ball, 1924
Red Bug, 1928
Red Devil Steamer, 1866
Red Jacket, 1907
Redshield, 1911
Red Wing, 1928
Reed, 1909
Reese, 1921

269

Automobiles of America

Reeves, 1897, 1908-11
Regal, 1908-18
Regas, 1903-5
Regent, 1917
Rehberger Truck, 1924
Reid, 1903-5
Reiland & Bree, 1928
Reinertsen, 1902
Relay, 1904
Relay Truck, 1921
Reliable, 1906-9
Reliable-Dayton, 1908-9
Reliance, 1903-9, 1917
Remel-Vincent Steam, 1923
Remington, 1901-4, 1912, 1915-16
Rennoc, 1918
Reno, 1908
Renville, 1911
Reo, 1904-36
Reo Truck, 1908-67
Republic, 1911-15
Republic Truck, 1914-31
Revere, 1917-25
Rex, 1914-15
Reya, 1918
Reynolds, 1920
Rhodes, 1908
Richard, 1914-18
Richards, 1914
Richelieu, 1922-23
Richmond, 1908-12, 1915
Richter, 1902
Rickenbacker, 1922-27
Ricketts, 1902
Ricketts Diamond, 1909
Rickmobile, 1948
Riddle, 1916, 1922-24

Rider-Lewis, 1908-9
Riess-Royal, 1922
Riker Electric Stanhope, 1896-99
Riker Gasoline, 1900
Riley & Cowley, 1902
Rinker Electric, 1898
Riper, 1917
Ripper, 1903
Ritz, 1915-16
Riviera, 1907
R & L Electric, 1920
R.M.C., 1908
R.O., 1911
Roadable, 1946
Road Cart, 1896
Roader, 1911-12
Road King, 1922
Road Plane, 1945
Roadster, 1903, 1915
Roamer, 1916-25
Robe, 1923
Roberts, 1904
Roberts Six, 1921
Robie, 1914
Robinson, 1900-2, 1914
Robson, 1908-11
Roche, 1920-26
Rochester, 1901
Rockaway, 1902-3
Rockcliff, 1905
Rocket, 1913, 1924
Rockette, 1946
Rock Falls, 1920
Rockford, 1903, 1908
Rock Hill, 1916
Rockne, 1931-33
Rockwell, 1908

roll call

Rodgers, 1903-5, 1921
Roebling, 1909
Roger, 1903
Rogers, 1895, 1911-12
Rogers & Hanford, 1901-2
Rogers Steamer, 1899
Rollin, 1923-25
Rolls-Royce (U.S.), 1920-31
Roman, 1909
Romer, 1921-24
Roosevelt, 1929-31
Root & Van Dervoort, 1904
Roper-Steamer, 1865
Roper Steam Vehicle, 1894
Ross, 1905-9, 1915-18, 1929
Rossler, 1907
Rotarian, 1921
Rotary, 1904-5, 1916-17, 1922
Rovan, 1914
Rovena Front-Drive, 1926
Rowe, 1911
Rowe-Stuart, 1922
Royal, 1904, 1914
Royal Electric, 1905
Royal Tourist, 1904-12
Rubay, 1922-24
Rugby Truck, 1927
Ruggles, 1905
Ruggles Truck, 1921
Ruler, 1917
Rumley, 1920
Runabout, 1902
Runner, 1913
Rush, 1918
Rushmobile, 1902
Russell, 1902-3, 1910
Russell-Knight, 1914

Rutenber, 1903
Ruxton, 1929-31
R & V Knight, 1919-24
Ryder, 1908-11
Rylander, 1914

Safety, 1909, 1917
Safety Steamer, 1901
Safeway, 1925
Saf-T-Cab, 1926
Saginaw, 1916-17
St. Cloud, 1921
St. Joe, 1909
St. Johns, 1903
St. Louis, 1899-1907, 1922
Salisbury Motorcycle, 1895
Salter, 1909
Salvador, 1914-15
Sampson, 1904-11, 1919
Sampson Electric Truck, 1907
Samson, 1919-23
Sanbert, 1911
Sandow Cab, 1925
Sandow Truck, 1915
Sandusky, 1903-4, 1911
Sanford-Herbert, 1911
Sanford Truck, 1918
Santos Dumont, 1902-4
Savage, 1912
Sawyer, 1913
Saxon, 1914-22
Saxon-Duplex, 1920
Sayer, 1917
Sayers & Scoville, 1907-24
Scarab, 1935-40, 1946
Schacht, 1905-13
Schaefer, 1910
Schaum, 1900-1

271

Schebler, 1908
Schleicher, 1895
Schloemer, 1889
Schlosser, 1912
Schlotterback, 1912
Schmidt, 1910
Schnader, 1914-18
Schoening, 1895
Schwartz, 1920
Scientific, 1921
Scioto, 1911
Scootmobile, 1947
Scott, 1901, 1921
Scott-Newcomb Steam, 1921
Scout, 1961—
Scripps, 1911
Scripps-Booth, 1914-22
Scripps-Booth Cyclecar, 1914
Seagrave, 1912, 1921
Searchmont, 1900-3
Sears, 1908-11
Sebring, 1909-12
Seitz, 1911
Sekine, 1923
Selden, 1906-14
Selden Truck, 1913
Sellers, 1909
Sellew-Royce, 1909
Seminole, 1928
Senator, 1906-11
Seneca, 1917-24
Serpentina, 1915
Serrifile, 1921
Service Truck, 1919
Servitor, 1907
Seven-Little-Buffaloes, 1908
Severin, 1920-22
S.F., *see* Ess Eff

S.G. Gay, 1915
S.G.V., 1910-15
Sha, 1920
Shadburn, 1917-18
Shad-Wyck, 1917
Shain, 1902-3
Shamrock, 1917
Sharon, 1915
Sharp, 1915
Sharp-Arrow, 1909-11
Shaum, 1905-8
Shavers Steam Buggy, 1895
Shaw, 1900, 1914-21
Shawmut, 1905-9
Shelby, 1902-3, 1917
Shelby American, 1965-69
Sheldon, 1905
Sheridan, 1921
Shoemaker, 1908-9
Sibley, 1911
Sibley-Curtis, 1912
Siebert, 1907-9
Sigma, 1914
Signal, 1915
Signet, 1913
Silent, 1906
Silent Knight, 1912
Silent Sioux, 1910
Silver Knight, 1906
Simmons, 1910
Simms, 1920
Simonds Steam Wagon, 1895
Simplex, 1905-19
Simplex-Crane, 1915
Simplicity, 1907-11
Simplo, 1909-10
Sinclair, 1921
Sinclair-Scott, 1906-7

roll call

Singer, 1914-21
Single Center, 1908-10
Sintz, 1897, 1903-4
Six-Wheel Truck, 1921
Sizer, 1911
S.J.R., 1915-16
Skelton, 1920-23
Skene, 1900-1
S. & M., 1913
Small, 1915, 1919-22
Smith, 1905-12
Smith & Mabley, 1905-7
Smith Motor Wheel, 1909
Smith Spring Motor, 1896
S.N., 1921
Snyder, 1908-9
Sommer, 1908
Soules, 1905-8
South Bend, 1919
Southern, 1908-10, 1922
Southern Six, 1921-22
Sovereign, 1907
Spacke, 1915-19
Spartan, 1907
Spaulding, 1902-3, 1911-16
Special, 1906
Specialty, 1898
Speed Wagon, 1918
Speedway, 1904
Speedway Special, 1918
Speedwell, 1907-15
Spencer, 1914, 1921
Spencer Steamer, 1862, 1901
Spenny, 1915
Sperling, 1921
Sperry, 1903
Sphinx, 1914-16
Spicer, 1903
Spiller, 1900
Spillman, 1907
Spoerer, 1909-14
Sport, 1921
Spracke, 1921
Sprague, 1896
Springer, 1904-6
Springfield, 1900-1, 1903-4, 1909-10
Sprite, 1914
Squier Steam 1899
S.S.E., 1917
S & S Hearse, 1907
Stafford, 1911-15
Stahl, 1910
Standard, 1902-5, 1909, 1916-23
Standard Eight, 1917
Standard Electric, 1911-14
Standard Electrique, 1903
Standard Six, 1910-11
Standard Steamer, 1900
Standish, 1925
Stanhope, 1903, 1905
Stanley, 1903
Stanley Steamer, 1897-1924
Stanley-Whitney, 1899-1902
Stanmobile, 1901
Stanton-Steam, 1901
Stanwood, 1920-22
Star, 1904, 1914, 1917, 1922-28
Starbuck, 1914
Star-Flee Truck, 1927
Starin, 1903
States, 1915-16, 1918
Static, 1923
Staver, 1907-14

273

Steamobile, 1901-2
Steam Vehicle, 1900-3
Stearns, 1898-1929
Stearns-Electric, 1900-4
Stearns-Knight, 1911
Stearns Steam Car, 1900-4
Steco, 1914
Steele, 1915
Steel Swallow, 1907-8
Stegeman, 1911
Steinhart-Jensen, 1908
Stein-Koenig, 1926
Steinmetz, 1920
Stephens, 1916-24
Stephenson, 1910
Step-N-Drive, 1929
Sterling, 1909-11, 1915, 1921-23
Sterling-Knight, 1921-25
Sternberg, 1909
Stetson, 1917
Stevens, 1915
Stevens-Duryea, 1902-15, 1919-24
Steward Truck, 1912
Stewart, 1895, 1915
Stewart-Coates, 1922
Stickney Motorette, 1913
Stilson, 1908-10
Stoddard, 1911
Stoddard-Dayton, 1904-13
Storck, 1902
Storms, 1915-16
Stoughton, 1919-31
Stover, 1909
Strathmore, 1900-1
Stratton, 1901-2, 1908-9, 1923

Streator, 1905-8
Stringer Steam, 1901
Strobel & Martin, 1910
Strong & Rogers, 1900
Strouse Steam, 1915
Struss, 1897
Studebaker, 1902-66
Sturges, 1895
Sturgis-Erie, 1898
Sturtevant, 1904-7
Stutz, 1912-34
Stuyvesant, 1911-12
Suburban, 1910-12
Success, 1906-9, 1920
Sullivan, 1904
Sullivan Truck, 1910
Sultan, 1906-12
Sultanic, 1913
Summit, 1907
Sun, 1915-17
Sunset, 1906-7
Super Cooled, 1923
Superior, 1908, 1918
Super Kar, 1946
Super Traction, 1923
Super Truck, 1920-28
Supreme, 1917, 1922, 1930
Swanson, 1911
Sweany Steam Carriage, 1895
Synnestvedt, 1904-8
Syracuse, 1899, 1905

Taft Steam, 1901
Tait, 1923
Tally-Ho, 1914
Tarkington, 1922
Tarrytown, 1914
Tasco, 1947

Taunton, 1901-2, 1904
Taylor, 1921
Teel, 1913
Templar, 1918-25
Temple, 1899
Templeton-Dubrie, 1910
Tennant, 1915
Terraplane, 1932-39
Terwilliger Steam, 1904
Tex, 1915
Texan, 1919
Texas, 1918-21
Texmobile, 1921
Thermot Monohan, 1919
Thomart, 1921
Thomas-Detroit, 1906-8
Thomas Flyer, 1902-12
Thomas Truck, 1907
Thompson, 1902-4, 1907-8
Thomson, 1901-8
Thor VI, 1909-10
Thorne, 1929
Thornycroft, 1901-3
Thorobred, 1901
Thresher, 1900
Thunderbird, 1954—
Tiffany, 1913
Tiffin, 1914
Tiger, 1914
Tiley, 1904, 1907-10
Tincher, 1904-9
Tinkham, 1899
Titan, 1916, 1919
Titan Truck, 1917
Titan Vim, 1925
Tjaarda, 1934
Toledo, 1902, 1909-10, 1915
Toledo Steamer, 1903

Tonawanda, 1900
Toquet, 1905
Torbensen, 1902-8
Touraine, 1912-16
Tourist, 1903
Tower, 1918
Town Car, 1909
Towne Shopper, 1948
Trabold, 1921
Tractmobile Steam, 1900
Traffic, 1914
Transit, 1912
Transport Truck, 1923
Trask-Detroit, 1922
Traveler, 1914-15, 1924
Traveller, 1906-7, 1910
Traverse City, 1918
Traylor, 1920
Trebert, 1907
Triangle, 1918
Tribune, 1913
Tri-Car, 1907, 1955
Tricar, 1912
Tricolet, 1905
Tri-Moto, 1901
Trinity Steam, 1900
Triple Truck, 1909
Triplex, 1905
Triumph, 1900-1, 1906-11, 1920
Trojan, 1916
Trombly, 1911
Troy, 1908-9
Trumbull, 1914-16
Tucker Mobile, 1900
Tucker Torpedo, 1946-47
Tudhope, 1913
Tulcar, 1915

Tulsa, 1917-21
Turnbull, 1918
Turner, 1902-4
Twin City, 1910
Twin Coach, 1927
Twombly, 1910, 1914-16
Twyford, 1902-8

Ultimate, 1920
Ultra, 1908-11, 1918
Union, 1902-5, 1908-9, 1912, 1917
Union Truck, 1902-4
United, 1902-4, 1916
United Motor, 1902
Unito, 1908
Universal, 1912, 1917, 1919
University, 1907
Unwin, 1907
Upton, 1903-6
Urgan, 1913
U.S., 1908
U.S. Auto, 1899-1918
U.S. Carriage, 1910-18
U.S. Long Distance, 1900-4
U.S. Motor Car, 1908
U.S. Motor Vehicle, 1899-1901
Utility, 1910, 1918

Valley Dispatch, 1927
Van, 1904
Van Auken, 1914
Vanderbilt, 1921
Van Dyke, 1912
Vanell Steam Carriage, 1895
Van L., 1911
Van Wagoner, 1900

Vaughn, 1905, 1913-14, 1923
V.E.C., 1903
Veerac, 1911
Velie, 1908-29
Vernon, 1916-20
Verrett Motor Wagon, 1896
Versare, 1928
Vestal, 1914
Veteran, 1921
Viall, 1917
Victor, 1906-15, 1921
Victoria, 1900
Victors, 1923
Victor Steamer, 1900
Victory, 1920
Viking, 1908, 1929-30
Vim Cyclecar, 1915
Vim Truck, 1914
Virginian, 1911
Vixen Cyclecar, 1914-16
Vogel, 1909
Vogue, 1918-22
Vogul, 1918
Voiturette, 1914
Voltra, 1917
Voltz, 1915
Vreeland, 1920
Vulcan, 1913-15, 1920

Wachusett Truck, 1921
Waco, 1915
Wade, 1913
Wagenhals, 1910-15
Wagner, 1902
Wagonette, 1901
Wahl, 1914
Waldron, 1909-11
Walker, 1911

roll call

Walker Truck, 1905-6
Wall, 1901-4
Wallworth, 1905
Walter, 1904-9, 1921
Walter Truck, 1914
Waltham, 1898, 1900-9, 1922
Waltham Orient, 1901
Walther, 1903
Walton, 1902
Walworth, 1905
Ward, 1920
Ward Electric, 1914-16
Ward La France, 1919
Ward Leonard, 1901-3
Ware, 1918
Warner, 1903
Warner Electric, 1895
Warren, 1905, 1911
Warren-Detroit, 1909-13
Warwick, 1901-4
Washington, 1907-12, 1921-23
Wasp, 1920
Waterloo, 1904-5
Waterman Arrowbile, 1937
Waterville, 1911
Watrous, 1905
Watson, 1907, 1916
Watt Steam, 1910
Waukesha, 1908
Waverly Electric, 1898-1917
Wayne, 1904-08
Webb, 1904
Webberville, 1920
Webb-Jay Steam, 1908
Weber, 1905
Weeks, 1908
Wege, 1917

Weier-Smith, 1917
Welch, 1904-9
Welch-Detroit, 1911
Welch & Lawson, 1895
Welch-Marquette, 1904
Welch-Pontiac, 1911
Werner Truck, 1926
Westcott, 1910-24
Western, 1901-11
Westfield Steam, 1910
West Gasoline Vehicle, 1895
Westinghouse, 1901
Westman, 1912
Weston, 1896
West Steamer, 1897
Weyher, 1910
W.F.S., 1912
Whaley-Henriette, 1900
Wharton, 1921-23
Wheel, 1902
Wheeler, 1903
Whippet, 1926-31
Whitcomb, 1928
White, 1901-19
White Hall, 1911
White Hickory, 1906, 1917
Whiteside, 1911
White Star, 1910-12
White Truck, 1902—
Whiting, 1905-7
Whitman, 1908-9
Whitney, 1898-99
Wichita, 1912
Wichita Truck, 1918
Wick, 1902
Wilcox, 1907-12
Wilcox Truck, 1910-27
Wildfire, 1953

277

Wildman, 1902
Willard, 1905
Willet, 1912
Williams, 1907
Willingham, 1916
Wills St. Clair, 1921–27
Will Truck, 1928
Willys, 1930–62
Willys-Knight, 1913–32
Willys-Overland, 1908–51
Wilson, 1903–5
Wilson Truck, 1915
Windsor, 1906–11, 1929–30
Wing, 1896, 1922
Winkler, 1911
Winner, 1899
Winther, 1920–23
Winther Truck, 1917
Winton, 1896–1925
Wisco, 1910
Wisconsin, 1899, 1910–11
Wisconsin Truck, 1921
Witt Thompson, 1921–23
Witt Will, 1917
Wizard, 1914, 1921
Wolfe, 1907
Wolverine, 1896, 1905–6, 1913, 1917–21, 1927
Wolverine-Detroit, 1912
Woodburn, 1912

Woodruff, 1902–5
Woods, 1899–1919
Woods Magnetic, 1917
Woods-Mobilette, 1907
Wood Truck, 1905
World Truck, 1927
Worth, 1907–8
Worthington, 1904–6
Wright, 1925
Wyeth, 1913

Xenia, 1915

Yale, 1903, 1917, 1921
Yankee, 1910
Yankee Cyclecar, 1914
Yellow Cab, 1921
Yellow Coach, 1921
Yellow Knight, 1928
York, 1904–10
York-Pullman, 1908–17
Young, 1921

Zeitler & Lamson, 1917
Zent, 1906–7
Zentmobile, 1903
Zephyr, 1936–40
Zimmerman, 1907–16
Zip, 1913

highlights

The story of highway transportation in America and its influence on the American people and their way of life can sometimes be most succinctly told in terms of pure facts and figures. These cold numbers in the following tables actually are the highlights of that story.

Historical Motor Vehicle Statistics

MOTOR VEHICLE REGISTRATIONS

Year	Passenger Cars (Thousands)	Buses[1] (Thousands)	Trucks[3] (Thousands)	Total[3] (Thousands)
1900	8	—	—	8
1905	77	—	1	79
1910	458	—	10	469
1915	2,332	—	159	2,491
1920	8,132	—	1,108	9,239
1925	17,481	18	2,570	20,069
1926	19,268	24	2,908	22,200
1927	20,193	28	3,082	23,303
1928	21,362	32	3,294	24,689
1929	23,121	34	3,550	26,705
1930	23,035	41	3,675	26,750

NOTE: Registrations shown here are not synonymous with vehicles in use since the latter implies a count of vehicles in operation on a specific date or an average for a period of time, while registrations are a count of transactions (with transfers eliminated) during a specified period. (1) Incomplete. Buses are not segregated from passenger cars or trucks in earlier years. Also included are municipally owned buses engaged in public transit. Due to new method of counting buses in 1959, the bus data for earlier years are not strictly comparable. (2) Alaska and Hawaii data included since 1959. (3) Data excludes farm trucks registered at a nominal fee in certain states and restricted to use in the vicinity of the owners' farms. There were 29,543 such trucks in the 1968 count.   *Preliminary

MOTOR VEHICLE REGISTRATIONS (CONTD.)

Year	Passenger Cars (Thousands)	Buses[1] (Thousands)	Trucks[3] (Thousands)	Total[3] (Thousands)
1931	22,396	42	3,656	26,094
1932	20,901	43	3,446	24,391
1933	20,657	45	3,457	24,159
1934	21,545	52	3,665	25,262
1935	22,568	59	3,919	26,546
1936	24,183	63	4,262	28,507
1937	25,467	83	4,509	30,059
1938	25,250	88	4,476	29,814
1939	26,226	92	4,691	31,010
1940	27,466	101	4,886	32,453
1941	29,624	120	5,150	34,894
1942	27,973	136	4,895	33,004
1943	26,009	152	4,727	30,888
1944	25,566	153	4,760	30,479
1945	25,797	162	5,076	31,035
1946	28,217	174	5,982	34,373
1947	30,849	187	6,805	37,841
1948	33,355	197	7,534	41,086
1949	36,458	209	8,023	44,690
1950	40,339	224	8,599	49,162
1951	42,688	230	8,994	51,913
1952	43,823	240	9,199	53,262
1953	46,429	244	9,544	56,217
1954	48,468	248	9,789	58,505
1955	52,144	255	10,289	62,689
1956	54,211	259	10,679	65,148
1957	55,918	264	10,943	67,125
1958	56,891	270	11,136	68,297
1959[2]	59,454	265	11,635	71,354
1960	61,682	272	11,914	73,868
1961	63,417	280	12,261	75,958
1962	66,108	285	12,780	79,173
1963	69,055	298	13,360	82,714
1964	71,983	305	14,013	86,301
1965	75,251	314	14,795	90,360
1966	78,123	322	15,517	93,962
1967	80,414	338	16,179	96,931
1968	83,592	352	16,941	100,885
1969	86,861	364	17,871	105,096

highlights

MOTOR VEHICLE REGISTRATIONS (CONTD.)

Year	Passenger Cars (Thousands)	Buses[1] (Thousands)	Trucks[3] (Thousands)	Total[3] (Thousands)
1970	89,231	379	18,748	108,376
1971	92,799	398	19,602	112,949
1972*	96,397	—21,209—		117,606

MILES OF TRAVEL, TAXES, AND EXPENDITURES

Year	Vehicle Miles of Travel (Billions)	Special Motor Vehicle Taxes (Millions)	Highway Expenditures (Millions)
1925	122		$ 1,755
1926	141		1,825
1927	158		2,049
1928	173		2,196
1929	198		2,249
1930	206	$ 851	2,541
1931	216	882	2,404
1932	201	915	1,904
1933	201	1,051	1,703
1934	216	1,119	2,020
1935	229	1,212	1,773
1936	252	1,363	2,491
1937	270	1,504	2,313
1938	271	1,445	2,675
1939	285	1,576	2,501
1940	302	1,743	2,378
1941	334	2,041	2,155
1942	268	1,942	1,769
1943	208	1,555	1,344
1944	213	1,613	1,349
1945	250	1,809	1,429
1946	341	2,414	2,043
1947	371	2,891	2,866
1948	398	3,259	3,444
1949	424	3,590	3,913
1950	458	4,094	4,155
1951	491	4,415	4,556
1952	514	4,969	5,051
1953	544	5,588	5,621

MILES OF TRAVEL, TAXES, AND EXPENDITURES (CONTD.)

Year	Vehicle Miles of Travel (Billions)	Special Motor Vehicle Taxes (Millions)	Highway Expenditures (Millions)
1954	561	5,844	6,580
1955	603	6,762	6,941
1956	628	7,242	7,938
1957	647	8,081	8,804
1958	665	7,816	9,793
1959	700	8,852	10,277
1960	719	9,717	10,161
1961	738	9,752	10,824
1962	767	10,591	11,623
1963	805	11,397	12,329
1964	847	12,216	12,985
1965	888	12,723	13,456
1966	931	12,943	14,783
1967	962	13,423	15,527
1968	1016	14,686	16,912
1969	1071	16,231	17,604
1970	1121	17,078	19,583
1971	1186	18,068	21,169
1972*	1250	16,970	21,652

*Preliminary

Source: U.S. Department of Transportation, Bureau of Public Roads.

highlights

Motor Vehicle Factory Sales, U. S. Plants

	PASSENGER CARS		MOTOR TRUCKS AND BUSES		TOTAL	
	Number	Value (000)	Number	Value (000)	Number	Value (000)
1900	4,192	$ 4,899			4,192	$ 4,899
1901	7,000	8,183			7,000	8,183
1902	9,000	10,395			9,000	10,395
1903	11,235	13,000			11,235	13,000
1904	22,130	23,358	700	$ 1,273	22,830	24,630
1905	24,250	38,670	750	1,330	25,000	40,000
1906	33,200	61,460	800	1,440	34,000	62,900
1907	43,000	91,620	1,000	1,780	44,000	93,400
1908	63,500	135,250	1,500	2,550	65,000	137,800
1909	123,990	159,766	3,297	5,334	127,287	165,099
1910	181,000	215,340	6,000	9,660	187,000	225,000
1911	199,319	225,000	10,681	21,000	210,000	246,000
1912	356,000	335,000	22,000	43,000	378,000	378,000
1913	461,500	399,902	23,500	44,000	485,000	443,902
1914	548,139	420,838	24,900	44,219	573,039	465,057
1915	895,930	575,978	74,000	125,800	969,930	701,778
1916	1,525,578	921,378	92,130	161,000	1,617,708	1,082,378
1917	1,745,792	1,053,506	128,157	220,983	1,873,949	1,274,488
1918	943,436	801,938	227,250	434,169	1,170,686	1,236,107
1919	1,651,625	1,365,395	224,731	371,423	1,876,356	1,736,818
1920	1,905,560	1,809,171	321,789	423,249	2,227,349	2,232,420
1921	1,468,067	1,038,191	148,052	166,071	1,616,119	1,204,262
1922	2,274,185	1,494,514	269,991	226,050	2,544,176	1,720,564
1923	3,624,717	2,196,272	409,295	308,538	4,034,012	2,504,810
1924	3,185,881	1,970,097	416,659	318,581	3,602,540	2,288,677
1925	3,735,171	2,458,370	530,659	458,400	4,265,830	2,916,770
1926	3,692,317	2,607,365	608,617	484,823	4,300,934	3,092,188
1927	2,936,533	2,164,671	464,793	420,131	3,401,326	2,584,802
1928	3,775,417	2,572,599	583,342	460,109	4,358,759	3,032,708
1929	4,455,178	2,790,614	881,909	622,534	5,337,087	3,413,148
1930	2,787,456	1,644,083	575,364	390,752	3,362,820	2,034,835
1931	1,948,164	1,108,247	432,262	265,445	2,380,426	1,373,691
1932	1,103,557	616,860	228,303	137,624	1,331,860	754,485
1933	1,560,599	773,425	329,218	175,381	1,889,817	948,806
1934	2,160,865	1,140,478	576,205	326,782	2,737,070	1,467,260
1935	3,273,874	1,707,836	697,367	380,997	3,971,241	2,088,834
1936	3,679,242	2,014,747	782,220	463,719	4,461,462	2,478,467
1937	3,929,203	2,240,913	891,016	537,315	4,820,219	2,778,227
1938	2,019,566	1,241,032	488,841	329,918	2,508,407	1,570,950
1939	2,888,512	1,770,232	700,377	489,787	3,588,889	2,260,018

Automobiles of America

	PASSENGER CARS		MOTOR TRUCKS AND BUSES		TOTAL	
	Number	Value (000)	Number	Value (000)	Number	Value (000)
1940	3,717,385	2,370,654	754,901	567,820	4,472,286	2,938,474
1941	3,779,682	2,567,206	1,060,820	1,069,800	4,840,502	3,637,006
1942	222,862	163,814	818,662	1,427,457	1,041,524	1,591,270
1943	139	102	699,689	1,451,794	699,828	1,451,896
1944	610	447	737,524	1,700,929	738,134	1,701,376
1945	69,532	57,255	655,683	1,181,956	725,215	1,239,210
1946	2,148,699	1,979,781	940,963	1,043,247	3,089,662	3,023,028
1947	3,558,178	3,936,017	1,239,443	1,731,713	4,797,621	5,667,730
1948	3,909,270	4,870,423	1,376,274	1,880,475	5,285,544	6,750,898
1949	5,119,466	6,650,857	1,134,185	1,394,035	6,253,651	8,044,892
1950	6,665,863	8,468,137	1,337,193	1,707,748	8,003,056	10,175,885
1951	5,338,435	7,241,275	1,426,828	2,323,859	6,765,263	9,565,134
1952	4,320,794	6,455,114	1,218,165	2,319,789	5,538,959	8,774,903
1953	6,116,948	9,002,580	1,206,266	2,089,060	7,323,214	11,091,640
1954	5,558,897	8,218,094	1,042,174	1,660,019	6,601,071	9,878,113
1955	7,920,186	12,452,871	1,249,106	2,020,973	9,169,292	14,473,844
1956	5,816,109	9,754,971	1,104,481	2,077,432	6,920,590	11,832,403
1957	6,113,344	11,198,379	1,107,176	2,082,723	7,220,520	13,281,102
1958	4,257,812	8,010,366	877,294	1,730,027	5,135,106	9,740,393
1959	5,591,243	10,534,421	1,137,386	2,338,719	6,728,629	12,873,140
1960	6,674,796	12,164,234	1,194,475	2,350,680	7,869,271	14,514,914
1961	5,542,707	10,285,777	1,133,804	2,155,753	6,676,511	12,441,530
1962	6,933,240	13,071,709	1,240,168	2,581,756	8,173,408	15,653,465
1963	7,637,728	14,427,077	1,462,708	3,090,345	9,100,436	17,517,422
1964	7,751,822	14,836,822	1,540,453	3,223,569	9,292,275	18,060,391
1965	9,305,561	18,380,036	1,751,805	3,733,664	11,057,366	22,113,700
1966	8,598,326	17,554,326	1,731,084	3,953,473	10,329,410	21,507,799
1967	7,436,764	15,653,436	1,539,462	3,592,049	8,976,226	19,245,485
1968	8,822,158	19,352,035	1,896,078	4,670,325	10,718,236	24,022,360
1969	8,223,715	18,751,176	1,923,179	4,936,683	10,146,894	23,687,859
1970	6,546,817	14,630,217	1,692,440	4,819,752	8,239,257	19,449,969
1971	8,584,592	21,409,824	2,053,146	5,963,525	10,637,738	27,373,349
1972*	8,823,938	23,133,051	2,446,807	7,654,180	11,270,745	30,787,231

NOTE: A substantial proportion of the trucks and buses consists of chassis only; therefore the value of the bodies for these chassis is not included. Value is based on vehicles with standard equipment. Prior to July 1, 1964 certain firms included tactical vehicles in factory sales data. After July 1, 1964 all tactical vehicles are excluded. Federal excise taxes are excluded. *Preliminary.

highlights

Automobiles Owned by 83 Percent of U.S. Families

Year	Number Families (Millions)	Percent Owning Automobiles	Number Owning Automobiles (Millions)
1941	—	51	—
1948	42.5	54	23
1949	44.1	56	25
1950	45.7	60	27
1951	46.3	65	30
1952	47.2	65	31
1953	48.0	65	31
1954	48.7	70	34
1955	49.3	71	35
1956	50.4	73	36
1957	51.2	75	39
1958	52.0	73	38
1959	52.5	74	39
1960	53.4	77	41
1961	54.2	76	41
1962	54.9	74	41
1963	56.5	80	45
1964	56.8	78	44
1965	58.4	79	46
1966	59.1	79	47
1967	60.2	78	47
1968	61.2	79	48
1969	62.1	79	49

SOURCE: "Survey of Consumer Finances," Survey Research Center, University of Michigan

36.7% OF CAR TRIPS RELATED TO EARNING A LIVING

36.7%
EARNING A LIVING
(To and From Work
Business Calls)

9.4%
EDUCATIONAL, CIVIC
AND RELIGIOUS

31.3%
FAMILY BUSINESS
(Shopping, Medical
and Dental, Etc.)

22.6%
SOCIAL & RECREATIONAL
(Pleasure Rides,
Vacations, Etc.)

SOURCE: National Personal Transportation Study, 1969–1970, U.S. Dept. of Transportation. FHWA.

Automobiles of America

Over 800,000 Businesses Dependent on Motor Vehicle Use

Type of Business	Establish-ments	Employees*	Payroll (000)	Sales or Receipts (000)
MANUFACTURING				
Motor Vehicles and Parts	1,855	686,100	$ 5,590,600	$ 38,919,800
Motor Truck and Bus Bodies	641	30,400	192,200	706,100
Motor Truck Trailers	179	22,900	147,100	713,900
Tires and Tubes	182	92,700	774,500	3,733,900
Storage Batteries	232	19,300	133,300	577,500
Petroleum Refining	437	106,700	965,000	20,293,900
Total Automotive Manufacturing	3,526	958,100	$ 7,802,700	$ 64,945,100
Total U.S. Manufacturing	311,125	19,398,000	$131,876,000	$555,863,000
Percent Automotive	1.1%	4.9%	5.9%	11.7%
WHOLESALE				
Automobiles and Other Motor Vehicles	4,783	93,956	$ 641,231	$ 31,329,583
Automotive Equipment	23,317	224,918	1,260,640	11,614,177
Tires and Tubes	3,114	36,483	224,652	3,178,398
Total Automotive Equipment	31,214	355,357	$ 2,126,523	$ 46,122,158
Petroleum Bulk Stations and Terminals	34,484	195,930	1,156,622	33,373,463
Total Automotive Wholesale	65,698	551,287	$ 3,283,145	$ 79,495,621
Total U.S. Wholesale Trade	311,464	3,641,266	$ 23,921,680	$459,475,967
Percent Automotive	21.1%	15.1%	13.7%	17.3%
RETAIL				
Motor Vehicle Dealers	62,023	785,868	$ 4,416,499	$ 48,635,589
Tire, Battery, and Accessory Dealers	29,189	158,799	604,432	4,235,752
Gasoline Service Stations	216,059	800,331	1,897,712	22,709,373
Total Retail Automotive	307,271	1,744,998	$ 6,918,643	$ 75,580,714
Total U.S. Retail	1,763,324	11,005,067	$ 36,174,723	$310,214,393
Percent Automotive	17.4%	15.8%	19.1%	24.4%
SELECTED SERVICES				
General Automobile Repair Shops	57,838	141,709	$ 384,375	$ 1,849,743
Top and Body Repair Shops	20,828	62,110	223,867	824,206
Other Automobile Repair Shops	31,280	93,250	335,042	1,411,591
Total Automobile Repair Shops	109,946	297,069	$ 943,284	$ 4,085,540

*Includes active proprietors of unincorporated businesses.   N.A.—Not Available.
(1) Establishments with payrolls only.
(2) Department of the Treasury, Internal Revenue Service, Statistics Income 1966, Business Income Tax Returns.
SOURCE: U.S. Department of Commerce, Bureau of the Census, 1967 Census of Business, Construction Industries and Manufacturing.

highlights

Over 800,000 Businesses Dependent on Motor Vehicle Use

Type of Business	Establish-ments	Employes*	Payroll (000)	Sales or Receipts (000)
MANUFACTURING				
Automobile Parking	10,606	37,442	$ 129,477	$ 483,809
Car, Truck Rental, Leasing Services, N.E.C.	18,691	106,927	395,027	2,458,860
Total Automotive Services, except Repair	29,297	144,369	$ 524,504	$ 2,942,669
Total Automotive Services	139,243	441,438	$ 1,467,788	$ 7,028,209
Motels, Motor Hotels and Tourist Courts	41,954	261,098	$ 622,583	$ 2,709,567
Trailer Parks	12,437	20,936	35,686	272,468
Drive-in Movie Theaters	3,384	21,999	59,389	313,012
Total Miscellaneous Auto Enterprises	57,775	304,033	$ 717,658	$ 3,295,047
Total Automotive Services and Miscellaneous Auto Enterprises	197,018	745,471	$ 2,185,446	$ 10,323,256
Total U.S. Selected Services	1,187,814	4,923,044	$ 17,524,045	$ 60,542,218
Percent Automotive Related	16.6%	15.1%	12.5%	17.1%
Highway and Street Construction Contractors	14,713	N.A.	N.A.	N.A.
Motor Freight Transportation and Related Services (2)	234,549	N.A.	N.A.	N.A.
TOTAL AUTOMOTIVE BUSINESSES IN U.S.A.	822,775	N.A.	N.A.	N.A.

index

"Roll call" is not indexed. Asterisks (*) indicate illustrations. Automobile is sometimes abbreviated auto.

a

A.A.A., 27, 131, 138
A.B.C. thread standard, 118
accessories, 70, 81; *see also* specific items: headlamps, radios, etc.
A.C.F. Motors, 81
Adams-Farwell, 39
advertising, 23, 56, 61, 63, 83, 85, 114, 197
Aerocar auto., 189
air bag safety device, 185, 188, 200, 202, 204
air cleaners, 75, 85, 144
air conditioning, 104, 132, 154, 205
air foils, spoilers, 182, 186, 187
Allison, James A., 33
Allstate auto., 127
aluminum, 20, 62, 143, 157, 193; *see also* individual parts: bodies, fenders, etc.
ambulances, 23
American Austin Car Co., 89
American Auto. Assoc., 27, 131, 138
American Bantam Co., 138
American LaFrance Fire Engine Co., 51
American Motor Car Manufacturers Assoc., 37
American Motor League, 14
American Motors Corp.: formed, 132; manufacturing moved to Wisconsin, 134; plant expansion, 152, 158, 162, 166, 168, 177; rebate, 155; Hornet, 186; expands facilities, 189; merges Kaiser Jeep, 193; buyer protection plan, 196; license for Wankel engine, 202
Amitrom auto., 184
Anderson, John W., 31
antifreeze solutions, 152
anti-theft protection, 151, 179, 185, 186, 189, 202
Apperson, Edgar, Elmer, 12, 207
Argonaut Motor Machine Corp., 145
Ariel auto., 37
Assoc. of Licensed Auto. Manufacturers, 31, 42, 53
atomic bomb tests, 130
Auburn auto., 180
Austin, Walter S., 208
Austin Bantam auto., 89, 90*
Autocar Co., 21, 43, 69, 129
"automobile" (use of term), 17
Automobile Blue Book, 25
Auto. Board of Trade, 53, 56
Auto. Club of America, 20, 22, 25, 29
Auto. Club of Great Britain & Ireland Reliability Trial, 32
Automobile Daily News, 82
Auto. Information Disclosure Act, 147
Auto. Manufacturers Assoc., 96, 97, 129, 132, 134, 138, 140, 143, 146, 150,

288

index

152, 153, 193, 195, 200
Automobile Topics, 23
Automotive Committee for Air Defense, 106
Automotive Council for War Production, 108, 109, 110
Automotive Golden Jubilee, 115
Automotive Information Council, 196
Automotive News, 82
Automotive Organization Team, 201
Automotive Products Trade Act, 170
Automotive Safety Foundation, 141
Automotive Service Industries Assoc., 148
Auto Wagon auto., 42*
Avanti Motor Corp., 172
axles, 89

b

back-up lights, 75
Baker, E. G., 78, 83
Baker electric auto, 162
Barnum & Bailey Circus, 16
Barthel, Oliver E., 16*
batteries, 38, 96, 101, 117, 175, 186, 200
Beck, C. D., & Co., 139
beds, convertible, 57, 98, 107*
Bendix, Vincent, 208
Bennett, Charles H., 31
Benz, Karl, 6
Besserdich, William, 46
Bezner, Frederick O., 39
bodies, 26, 27, 70; aluminum, 38, 62, 88; torpedo, 49; 4-door, 52, 76, 98; steel, 55, 77, 96; seating arrangement, 58, 59; double-cowl, 61; enclosed, 73, 75, 77, 81, 89; streamlining, 85, 94; closed percent of cars, 89; "No-Draft Ventilation," 94; doors wider, 96; sloping side windows, 99; unitized, 104, 145, 189; antirust protection, 144, 176; on-frame construction, 189; *see also* specific types: sedan, tonneau, etc.

body finishes, *see* paints
Borg-Warner Corp., 122
Brady, James J., 40
brakes, 40, 41; air, 35; hand, 58, 98; hydraulic, 67, 86; 4-wheel, 67, 70, 80, 85; vacuum, 85, 86; power, 89, 94; emergency, 99; self-adjusting, 116, 151, 154, 161; bonded, 120; suspended pedal, 128; aluminum drum, 144; flanged drum, 147; automatic release, parking, 151; dual, 156, 172; disc, 161, 168, 181, 190; skid-control, 185, 189, 193
Brayton, George B., 13
Breer, Carl, 24, 73, 85
Breer Engineering Co., 77
brick roads, 12
Briggs Mfg. Co., 131
Briscoe, Benjamin, 28, 50, 208
Briscoe, Frank, 28, 208
Briscoe auto., 61*
Brockaway, George, 55
Brockaway Motor Co., 55, 87, 139
Brockaway truck, 54*
Brownlow-Latimer Good Roads Bill, 33
Brush, Alanson P., 41
Budd, Edward G., 55
Buick, David D., 26, 208
Buick auto.: 6-cylinder, 59; 8-cylinder, 92; 3,000,000th, 99; model changeover in 10 days, 100; Dynaflow hydraulic torque converter, 118; hardtop convertible, 120*; XP 300 experimental, 125; Century, 133*; Special, 152
Buick Autovim and Power Co., 26
Buick Motor Co., 31, 45
bumpers, 39, 69, 82, 181, 193, 202
buses, 38, 87, 154, 158, 176, 197; *see also* makes: Reo, White, etc.

c

Cadillac auto.: first, 28; Dewar Trophy, 44, 56; electic starter, 54, 56; V-8

289

engine, 58; syncro-mesh transmission, 86; V-12, V-16 engines, 89; power brakes, 89; front wheel drive, 180
Cadillac Auto. Co., 28, 33
Cadillac Div. of G.M., 48, 163, 168
Cadillac Motor Car Co., 33, 48, 74
"California Top," 33
campers, 162, 167, 188, 197, 203
Canada-U.S. tariff agreement, 170, 179
carburetors, 11, 24; twin, 41; thermostatic control, 73; down-draft, 88; intake silencer, 89
Chadwick, Lee S., 209
Chalmers, Hugh, 210
Chandler auto., 86
Chapin, Roy D., 26, 39, 210
chassis: "simplified," 53; gold, 62; rubber springs, 89; without X-member, 98
Checker auto., 147, 164, 182
Checker Motors Corp., 147
Chevrolet, Louis, 47, 210
Chevrolet auto.: first, 47; 4-cylinder engine, 58; V-8 engine, 64; 6-cylinder engine, 87, 191; production highlights, 96, 102, 124, 155, 164, 170, 194; steel station wagon, 97*; vacuum operated gearshift, 102, truck, 138, 143, 148; Impala, 146*, Vega, 195
Chevrolet Div. of G.M. 67, 116, 130, 138, 199
Chevrolet Motor Co., 53, 56, 67
Chevrolet truck, 193
Chicago Times-Herald Race, 13
chokes, automatic, 93
Christie, John W., 211
chromium plating, 81
Chrysler, Walter P., 77, 211
Chrysler auto.: developed, 77; rubber-mounted engine, 93; automatic transmission, 96; Town & Country series, 119*; ignition key starting, 121; turbine, 133, 140, 155, 165, 170
Chrysler Corp.: formed, 82; dividends, 86; purchases Dodge Bros., 87; Plymouth, DeSoto introduced, 87; 8-cylinder engine, 89; "Superfinish," 102; Silver anniversary, 124; Detroit Tank Arsenal, 128; proving grounds, 129, 134; purchases Briggs auto plants, 131; loan from Prudential Insurance, 132; buys Universal Products Co. 135; plant expansion, 118, 136, 152, 173, 177; 25 millionth, 144; purchases stock in Simca, 145; divisions realigned, 148; Chrysler-Plymouth Div., 158; purchases Lone Star Boat Co., 173; purchases share of Mitsubishi Motors, 197
cigar lighters, 81
circuses, 16, 65
Clarke, Louis S., 19, 28
Clark Equipment Co., 167
Clifton, Charles, 65, 212
clocks, 200
clutches: centrifugal, 35; multiple disc, 53; vacuum-operated, 93; automatic, semi-automatic transmission, 106; suspended pedal, 128; E-stick automatic transmission, 156; interlock, 156
Coffin, Howard E., 39
colors, see paints
Columbia Electric truck, 32
Commercial Car Manufacturers Assoc., 46
compact cars, 144, 150, 186
Compac-Vans, 173
Comuta auto., 179
concrete mixers, truck, 86
concrete pavement, 47
Continental auto., 135*
Continental Motors Corp., 126, 162
convertible bodies, 33, 59, 70, 92, 102*
cooling, 28, 37, 158, 186; see also radiators
Cord auto., 90*, 100*, 162, 172, 176
Cortez mobile home, 167

index

Cosmopolitan Race, 16
Couzens, James, 31
Crocker, Sewall K., 30*
Crosley, Powell, Jr., 103*
Crosley auto., 103*, 115*, 123, 128
Crosley Corp., 112, 122, 123, 128
cross licensing, 63
Cugnot, Nicolas, 5
Cummins, Clessie L., 196
Curtiss-Wright Corp., 150, 158, 192, 196
cyclecars, 58
cylinder casting, 48

d

Daimler, Gottlieb, 6
dashboards, *see* instrument panels
Day, George H., 31
dealers, dealerships, 20, 21
Dearborn Motors Corp., 129
defrosters, 99, 190
design, *see* bodies
DeSoto auto.: introduced, 87; vacuum-operated clutch, 93; "Airflow," 95; automatic transmission overdrive, 96; 9-passenger station wagon, 121; V-8 engine, 128; discontinued, 155
Detroit, early auto industry, 25, 40
Detroit Diesel Engine Div., 158
Detroit Tank Arsenal, 128
Dewar Trophy, 44, 56
Diamond T Motor Car Co., 38, 53, 145, 180
diesel trucks, 88, 128, 149, 158, 187
Dietz, R. E., Co., 23
disabled veterans, 115
Divco Truck Div., 139
Double, Abner, 212
Dodge, Horace, John, 29, 58, 213
Dodge auto., 58, 77, 120, 121, 130*; truck, 123, 182, 192
Dodge Bros. Co. 87; Div., 167
Dorris, George P., 214
Dort auto., 71*

Drake, J. Walter, 74
"drive-it-yourself," 82
driver education, 117, 118, 127, 137
drivers' licenses, 21, 23, 137, 159, 186
drunk drivers, 194, 202
dual-control, 118
Dual Motors Corp., 136, 138
Duesenberg, Frederick S., 198
Dusenberg auto., 70, 91*, 168
duPont, Pierre S., 70
Durant, William C., 43, 70, 76, 214
Durant Motors, 76, 77*
Duryea, Charles E., 10*, 13, 215
Duryea, J. Frank 10*, 13, 15*, 216
Duryea auto., 10*, 15, 17
Duryea Motor Wagon Co., 13, 15
Dyke, A. L., 21, 216

e

Earl, Harley, 216
Eaton, William, 43
economy runs, contests, 42, 63, 187
Edgar, Graham, 84
electrical systems, 128, 132, 152, 181
Electric Autolite Co., 158
electric autos., 16, 23, 53, 78, 148, 162, 179, 182, 188, 197
Electric Fuel Propulsion, Inc., 188
Electric Vehicle Co., 26, 29
electrochemical fuel conversion, 148
Electrovair auto., 175, 179
Electrovan, 175
Ellerbeck, B. B., 92
Elliott, Sterling, 29
engine mountings, rubber, 72, 82, 92, 93
engines: air-cooled, 20, 37, 40*, 150: under hood, 23, 29; valve-in-head, 20, 31; 6-cylinder, 39, 40, 79, 132, 194; rotary, 39, 150, 192, 196, 202; 12-cylinder, 39, 61, 89, 94, 149; 8-cylinder, 42, 58, 70, 80, 88, 89, 132; sleeve-valve, 46, 51, 73*; V-8, 42, 58, 62, 93*, 118, 126*, 128, 132, 135,

291

137, 152; L-head, 77; V-16, 89; superchargers, 95; interchangeable 6- or 8-cylinder, 106; high-compression, 118; gas turbine, 126, 133, 140, 143, 148, 155, 159, 161, 162, 170, 171, 195, 200, 202; free-piston, 139; V-4, 140; aluminum, 150, 152, 191; fluid injected turbo-charged, 160; positive crankcase ventilating, 161: preheaters, 175: diesel, 182; mid-engine design, 184; 4-cylinder, 194
Erskine, Albert R., 217
Erskine auto., 84
Essex auto., 68*
Essex Motor Car Co., 64
Ethyl Corp., 80
Euclid Road Machinery Co., 130
Evans, Oliver, 5
exhaust emission control, 151, 161, 177, 181, 193, 194
experimental safety vehicles, 192, 198, 204

f

factories, reinforced concrete, 31
Fageol Motors Co., 81, 85
Federal Aid Highway Act, of 1970, 194
Federal Aid Road Act, 63
fenders: aluminum, 62; full-skirted, 93; covers for rear, 94, 96; middle of front door, 106
Ferguson, Harry, Inc., 129
filters, 80, 85
financing, see installment buying
fire-fighting apparatus, 51
firsts, auto., see subjects: magazines, purchase, roads, etc.
Fischer auto., 35
Fisher, Alfred J., 217
Fisher, Carl G., 33, 48, 57
Fisher, Charles T., Frederic J., 46, 217
Fisher, Howard A., Lawrence P., 217
Fisher Body Co., 46, 69, 82, 84
Flanders, Walter E., 218

"flat-rate" repair system, 68
Fleet Owner, 87
Fleetwood Body Corp., 82
Flint auto., 79*
fluidic controls, 184
flying autos., 100, 110, 147, 189
Ford, Edsel B., 69
Ford, Henry, 15*, 29, 69, 185, 219
Ford, Henry, II, 112*
Ford auto.: Quadricycle, 15*; "999," 30*, 32; Model T, 43*, 55*, 79*, 85, 144; Model A, 84*, 93; V-8, 93*, 119*, 142*; Thunderbird, 145*; turbine car, 165; Maverick, 186, 188
Ford Motor Co.: incorporated, 29; first branch, 35; Selden Patent Case, 32, 47, 52; Highland Park plant, 42, 51; production highlights, 56, 58, 68, 72, 78, 80, 106, 144, 159, 164, 180; $5.00 daily wage, 58; rebate plan, 58, 61; Rouge plant, 63; financial crisis, 72; buys Lincoln Motor Co., 76; prices reduced, 76; weekly purchase plan, 77; manufactures accessories, 80; 5-day work week, 84; $7.00 daily wage, 88; in National Auto Show, 97, 106; plant expansion, 102, 118, 130, 134, 135, 163, 166, 168, 173, 177; production resumed after WW II, 112*, 113; Ford Div., 120; proving grounds, 134; stock offered to public, 138; joins AMA, 140; purchases Sherman Products, 152; Philco, Electric Autolite plants, 158; Industrial & Chemical Products Div., 179; U.S.S.R. factory proposal, 192; Autolite divestiture, 196
Ford Motor Credit Co., 149
Ford of Europe; Ford, Philippines, 180
Fordson tractor, 63
foreign activities, U.S. automakers, 74
four-wheel drive, 46, 50, 57
Four Wheel Drive Auto Co., 50, 145
frame construction, pressed steel, 31
Franklin, Herbert H., 219

index

Franklin auto., 40*
Frazer, E. M., 85
Frazer, Joseph W., 110, 220
free-wheeling, 89, 92, 93
front-wheel drive, 34, 173, 180
Fry, Vernon, 31
fuel economy, 94
fuel injection, 140
Furber, Frederick, 65

g

Gabelich, Gary, 193
garages, *see* service stations
gas, liquified petroleum (LPG), 128
gas turbines, *see* engines
gasoline: ethyl, 75, 77, 80; octane scale, 84; high-octane, 118; lead-free, 192
gasoline-electric autos., 45
gasoline gauges, 76
gasoline stations, *see* service stations
gasoline tanks, plastic, 190
gears, 46, 56, 83
gearshifts: "H" slot, 29; on dashboard, 96, 107, 134; finger-tip control, 97, 101; automatic, 101; vacuum-operated, 102
General Motors Acceptance Corp., 69
General Motors bus, 158; truck, 53, 62, 132
General Motors Co., 43; Corp.: acquires Buick, Oldsmobile, Oakland, Rapid Motor Vehicle Co., 46, 47; Cadillac, 48; stock dividends, 48, 60, 85; Chevrolet, 67; buys interest in Fisher Body Co., 69; GM building, 74; proving grounds, 80, 125, 129, 182; Yellow Truck & Coach Co., 81; Fisher Body Corp., 84; all-steel turret tops, 96; plant expansion, 118, 163, 166, 168, 173, 177; Transportation Unlimited show, 120; Euclid Road Machinery stock, 130; transmission plant fire, 131; production highlights, 134, 159, 167, 180; GM Parts Div., 187; Progress of Power show, 187; purchases part of Isuzu Motors, 197
General Motors Research Corp., 70
General Motors Truck Co., 53
General Tire & Rubber Co., 128, 160
generators, 96, 150
glass, safety, 82
Glassic auto., 180
Glidden, Charles J., 35, 220
Glidden Tours, 35, 37*, 45, 48
Goodyear Tire & Rubber Co., 158, 160, 166
governors, 24
Grabowsky, Max, 28
Graham, Joseph B., Roy A., Robert C., 221
Graham-Paige Motors Corp., 85, 109, 110, 117
Gramm, B. A., 32
Gray, John S., 31
grilles, *see* radiators
guarantees, *see* warranties

h

Hall, E. J., 64
Hammond, E. T., 31
Harroun, Ray, 53
Haynes, Elwood G., 12, 13*, 76, 221
Haynes-Apperson auto., 20
Haynes auto., 12, 13*, 20
headlamps, 33, 83; kerosene, 23; acetylene, 33; standard equipment, 35; electric-acetylene, 49; tilt-beam, 60; prism lenses, 61; dimming, 77, 128, 181; two-filament bulb, 80; sealed-beam, 104, 134, 138; concealed in front fenders, 107, 166, 188; dual-headlighting, 134, 138, 140, 143, 150; automatically turned on, 151, 166; warning buzzer, 181; "Superlite," 186; washers, 186; delayed, 190
heating, ventilation, 65, 70, 84, 101, 104, 134; *see also* air conditioning
Hercules Engine Div., 177

293

Herrington, Arthur W., 93, 104
Hewitt Motor Car Co., 42, 53
Highway Act, 139, 194
Highway Emergency Locating Plan, 171
Highway Products, Inc., 173
Highway Research Board, 72
highways, *see* roads, turnpikes
Highway Safety Act, 174
Highway Trust, 194
hill climbs, 20, 42
Hines, Edward N., 53
Holcomb, Bert, 19*
hoods, lock releases, 103
horns, 38, 46, 181
Horseless Age, 14
horse power formula, 42
Howe, Robert G., 104
Hudson auto., 47*, 53, 80, 97, 99, 143
Hudson Motor Car Co., 48, 132
Hupmobile auto., 69*, 92, 95, 97
Hupmobile Motor Car Corp., 88, 121

i

ignition systems, 11, 48, 121, 124, 151, 161, 198, 202
Imperial auto., 149*
Indianapolis 500-Mile Race, 53, 180, 193, 204
Indianapolis Speedway, 48
Indiana Truck Corp., 87, 94
installment buying, 37, 56, 77, 106, 121, 124, 126
instrument panels, 69, 134, 151, 168
insurance 19, 76
International Harvester Co., 41, 102, 153, 166, 177, 204
International Harvester Scout, 204
International motor truck, 42*, 128, 166, 167, 182, 187

j

Jackson, H. Nelson, 30*, 31

"Jeep," 104, 108; *see also* Willys Overland
Jeffery, Thomas B., 24, 221; Co., 28, 62
Jeffery Auto., 58
jitneys, 60
Jordan, Edward, 84, 222
Jordan Motor Car Co., 83*, 84
Joy, Henry B., 222

k

Kahn, Albert, 31
Kaiser, Henry, 110
Kaiser auto., 116*
Kaiser-Frazer Corp., 113, 114, 117, 118, 129
Kaiser Industries Corp., 136
Kaiser Jeep Corp., 164, 193
Kaiser Motors Corp., 134, 136
Keeshin Transcontinental Run, 98
Kelly Springfield Co., 65
Kelsey, C. W., 223
Kelvinator Corp., 99
kerosene, 66
Kettering, Charles F., 54, 70, 118, 223; Award, 180
King, Charles B., 14, 16*, 28, 224
Kissel auto., 56, 71*
Knight, Charles Y., 46
Knight sleeve-valve engine, 46, 51, 73*
Knudsen, William S., 104, 224
Kurtis-Kraft, Inc., 122

l

labor strikes, 69, 113
Lafayette Motors Corp., 80
Lanchester vibration dampener, 70
latches, trunk, door, 137, 138, 141, 147, 151, 189
laws, legislation, 18, 26, 28, 33, 38, 42, 55, 63, 67, 109, 139, 147, 179, 185; *see also* specific laws: Federal Aid, Red Flag, etc.

index

leasing, 82
Lee, Gordon, 74
Leland, Henry M., 64, 225
Leland & Faulconer Mfg. Co., 33
Leonardo da Vinci, 5
Levacar, 156
Levassor, Emile, 6
Liberty aircraft engines, 64
Liberty Bell, 60
licenses, vehicle, 26; *see also* drivers'
lights, emergency flashing, 150; *see also* headlamps, tail lamps, side lamps
Lincoln auto., 96*
Lincoln Highway, 57
Lincoln-Mercury Div., 129
Lincoln Motor Co., 64, 76
Little Motor Car Co., 56
locks, *see* latches
Locomomobile auto., 29
Loomis, Gilbert, 19
Laughead, Malcolm, 67, 70, 86
LPG, 128
lubrication, 35, 56, 84, 135, 154
lunar rover vehicle, 192

m

Macauley, Alvan, 225
Mack Bros. Motor Car Co., 22, 53, 85
Mack bus, 22, 143; truck, 52*, 72, 163
Mackinac Bridge, 143
Mack Truck, 193
Mack Truck, Inc., 124, 139, 143, 177, 195, 199
magazines, 14, 21, 31, 80, 82
magnetos, 26, 48
Major Award Trophy, 80
Malcolmson, Alex Y., 29
manifolds, 64, 89, 98
Markette auto., 179
Marmon, Howard C., 226
Marmon, Walter C., 93
Marmon auto., racer, 53, 62
Marmon-Herrington Co., 123, 163

Marquette auto., 87*
Marriott, Fred, 38, 39*
Mason, George W., 100, 226
Matheson, Charles W., Frank, 227
Matter, Louis, 134
Maxim, Hiram P., 13, 16, 19*
Maxwell, Jonathan D., 12, 28, 227
Maxwell auto., 41*
Maxwell-Chalmers Corp., 79, 82
Maxwell Motor Co., 72
Maybach, Wilhelm, 6
mechanics, schools, 33; *see also* service men
Mercer auto., 185
Mercury auto., 101
Mercury-Edsel-Lincoln Div., 145
metric system, 205
Metropolitan auto., 122
Metz, Charles, 228
Metzger, William E., 20
Michigan International Speedway, 185
Michigan State College, 128
Midgley, Thomas, Jr., 75
Miles, Samuel H., 228
Minibus, Inc., 177
mirrors, 53, 81, 144, 147, 151, 184
mobile homes, 162, 167
Mobile Steamer, 21*
Mobile Oil Economy Run, 187
model announcement dates, 91, 97, 98, 122
Montpelier Mfg. Co., 149
Morgan, William, 19
Morill, George H., Jr., 15
Morris & Salom Electrobat, 17
Motocycle, 14
Motor, 31, 80
Motor Age, 21
Motor Vehicle Manufacturers Assoc., 200
Mott, C. S., 229
Mueller, Oscar, 14
Mueller-Benz auto., 14
mufflers, 154
Murdock, J. M., 45*

295

Murphy, Edward M., 41

n

Nader, Ralph, 196
Narragansett Park Race, 16*, 17
Nash, Charles W., 62, 100, 229
Nash auto., 64*, 88, 98, 104, 107*, 122, 143
Nash-Kelvinator Corp., 99, 122, 123, 132
Nash Motors Co.: formed, 62; trucks for U.S. Army, 67; interest in Seaman Body, 69; Lafayette Motors Corp., 80; stock held by employees, 85; merges with Kelvinator, 99
National Assoc. of Auto. Advertising Men, 56
National Assoc. of Auto. Manufacturers, 24, 56
National Assoc. of Retail Auto. Dealers, 35
National Auto. Chamber of Commerce, 56, 59, 63, 74, 89, 91, 96
National Auto. Dealers Assoc., 67
National Driver Registration Service, 159
National Traffic & Motor Vehicle Safety Act, 174
New York & Ohio Co., 21
New York Stock Exchange, 53
New York-to-Buffalo endurance run, 24*, 25
New York-to-Paris Race, 44*, 45
New York-to-Portalnd Race, 37
New York-to-St. Louis tour, 34*, 35
nickel plate trim, 42
Nic-L-Silver Battery Co., 148
Nixon, Richard M., 140
Northern auto., 28
NSU Werke, 150
noise, 193

o

Oakland Motor Car Co., 41, 45, 91
odometers, 187, 189, 190, 204

Ohio Auto. Co., 28
Oldfield, Berner Eli, 30*, 32
"Old Pacific," 31
Olds, Ransom E., 18, 20, 33, 230
Oldsmobile auto., 18, 19, 27*, 36*, 76, 92, 93, 105*, 120, 121, 126*
Oldsmobile Div., 45, 158
Olds Motor Vehicle Co., 19
Olds Motor Works, 20, 28, 33
Oliver Corp., 152
Otto, Nikolaus A., 5
Overland auto., 32*
Overland Auto. Co., 46
Owen, Percy, 21
Owen, auto., 49*

p

Packard, J. W., W. D., 21, 230
Packard auto., 21, 59, 61, 73, 92*, 136*, 140, 145
Packard Motor Car Co.: "H" slot gearshift, 29; moves, 31; straight "8" engine, 77; hypoid gears, 83; test track, 85; millionth, 117; merges with Studebaker, 132
Paige, Fred O., 231
Paige-Detroit Motor Car Co., 85
paints, finishes: baked enamel, 46; pyroxolin, 81; color ranges, 103; with wax, 147; electrocoating process, 168; medium blue popular, 179; reflective racing stripes, 180; wood-like panel appliques, 182
parades, 55
Paradynamics, Inc., 145
parts, 21, 49, 80, 102, 118, 128
patent licensing agreements, 63
Peerless auto., 31, 75*
Pennington, Edward J., 12
periodic inspection laws, 179
phaeton bodies, 76, 92*
Philadelphia wagon parade, 55
Philco, Corp., 158
Phillips, (Mrs.) John H., 21

index

Pierce, George N., 25*, 231
Pierce, Percy, 37
Pierce-Arrow auto., 25*, 37, 45, 93; truck, 53
Pierce-Arrow Motor Car Co., 87
"piggy-back" R.R. service, *see* trucks

Pikes Peak, 23
pistons, 59, 89, 107
Pittsburgh Motor Vehicle Co., 19, 21
Plymouth auto.: introduced, 87; "floating power," 92; vacuum-powered convertible top, 102; 4 millionth, 106; steel station wagon, 121; gas turbine model, 133; 10 millionth, 141; Cricket introduced, 192
Pontiac auto., 89, 91, 101, 140, 152; introduced, 83; production highlights, 98, 148, 187, 194; taxicabs, 104
Pope, Albert A., 231
Pope-Columbia auto., 19*
Pope-Hartford auto., 35; truck, 54
Pope Mfg. Co., 13, 16, 19
Porter, Finley R., 232
Post, Augustus, 35
postage stamps, commemorative, 128, 154, 185
power take-off, 32
Presidents (U.S.), 23, 73, 98, 154, 182
President's Action Committee for Highway Safety, 134
press previews, 18
Prest-O-Lite Co., 33
prices, pricing, 63, 147
production, millions of vehicles: 25, 82; 50, 92; 75, 102; 100, 118; 250, 186; 100 million passenger cars, 127
Prudential Insurance Co., 132
purchase of first car, 16

r

races, racing, 13, 15*, 17, 34*, 138, 185; *see also* names: Chicago Times-Herald, Indianapolis 500, etc.
Rackham, Horace H., 31
radiators: cellular replaces tubular, 48; shutter, 65; locking cap, 81; pressed steel grille, 92; V-shaped grille, 94; aluminum grille, 157; *see also* cooling
Radio Corp. of America, 131
radios, 77, 88, 96, 104, 144, 171, 186
railway box cars, 59
Rambler auto. (Nash-Kelvinator Corp.), 123; (T. J. Jeffery Co.), 24, 28, 58
Ramsey, (Mrs.) John R., 46*, 47
Rapid Motor Vehicle Co., 28, 46, 53
rationing, 109, 110
rebates, 58, 61, 155
record players, 138
recreational vehicles, *see* campers
"Red Flag" law, 18
Reeves, Alfred P., 232
registrations, 167, 182
Reliance Truck Co., 53
rentals, 82
Reo auto., 84, 86*, 95, 97, 99; bus, 80, 99; truck, 50, 99
Reo Motor Car Co., 33, 99, 123
Reo Motors, Inc., 143
restrictions during war, 66, 109, 110
Reuther, W., 194
Rickenbacker auto., 80, 82, 83
Rickenbacker, E. V., 232
Riker, Andrew L., 232
Riker Electric auto., 17
road maps, 57; signs, 26
roads, 12, 33; first mile of concrete, 47; center lines, 53; Lincoln Highway, 57; building codes, 59; federal aid to, 63, 67, 72, 115, 139, 145; research on, 72, 136, 137, 170; uniform numbering, 82; Interstate Highway System, 139, 140, 145, 153, 177; travel exceeds trillion vehicle miles, 182; *see also* turnpikes
roadster-coupe bodies, 75
roofs, sliding, 199

297

running boards, 104, 106
rust prevention, 144, 176

S

safety: police instruct in, 69; electronic steering, braking, 131; President's Action Committee, 134; door latches, 137; radar warning devices, 148; "electric fence," 152; AMA grants for promotion, 153, 170; National Traffic & Motor Safety, Highway Safety acts, 174; experimental safety vehicles, 192, 204
salesrooms, 21
Sampson truck, 54
San Francisco earthquake, 38
Saurer truck, 52
Saxon auto., 60*
Schacht, G. A., 69
Schacht truck, 51, 69
Schwab, Charles M., 76
Scott, John, Medal, 76
scrappage of cars, 89
Seaman Body Corp., 47, 69
Sears, Roebuck & Co., 127
seat belts: on Rambler, 123, 156; emphasized, 137; anchors for installation, 154, 161; front, standard, 166; rear, standard, 171; buzzer and light reminders, 199; engine interlock system, 201, 205
seats: adjustable, 58, 101; movable, 59; rumble, 64, 81, 86*; safety padding, 101; "Airfoam" cushions, 103; hydraulically operated, 117; swivel, front, 147; lock, 148; electric heating, 170; safety, for children, 181
sedan bodies, hardtop, 120, 122
Selden, George B., 13, 14*, 233
Selden Patent, 13, 26, 32, 47, 52; license plate, 31*
service men, 33, 146, 184, 189
service stations, 21, 27, 51
Shelby American auto., 160, 173, 180

Sherman Products, 152
shock absorbers, 32, 190
shoulder harnesses, 183*
shows, Detroit, 150, 153*, 154, 162; New York, 22, 97, 140
side lamps, 49
side marker lights, 181
Sintz, Clark, 13
Skelton, Owen R., 73, 77
Slick Airways, Inc., 136
Sloan, Alfred P., Jr., 63, 78, 234
snow removal equipment, 76
Soap Box Derby, 199
"sociable" body, 59
Society of Auto. Engineers, 37, 50, 59, 63, 64; Automotive Engineers, 64, 80
"Somewhere West of Laramie," 78
Sorensen, Charles E., 234
Souther, Henry, 50
spark plugs, 28, 176
Spaulding auto., 57
speedometers, 26, 102, 141
speed records, 38, 182, 193, 197
Springfield Body Corp., 77
springs, suspension: "Duflex" rear, 101; coil, in rear, 101; all-coil suspension, knee-action, 104; ball joint front wheel suspension, 128; air suspension, 131, 144; torsion bar, 140, 151; single leaf rear, 156; pneumatic load leveller, 181
standardization of parts, 49, 80, 118
Stanley, F. E., F. O., 18*, 20, 235
Stanley Bros., 20, 21
Stanley Steamer auto., 18*, 20, 38, 39*, 185
Star auto., 77*
starting devices, 47, 52, 54; accelerator pedal, 94; ignition key, 121
station wagons, 77*, 97*, 105*, 116, 118*, 121, 124, 125*, 143, 151, 172, 181
steam cars, 20, 78, 188
steel, 31, 45, 48, 72, 152, 176